I Am A Black Man

The Evolution of a Dangerous Negro

Demetrius Walker

Capitalize The B Publishing

Copyright © 2017 by Demetrius Walker
All rights reserved. This book or any portion thereof may not be reproduced or used in any manner whatsoever without the express written permission of the publisher except for the use of brief quotations in a book review.

Printed in the United States of America

First Printing, 2017

ISBN 978-0-9990236-0-0

Capitalize The B Publishing
3055 Walnut Bend Lane
Unit 33
Houston, TX 77042

www.CapitalizeTheB.com

Some names and identifying details have been changed to protect the privacy of individuals.

I wrote this book for you, my son, Hunter Warren Walker, so that you will never question your Daddy's love, motives, and dedication to helping you find fulfillment in life.

And to my mother Esrenée, thank you for setting me on my literary journey by critiquing my writing as far back as elementary school. Your sacrifices for my education and well-being are appreciated more than I can express.

To my father, Don, my first superhero, thank you for inspiring me to break the cycle.

Finally, Sabree, my "twin" sister, thank you for never giving up on your brother. I love you.

I Am A Black Man 4

TABLE OF CONTENTS

SKULLY	7
CROOKLYN DODGER	17
SECTION 5	37
MEEK THA FREAK	53
BECOMING A BLACK MAN IN BOARDING SCHOOL	79
BLACK GUY AT A PWI	131
THE PLANTATION	171
dangerousNEGRO	193
ROCK BOTTOM	217
THE LIGHT	229
BREAKING INDUSTRY RULE #4080	241
ASHES	255
THERAPEUTIC IGNORANCE	271
JANTEENTH	279
REFERENCES	291

I Am A Black Man 6

CHAPTER ONE

SKULLY

> The works I've done,
> Sometimes it seems so small,
> It seems like I've done nothing at all.
> Lord I'm (leaning) and depending on You,
> If I do right You're gonna see me through;
> May the works (the works I've done),
> Let it speak for me (for me).
> -Keith Wonderboy Johnson "May The Works I've Done (Speak For Me)"

We took turns staring out the living room window. Apartment 11H gave us a bird's-eye view of the graffiti covered 2 and 5 trains, which pulled into the Jackson Avenue station like clockwork. We called them "Beat Street" trains. With enough squint and strain we pinpointed the twenty-plus story buildings of Co-op City at the edge of the northern horizon. Across the East River to the right, were the barbed wire walls of Rikers Island and its industrial maze of buildings. "If you don't leave me alone, they're gonna send you over there with Cousin Ed!" I'd tell my little sister Sabree. She wasn't easily persuaded to step down from the plastic covered recliner though. With her knees in the seat and stomach pressed against the seat back, she'd stare past Rikers and watch the planes take off and land at LaGuardia.

A hundred feet below the brick windowsill was "the big park." Two full length basketball courts, equipped with metal backboards and double rims, took up most of the real estate in this, the larger of St. Mary's project parks. Along the southern border was a handball court where Spanish-speaking kids smacked navy blue orbs against a twenty-foot concrete slab covered in graffiti. The portion of the park that bordered East 156th Street boasted a few slides, swings, and wooden benches. We'd watch the neighborhood drink 40s, smoke blunts, and cypher there.

Momma was always overprotective, so we didn't go to "the big park" often. We spent most of our time in "the little park," next to her building, a few hundred feet away from "the big park." "The little park" had two metal monkey bar setups (one shaped like a turtle shell, the other more linear - something like what you'd expect soldiers to train on), a concrete four-legged apparatus, (which somewhat resembled a dinosaur), plus painted outlines for hopscotch, and my personal favorite, skully (pronounced skelly in St Mary's Projects). There were wooden benches lining the chain-link fence of the "little park." Most of the younger kids played there. While my sister played double dutch, I was mastering skully, flicking bottle caps across the black pavement with enough precision to knock competitors out their numbered squares. The art of trash talking was perfected here.

Momma would sit on the green wooden benches and chat with her best friend, Aunt Dot, and other elderly acquaintances. Mr. Willy would sit next to them and feed the pigeons peanuts. Every so often an unfamiliar figure got within cane's length of us and Momma would announce, "I'll bust you in the head," extending her cane like a scepter to obstruct further motion.

Born to sharecroppers Robert T. and Cora V. Edmonds in Merchant, Virginia on July 7, 1919, Momma was a Southern girl, skeptical of New York City's unpredictable strangers. In line with Old South tradition, Momma's baptism at Meharrin Baptist Church occurred at an early age. God and grinding were the themes of the day. Generations of farming preceded her proclivity for hard work. An excellent fisher, Momma feared few of God's creations, as she caught meals for her family growing up. Dogs however, she approached with caution. Walks home from the schoolhouse might include the added suspense of being terrorized by White people's canines, who Momma swore were trained to hate Black people.

In 1936, after my great-great grandparents could finally save up enough money to buy their way out of sharecropping, they fled Merchant to purchase a forty acre farm in Lawrenceville, Virginia. They could wait no longer for William T. Sherman's empty, post-Civil War reparations promise. Momma would pick tobacco and cotton, like she had all her life, on this farm too. With Christianity being central to her life, she joined local Oak Grove Baptist Church. There, she met a crafty womanizer, my great-grandfather, Thomas H. Walker. His wide footed waddle earned him the nickname, Duck. They married in 1938 and ended up having four children - three girls and a boy. Their only son, and youngest child, died at four months from complications of premature birth.

Domestic violence forced Momma to leave my great-grandfather in the Jim Crow South in 1954. With no assets, she also left behind her three daughters Vye, Agnes, and Constance, to establish a foundation in the North. By this time, Harlem had become Black Mecca. A couple of Momma's sisters had already established themselves there, giving Momma confidence her skills as a seamstress and tailor would open countless opportunities to generate income. Endless competition made landing a job in her preferred field daunting though. She worked a series of menial jobs cleaning houses for White folks, before landing a job as a hatmaker at the Faye Hat

Co. on 163rd St and 3rd Avenue, in The Bronx. After years of working and saving, Momma sent for her daughters. Her youngest, Constance, my grandmother, made it to New York in 1960 at age fourteen.

    Connie immediately fell in love with New York. There was no tobacco to pick. She didn't have to worry about the repercussions of stuffing rocks into her cotton sack to cheat Virginia's ten cents per pound market rate. No longer would she have to tend to pigs, horses, and chickens. Walking all the way to the spring to draw up buckets of water was no longer a necessity. In fact, she enjoyed not having to walk much at all in New York. There were buses, trains, and cabs galore. Within minutes Connie could travel miles away from home, observing exquisitely dressed strangers along the way. Growing up on a farm in Virginia didn't require one to be fashion forward; Connie only had a few outfits when she arrived. That changed overnight. By the summer, the young teen would dress elegantly enough to capture the eye of Mr. William Harold Thompson, a tall, charming, light-skinned man with wavy hair, seven years her senior. She'd never seen a man so handsome. T, as everyone called him, lived across the street from Momma's 236 West 123rd Street, Harlem residence. Connie was smitten. A whirlwind romance ensued. On March 3rd, 1961 she gave birth to my father, Leland Darnell Walker. A year later, Connie and T welcomed my uncle, Gregory Walker, into the world. Shortly thereafter, T abandoned his new family.

***

    The streets renamed my father Donnie, or Don for short. Gregory shortened to Greg. They both called their young mother, Connie, by her first name. Connie realized the importance of having a father figure, so she'd send Donnie and Greg to stay with their grandfather, Duck, in Virginia many summers.

All Walker kids looked forward to summers with Duck. Dodging snakes and tending to pigs on Duck's farm was enough to fuel their adrenaline rush. Dad, Uncle Greg, and ten of their cousins would somehow squeeze into Duck's two-bedroom shack for country adventure. In the living room was a metal bathtub that doubled as a large sink for rinsing produce. After every four baths, the tub was refilled with fresh water for the next set of bathers. Under the house, below the wooden floor, Duck would let his corn whiskey and peach wine ferment. Sips of the bootleg liquor were snuck by the kids as early as five or six. Duck didn't mind. My father says he never saw Duck sober, his eyes were always bloodshot and glazed over from drinking. His soulmate, Lorraine, was as big of a drunk as he was.

On the weekends, Duck, a Negro League umpire, would pile all the grandkids into his station wagon to attend his games. Watching intently, my dad would study each batter's stance. He'd store the observations for future use. Donnie's love for baseball was one of the few traits he could attribute to his genetic lineage.

***

At fourteen and thirteen, Donnie and Greg finally met their father, T. While they always had a relationship with T's mother, their grandmother, Grace, nobody ever told them the reason they had never met their father. One day after being invited over for a meal at Grace's apartment in Harlem, T randomly showed up. So happy to meet their father for the first time, my father and Greg did not interrogate him about where he'd been all their lives. They relished the moment. They would soon learn that T was a gangster, known to make a living pulling off large scale burglaries of warehouses, department stores, and the like. From furs to jewelry, T only dealt with "big jobs." He wasn't one of the lowly wig snatchers who headlined the evening news. Besides robbing and hustling, it's doubtful T ever held a legitimate job.

I only remember meeting T twice. Once, when my father and I were walking through Harlem, he looked up at the street sign and said, "My father lives on this block, I wonder if he's home." We proceeded down the street until my father's eyes pinpointed a third floor window. Cupping his hands around his mouth he shouted, "T!..... T!"

A wiry light-skinned dude lifted the window and peeked out. "What's up Donnie? What you doing round here?"

My father put his hand on my head. "I was just passing by with your grandson, Meek!"

I was nine years old. Three years later I would see T again, at his funeral. A couple weeks prior, my dad received a random phone call from one of T's friends saying he was in the hospital and wasn't doing too well. My father rushed to Harlem Hospital to find out what was going on. He questioned the front desk on the whereabouts of Harold Thompson and found no person admitted by that name. Devastated, my dad figured he was too late and T had already died. Then, he called Connie to ask if she had any ideas. She told him T's full name was *William* Harold Thompson. Realizing he didn't even know his father's full name, deep embarrassment consumed him.

After checking under William Harold Thompson, my dad discovered T was indeed at Harlem Hospital. He was in a coma on life support - a vegetable. A heroin overdose two days prior led to his admission. No other family came to T's bedside to advise on what to do in this circumstance. Another forty-eight hours went by and it was apparent that T would not recover. My father and Greg decided to pull the plug on their father, T, a man they had seen less than ten times in twenty years. They would never get to ask why he abandoned them. They could only deduce T was too busy being a gangster to make his sons a priority.

Being a professional gangster came with no health benefits or life insurance. With no one else to assist with funeral expenses, my father scraped together a few thousand dollars to bury T. T didn't own a suit, so my father dressed him in one of his own for the casket. The only time I ever saw my dad cry was at T's wake, in a small church housed out of a Harlem brownstone. A stranger, I resolved not to shed a tear for T.

T wasn't there when my father, Greg, and Nana lived in a condemned building on Crotona Park East, in the South Bronx. Buckets filled with fire hydrant water supplied their household needs. With no funds to move out like the rest of the residents, they endured brutal New York winters with no heat. Occasionally, they would wake up coughing from smoke that had inundated the building. Squatters, many heroin and glue addicts, would haphazardly allow their fires to grow uncontrollable. My father would watch the flames light up the freezing night in awe. After the fire department would extinguish the flames, everybody would go back into the abyss. Business as usual. The profundity of their poverty wasn't easily apparent - this was just life in the South Bronx. With Connie laboring at the Post Office during the day and away at night school in the evenings, the streets became my father and Greg's primary custodian.

When the weather broke, Hip Hop would sprout from these dangerous streets and dilapidated buildings. Donnie and Greg only had to step outside to hear random disco beats and foreign tunes echo through Crotona Park. As early as twelve, they'd pay fifty cents to get into Harlem house parties where Spoonie G or Kurtis Blow would play records on Technics B10 turntables. Fascinated, my father and Greg saved up enough to purchase their own pair of B10s and a small mixer. The B10s were coveted because they were belt driven, perfect for backspinning. They swiped the subwoofers from Momma's HiFi console to create their own speakers. Momma so rarely cranked up the system, she never even realized they disappeared. With a little more ingenuity they also rigged Momma's old, 1920s era amplifier to work with the homemade speakers. Donnie and Greg declared themselves DJs and spent hours a day honing their skills.

 Back then, the key to being a memorable DJ was introducing the audience to new music, which was really re-purposed old music. Like many of the first DJs to emerge, my dad frequented Downstairs, a hole in the wall record store in the 42nd Street Subway station. Standing room only, Downstairs was run by two enterprising Jews who imported European LPs from the likes of Kraftwerk and Fausto Papetti. My father studied the records in search of breakbeats, looping the beats by spinning back to their point of origin on one turntable, while the beat played on the other. In little to no time, my father became the self proclaimed "King of the Backspin."

 In 1975 Connie married Ralph, a coworker from the Post Office, and moved Donnie and Greg to Coney Island. Quickly, my father developed a reputation for having the most extensive catalogue in the neighborhood. The handful of DJs living there never ventured all the way to Downstairs in Midtown. My dad was the first to bring break records to Coney Island, making him popular amongst Coney Island's burgeoning Hip Hop community. Friends would spend days in Connie's duplex apartment listening to Donnie and Greg cut and scratch. Forty ounce bottles of Olde English littered the bedroom; the reefer smoke so thick people could barely see who they rubbed shoulders with. On the rare occasions they would open the window for much needed oxygen, people on the street below would mistake the billowing smoke for fire. Despite these facts, my dad maintained a reputation for being clean cut. He dressed neatly and spoke politely in public. His best friend, Eric Bullock, called him Richie C, in a nod to what The Fonz called *Happy Days'* straightlaced Richie Cunningham. My father would replace Richie with Don, to assume his DJ monicker, Don C. He would go out to Kaiser Park, where DJ Danny D Hollywood often drew a crowd, and jump on the wheels. Speakers stacked twenty feet high interrupted natural heart rhythms with thunderous bass. Eventually, my father, Don C's growing reputation led him to cross paths with Grandmaster JC, with whom he shared mutual friends. JC was more of an R&B DJ and Emcee; he needed my father to feed the Hip Hop needs of his crowds in Flatbush. Together, Don C and JC tore up the late 70s party and club scene in tandem.

  In 1980, Jimmy Carter issued a Presidential Proclamation mandating all males eighteen and older register for the draft to show strength to the Commies. Donnie and Greg, who were too young to fight in the Vietnam War, but old enough to remember people not making it back, feared they would be called up for an impending draft. The media made it seem all but certain a new draft would be enacted. Worried the Army or Marines would call them to combat against their will, Donnie and Greg proactively joined the Navy; they figured they could avoid the ground battles that killed and wounded several of their older friends. My father was commissioned to the USS O'Bannon, a destroyer, while Greg was sent to the USS Forrestal, an aircraft carrier.

  Traveling the world on the O'Bannon, my father was one of Hip Hop's first global ambassadors. Stopping at ports in Brazil, Norway, Portugal, and Germany he convinced local clubs and DJs to let him jump on the wheels. While my father introduced these crowds to mixing, scratching, and backspinning, other sailors breakdanced. The spectacle awed foreign discotecs. Club owners loved when the

US Navy was in town; they spread the gospel of Hip Hop beyond US soil before Blondie's "Rapture" would first appear on MTV.

CHAPTER TWO

CROOKLYN DODGER

> Panic, as another manic depressant
> Adolescent stares at death, now what's left
> When there ain't no guide, and a whole lot of pride
> It might be a homicide, so let the drama slide
> We don't want no problems, B
> Get your name in the obituary column sheet
> Cause life is too short and it just gets shorter
> I wish I had a quarter for all my people they slaughter
> -Special Ed (Crooklyn Dodgers) "Crooklyn"

A high school ski trip provided the chance encounter which brought my parents together. My father, the handsome Lincoln High School standout and DJ, was drawn to my Panamanian mother's golden skin, long legs, and smile. Esrenée was different, driven to succeed. Though she'd grown up in Brooklyn's notorious East New York, she hadn't let the streets limit her ambition. When it was time to choose a high school, she opted to enroll at Sheepshead Bay, an exceptional public school in the Italian neighborhood famous for rearing Vince Lombardi. Mature beyond her years from having to cook, clean, and manage a household of younger siblings, while her mother slaved at Kings County Hospital and attended night school, Esrenée was wifey material.

Like my father, Don, she also hadn't known her dad until well into adolescence. It wasn't until she checked into a dental appointment under her maiden name that she discovered she had siblings from her dad's side... living in Brooklyn of all places.

"I'm here for my check up," my mother told the receptionist.

"Last name?" the woman requested.

"Fischle," my mother voiced expecting her novel name to stand out on the appointment log.

"Which one?" the receptionist pried.

In thirteen years, my mother had never heard this question. Bewildered, she responded "There's another Fischle that goes here? I'm Esrenée, what's her name?"

Amused, the receptionist disclosed, "Maritza."

From there the stage was set for my mother to finally meet her father, who she believed to be somewhere in Panama, where her mother, Gloria, left him in 1962. Further investigation revealed her father, Alric Fischle, had also settled in Brooklyn and longed to see her for years. But Gloria had since married Joe, an iron and plastic factory worker from Alabama known for his temper. Joe forbade my mother's father, a, tall, attractive, caramel man with dimples, from showing his face anywhere near Gloria or Esrenée.

The void created by her father's absence forced my mother to lock away and suppress emotions... emotions that could only be unlocked by someone of familiar circumstance, like my father. The cold feet shared on the ski slopes of their senior trip transformed into warm feelings of forever. Naïve, immature, and inseparable, the Navy wasn't even powerful enough to destroy their bond. They married on October 17th, 1981 in a military wedding. Months prior, my mother visited the love of her life at his naval base in Germany, where they downed nickel beer and made up for lost time.

Nine months later I was cut from my mother, Esrenée Walker's, womb at 7:56am on January the 8th, 1982. The night before my birth, an angel appeared to my mother in a dream and told her to name me Demetrius. She listened. I took my first breath at Brooklyn Hospital, just a short walk from the Brooklyn Navy Yards. Connie made her way to the hospital as soon as she heard the news. Peering through the incubation window, she admired my little bald head, and another name came to mind: "That's my grandson - Meek." As quick as I became Meek, Connie became Nana. Due to his military deployment, I wouldn't bond with my dad until my first birthday.

Charleston, South Carolina. Portland, Maine. Fort Hamilton, New York. The Navy bounced us around the East Coast. I remember bits and pieces here and there; my dad playing The Mary Jane Girls' "All Night Long" back to back nonstop in Charleston; calling Nana on a chilly December night from the hospital in Portland to let her know my sister, Sabree, was born; the secret road at the end of the Verrazano Bridge that led us into the military base at Fort Hamilton; Loose End's "Hangin on a String." This all happened before I turned four-years-old.

My memory comes into clearer focus at 926 Belmont Avenue in East New York, Brooklyn. My parents rented a modest two bedroom apartment from Grandma Gloria, who purchased the building with Grandpa Joe years earlier. The apartment placed us four blocks away from them and just one block away from Great-Grandma Lillian on Fountain Avenue. The two-story, brown brick building housed four apartments. Ours was on the first floor at the end of the hall, just beyond the two-tiered staircase that led to the second floor. Slugs found shelter in this hallway whenever it rained. I avoided eye contact with the slime monsters as I tiptoed over them into our quaint apartment. Save for the lima bean colored vinyl tile in the living room, the unit had been modified little since the building's construction in the nineteen-twenties. Upon entering the apartment, there was a small bathroom immediately to the right with a rusty porcelain sink, toilet, and tub. A single light bulb with a beaded metal drawstring hung down from the ceiling. It always felt cold in there. Importing traditions from Maine, my parents would buy lobsters for the Super Bowl and leave them in the tub to stay cool. I'd cry because I thought it was inhumane for them to freeze before meeting their shrieking demise in a scorching cauldron. Moving past the bathroom was our cozy living room, equipped with a thirty-six inch Zenith TV and VCR. Our matching grey sofa and loveseat each took up a wall. In front of the sofa was a rectangular wood and glass coffee table. When guests visited, the table served as the place for razor blades to chop white blocks into lines of powder to be snorted through rolled up dollar bills. Fascinated by the ritual, I knew this was strictly adult shit. A few feet beyond the coffee table were my dad's speakers, receiver, and tape deck. On the weekends he might throw on a recording of Kool DJ Red Alert's KISS FM mix to let Doug E. Fresh, Kool Moe Dee, or Whodini echo through our apartment. He'd grab his perfectly rolled Bambú joint from behind his ear and soon the place would be cloudy with the sweet, skunky aroma of reefer. Next to one speaker was a twenty inch, hand-carved, wooden antelope brought back from a Navy stop in Lagos. Its ivory antlers looked exactly like my dad's joints. I'd dislodge an antler and put it between my little lips pretending to smoke with my dad. My mom, who I called Renée the way my dad called his mom Connie, didn't find this amusing at all. She chastised my dad for condoning this behavior. His vibe would be killed.

  Rarely did I enter my parents' bedroom. It was just large enough for their waterbed and a wooden dresser. A cuckoo clock my dad brought back from South America hung on the wall. If you slid its front panel to the right, an Argentinian dude with a Gaucho hat banged a chick doggystyle to the pendulum's rhythm. I assumed he was letting her know what time it was. Below the clock to the left was a window that overlooked a fenced backyard behind our building.

Although our apartment was on the first floor, we were still elevated eight feet off the ground in the rear of the building, due to there being a basement. Grandpa Joe never planted grass in the backyard, so a thin layer of brown dirt and dog feces blanketed the surface. Beyond the backyard in the distance, the view concluded with the seven-story buildings of Cypress Hills Projects, New York's roughest, most notorious public housing complex. Drug debts precipitated whole families being thrown off rooftops there. Ears grew desensitized to nightly shootouts.

 I'd stare at the projects from the top bunk in the small bedroom I shared with Sabree. There was only enough room for our bunk bed, an iron column radiator, and a toy box featuring sliding doors that doubled as chalkboards. The dark wooden floor lining our room had planks missing. Most of the time we were careful to step around the nail protruding from the missing floorboard in the doorway, though I impaled my right knee on it during a game of tag with Auntie Jonelle and Sabree one afternoon.

 My dad's wingspan spanned the length of our kitchen. The white cabinets above the sink usually held a few boxes of King Vitamin or Captain Crunch. The fridge always contained a minimum of three items: Kool-Aid, government Cheese, and bologna. Momma always looked out for us when we visited The Bronx; there was no way she would let us leave without at least taking a brick of government cheese to boot. Truth be told, government cheese made the best grilled cheese sandwiches, so I was grateful. Our stove was super old school, so anytime my mom wanted to use the range or oven she'd have to light a match and toss it under the pilot to get it lit. I would camp out to the right of the stove under our small "dining room" table pretending I was in exotic places while she cooked or washed dishes.

When my Dad had free time he'd take me and my sister to the nearest park, which was a few blocks away in Cypress Hills Projects. Like most of the parks in the concrete jungle of New York City, there was a metal swing set, a handball court, and a few slides. The swing set in Cypress was the biggest and best in Brooklyn. With swings suspended from twenty foot rope chains, it featured flat steel seats, which were easy to stand on, while thrusting one's hips to gain momentum. Kids would compete to see how high they could fly before jumping or flipping at their peak to land on the other side of the chain-linked fence that separated the swings from the rest of the playground. It was as graceful and competitive as Olympic high diving. One just had to be extremely careful not to land on the ever present remains of shattered Olde English and Colt 45 bottles.

Amongst this rugged terrain my father taught me to ride my first bike, a black and gold BMX - the kind the White boys used for tricks. If you didn't have a BMX your bike was wack. Consequently, they were a hot commodity and often stolen. Either my father didn't believe in training wheels or we couldn't afford them because I got a crash course in operating my BMX right there in Cypress. Running alongside me while he held the back of my seat, I quickly learned how to navigate the pavement chock-full of glass.

While playing in Cypress Hills, my father also introduced me to my first true love - baseball. There was a neglected field of grass just beyond the chain linked fence that encircled the playground. One morning we climbed through a hole in the fence someone conveniently carved with a bolt cutter. As we stood amongst stalks of ragweed, I could hear Joe Ski Love teaching everyone how to do the Pee-Wee Herman from a fourth floor boombox. Ignoring the sets of eyeballs staring down on us, my father fashioned a home plate from an assortment of sticks. I stood next to the makeshift plate blocking the sun's glare with my little hand. He showed me how to hold the

Louisville Slugger, right hand over left, while getting a wide stance. Backing away about twenty feet, he stood in front of me and encouraged me to keep my eye on the handball in his left hand. The fondest memory of my childhood is my father lobbing the ball underhand and my reflexes kicking in to blast it over his head. *I could hit!* My dad wore the widest smile, I had never seen him this proud of me. I had unexpected hand-eye coordination and an immediate dilemma - would I be a major league baseball player or a professional wrestler?

    The WWF was an important part of my life at this point. My father loved wrestling as much as I did. We subscribed to WWF Magazine, my Bret The Hitman Hart sunglasses were my favorite accessory, and I idolized Hulk Hogan. My mother even got in on the action. She once surprised us with tickets to SummerSlam at Madison Square Garden to see Hulk Hogan and Macho Man take on Andre The Giant and "The Million Dollar Man" Ted DiBiase. It would be an understatement to say I was a wrestling fan - I *lived* for professional wrestling… until I hit that home run in Cypress Hills. Then the Mets, Yankees, and WWF divided my attention. The rest of East New York couldn't care less about baseball though. There was no Little League to join. Everyone focused their attention on basketball or football. Baseball was becoming a White boy sport.

***

    Around the corner on Fountain Avenue, Grandma Lillian lived in a pale, yellow, two-family home. The first floor unit housed my parents' favorite couple Jay and Sheila, prior to my uncle Dwayne, his girlfriend Julie, and son Elijah occupying the space. Underneath their apartment was a scary basement my sister and I explored to test our will. Filled with dust covered antiques and a menacing furnace, it looked like the set of a Freddie Krueger movie. Upstairs, Grandma Lillian had a modest two bedroom apartment with a small kitchen, living room, and dining room. She stayed in the master bedroom, while her son, my great-uncle Eric, lived in a small room at the summit of the staircase. The first time I met Grandma Lillian the darkness of her skin struck me. She would never let me live down my first words to her: "Why are you soooo Black?" Knee slapping laughter ensued every time she told the story.

 A couple blocks north of Grandma Lillian's house, on the other side of Pitkin Avenue, was St. Lydia's Episcopal Church. There, I got my first taste of religiosity. Every time I entered the quaint brick building I found the smell of frankincense delightfully intoxicating. There were ten rows of pews, each lined with a kneel pad, Bible, and Catholic hymnal. "But I thought this was an Episcopal church," I'd probe my mother.

 "They're very similar. We even keep up with the Pope," she revealed.

 St. Lydia's was very traditional. Hymns of the week hung from a vintage letterboard. To avoid fidgeting in my seat and drawing the evil eye of an elder, I'd study the hymnals looking for insight. Rigidly structured, the congregation sang the hymns with little conviction. To stay awake I'd locate the most off key singers and laugh hysterically on the inside. Distracted, it was hard to devote my attention to the Lord. While we were supposed to be praying, I'd often keep one eye open to spy how many people were actively engaged versus going through the motions. Most people were faking the funk and I struggled to understand why they continued to attend. The worst part of the service was the pastor's snooze inducing sermon carried out in the thickest, incoherent West Indian accent imaginable. Save for the tasty cracker and thimble of grape juice we got during communion, everything about St. Lydia's was dry and uninspiring. But enduring a miserable service was a small price to pay for God's protection in East New York.

    Danger was ever present. One afternoon my mom picked me and my sister up from daycare early. She had a doctor's appointment and only worked a half day. She unlocked the top and bottom locks of our two-bedroom apartment and I enthusiastically pushed open the front door. Right away at twelve o'clock I noticed my parents' bedroom door curiously open. Focusing another ten feet beyond the open door I could see a man dressed in all black climbing out the window with our Zenith VCR. "What the hell are you doing?!!" Renée shouted. The burglar made solid eye contact with me before proceeding to climb down into the backyard. He quickly scaled the fence and hauled ass through the back alley. I wondered why God didn't stop him.

    That night and every night after, I would stare out my bedroom window from the top bunk. I'd scan the alley looking for the guy to come back. The boogeyman was real; I had looked him in the eye. So I slept with the miniature Louisville Slugger I got at bat day at Shea. I promised I would be ready when he returned. I prayed to God that I didn't fall asleep before he snuck into my window. Even after Grandpa Joe added Rottweilers to the backyard and we acquired an elderly Sheba, (my dad and Greg's old Coney Island mutt), I still stayed up as late as I could to watch for the burglar.

***

    Most of the kids that lived on my block were a few years older. I never got particularly close with any of them, but since we were closest in age, I considered John John my best friend. He was biracial (Black and White), very polite, and athletic. From my big wheel I'd watch John John, his buck-toothed cousin Bob, and Skip, a lanky brown-skinned dude, toss nerf footballs from the corner of Fountain Avenue to the corner of Crystal Street. I admired Skip because he treated us like equals even though we weren't teenagers. I imagined being cool like Skip when I turned thirteen; everyone liked him and he knew how to dress.

Cityline kept Skip fresh. Every once in awhile my parents would take me and my sister there to purchase new clothes or sneakers. An endless strip of storefronts on the border of Brooklyn and Queens, *everybody* in East New York shopped for deals at Cityline. One day my dad and I made the trek to Cityline to settle a debt. Earlier in the day he promised the toy of my choice if I didn't cry at the barbershop while getting a haircut. Until I was four, my mom would cornrow my hair. I loathed the hairstyle because people often mistook me for a girl. So my dad started taking me along with him to Bautista's Barbershop, two doors down from Grandma Gloria's house. I loved almost everything about the barbershop; the smell of clipper cooling spray, the camaraderie, the KRS-One vs MC Shan debates. I just couldn't get past the menacing buzz of cold steel on my head. Propped up on a milk crate, I balled like a baby and peed myself during my first haircut. My dad was deeply embarrassed. Though I controlled my bladder on subsequent visits, tears still rolled down my cheeks. Until the bribe. I could contain myself for a new toy. So, after I survived my first Caesar without incident, it was off to Cityline. I finally felt like a man, the logical choice was a weapon. We entered a store with a green awning on Liberty Avenue. A green flag with a big red circle hung from the ceiling. The store was a hodgepodge of miscellaneous trinkets, apparel, and products - the precursor to The Dollar Store. I walked past the tubs of bootleg sneakers and off brand laundry detergent to the toy aisle. "How about this?" my dad asked holding an action figure.

I sighed, "I already have He-Man."

My eyes kept scanning the aisle until they froze on a neatly packaged, shiny, black uzi. Embossed in plastic except for the trigger, I assumed the package suggested "Squeeze Here." A revving sound similar to the turning wheel on Wheel of Fortune erupted. My dad looked down at me and my Kool-Aid smile, "You sure that's what you want? I don't know about that Meek."

I nodded, "Don't worry Daddy, it has an orange tip. People won't think it's real."

My father reluctantly handed three dollars to the clerk and we made the trek back to Belmont Avenue. Flava Flav and the burglar who stole our VCR knew 911 was a joke. *I bet his ass won't be laughing when he sees this uzi though.*

Not too long afterwards, my cousin Greggy came over to spend the weekend. Everyone else called him Boo or Lil Greg. I'm not sure where or how I developed his exclusive monicker. Four months my senior, Greggy was my ace boon coon. I loved showing him my new toys, not to boast, but because I knew he'd share a mutual appreciation. Sometimes we would swap toys. "Meek I need this!" he smiled with front teeth giving away his thumb sucking addiction. As Greggy pointed the faux firearm, I made it clear the uzi was unswappable. Teddy Ruxpin or any of the Masters of the Universe were on the table, but not my gun.

Greggy's fascination led me to believe John-John, Skip, and Bob would find my submachine gun impressive as well. So one Saturday, while my parents slept in, I decided not to patrol the block on my precious big wheel, I would lay down the law with my weapon instead. I creeped through the hallway and out the door to the street. Bingo… at twelve o'clock Skip was standing by the curb facing the street with his back to me. Somehow he didn't hear me come out the building, so I was able to sneak up behind him. I pushed the uzi into Skip's rib cage. "Run your pockets," I shouted, attempting to put bass in my voice. He froze then slowly started taking his hands out of his black leather jacket. Right before I could shout, "Haha, I gotcha," he turned around and I realized it wasn't Skip. The error was potentially fatal. Mortified I confessed, "I'm sorry, I thought you were my friend. I was just playing."

Pissed, the stranger retorted, "You lucky you a little nigga. You almost got smoked. Don't nobody care if your gun got an orange tip on it. You better watch yourself out here you little motherfucker."

In the words of Jeru The Damaja, this was "Homicide Central - East New York." People were getting shot everyday. Sirens blared around the clock. The 80s crack epidemic turned East New York into a war zone. Despite hearing gunshots in the distance at night, I hadn't considered that myself, innocent, and far from being a gangster, could be a victim. The "Skip" incident was my wakeup call. Nobody's safe. I wasn't invincible. I didn't want to end up on Eyewitness News. So I started leaving the fake uzi in the toybox. Thinking back on the incident, I'm astonished toy guns that looked so authentic were so readily available. Perhaps we were being purposely desensitized to the instruments of Black genocide. Perhaps our plight was being exploited. All I know is I couldn't find toy uzis at FAO Schwartz in Manhattan.

***

I'd hold Renée's hand the entire seven blocks from our apartment on Belmont Avenue to the daycare on Pitkin, and I loved every minute. Nas once rhymed, "Your mother's the closest thing to God that you ever have kid." It was in these moments I felt that most. She'd kiss me goodbye and I'd watch her walk to the end of the block to catch the A train at Shepherd Avenue. I was always sad to see her go because I knew I wouldn't see her again until late in the evening. But she was determined to end the struggle for our family.

So my mother would whisk off to her administrative assistant job at Towers Perrin in Midtown. My dad had a long commute to his job at the VA Hospital in The Bronx, so him bringing me to school was never an option. He was long gone in our tinted Grand Prix before I awoke.

That would leave afternoon responsibilities to my mother's little sister, Jonelle. A street smart teenager, she'd pick me up from daycare after her school's dismissal. As we made our way down Pitkin Avenue to Grandma Gloria's house, she'd embrace the opportunity to toughen up her sensitive little cousin. I didn't want to be toughened up though. I just wanted to eat five cent swedish fish and pecan twirls. But we lived in East New York, Jonelle knew being a punk provided no benefits. She'd tease and taunt me all the way home. She'd use foul language. Jonelle was wild to me. She felt no shame in wearing a shower cap in public to protect her Jheri Curl. She's the first person I knew who didn't give a fuck. Sometimes I'd complain to Grandma Gloria about Jonelle's obscenities on the way home from school. Upon the realization snitching to Grandma would only intensify the torment, I learned to roll with Jonelle's behavior.

After growing some thicker skin, I even looked forward to heading home with her. I knew the afternoon shenanigans would ultimately culminate with watching Video Music Box, required viewing for young, Black Brooklynites. Every afternoon at 3pm DJ Ralph McDaniels would deliver the Hip Hop gospel. The latest dance moves, music videos, controversies, and Hip Hop politics invaded the screen. Video Music Box was sixty minutes of heaven for me and Jonelle. It's how we learned to do the Wop and the Roger Rabbit. Watching Whodini, Slick Rick, Rob Bass, Eric B. & Rakim, and all of the hottest artists in the game influence our culture was magical. And Video Music Box wouldn't only show their videos, it would also show highlights from their club performances and parties. It made me hate being too young to attend. I longed for the day I'd get to party with rappers, and wear the flashiest clothes, and give my friends shout outs on the microphone.

At daycare, me and the other kids would take turns reciting the latest raps we learned from Video Music Box, Kiss FM, and WBLS. Epifanio challenged me to recite a new rap every week. "I bet you don't know Top Billin" he'd say. I'd hit him with:

> "MC am I people call me Milk
> When I'm bustin' up a party I feel no guilt
> Gizmo's cuttin', up for the
> Suckers that's, down with me
> The One of us, that's how I feel
> To be down you must appeal
> To the Two, we're rated R
> We're gifted, and we're going far
> Down the road, to the bank
> While I'm here I'd like to thank
> Mom and dad, they knew the time
> Gizmo's scratching Milk Dee's rhyming
> Milk is chillin', Giz is chillin'
> What more can I say? Top billin.'"

Audio Two's "Top Billin" was the first rap song I memorized bar for bar. Despite my dad being a DJ, I fashioned I might make a decent emcee someday. Rappers seemed to get all the fame and love. Their opinions determined what was cool, what was wack, and what was played out. The excitement I felt when "Santa Claus" delivered my wish list requests of The Fat Boys' *Crushin* and The Beastie Boys' *License to Ill* is unquantifiable. Like Big said "I'd let my tape rock / til my tape popped." I'm sure I wore my parents thin with requests to relisten to the cassettes.

Most of the kids at the Pitkin Avenue Daycare didn't own their own cassettes. I saved every quarter I found on the curb and every dollar Grandpa Joe gave me to buy my own albums. That gave me an advantage in memorizing the latest tunes. Not only could I whoop all my classmates in Simon and Connect Four, I could turn into Milk Dee at the drop of a dime. I thought I was the coolest kid at daycare until a bully punched me in the mouth and busted my lip. Her name was Ramona Griffin. I did nothing to provoke her. I just remember being lined up behind her, as our teacher walked us down the hall from class to the recess room. Maybe she thought I touched her butt, I don't know. All I remember is her right hook connecting with my bottom lip. I ran to a nearby water fountain and saw the blood drip into the sink. "That's what you get messing with little girls," my teacher said. I was embarrassed. Everyone was tougher than me. Sick of being perceived as soft, I went home and practiced scowling in the mirror until I developed my Brooklyn face, my first line of defense.

Shortly thereafter, I enrolled at P.S. 345, one block behind the daycare center. Empty crack vials with Skittle colored plastic tops littered the school yard. Bobby McFerrin's "Don't Worry, Be Happy" was charting, though I delved further into Hip Hop. Through allowance I saved up enough money to buy Biz Markie's *Goin' Off* cassette, my first self album purchase. I really wanted a Walkman so I could listen to my tapes on the way to and from school, but my mom was adamant it'd make me go deaf. So I'd have to wait what seemed an eternity to get home and finally rap along to "The Vapors."

At school I liked my first grade teacher, Ms. Irizarry. She came up with a clever song to get my class' attention any time we were out of order. "Stop... Look... Listen to Ms. Irizarry talking..." she'd sing over and over until everyone focused their attention on her. I liked school and I would do whatever it took to earn Ms.

Irizarry's Teddy Grahams. In a school zoned for poor and lower income kids I became a target. P.S. 345 students knew how to fight better than they knew how to add and subtract. I was in a building full of Ramona Griffins. My Brooklyn scowl wasn't intimidating enough. To protect myself, I made up a story about being in a gang. On numerous occasions my dad had told me about being a member of the Baby Skulls while growing up in The Bronx. So I figured I'd not only impress him with my "gang initiation," I'd also convince my classmates I was a dangerous little man. I purchased a small gold rope chain from a twenty-five cent machine on the way home with Jonelle one afternoon. The chain looked authentic, the only thing that gave it away was the green ring it'd leave on your neck if you wore it longer than ten minutes. I was smart enough not to wear the chain around my neck. When my parents finally picked me up from Grandma Gloria's house I bragged about the new chain I was gifted for joining a gang at school. My dad grinned for half a second before my mom went ballistic. "What the hell is wrong with you?! You think this is a game Meek? Who are these guys?!" she screamed.

"Some kids that came up to me after school. They had on leather jackets and they said I could be down with their gang and they gave me this. I don't know their names," I explained.

"I know you're not stupid enough to join no gang! I'll be meeting with your teacher tomorrow morning," she fumed.

The very next day I tried to convince my mom that the gang thing wasn't a big deal and she should calm down. She wasn't having any of it. We made it to school in record time. Ms. Irizarry was shocked to learn of my new gang membership. She told my mom I was the most gifted student she had seen in years and it was probably a good idea for me to test for the gifted and talented program at P.S. 159. It was a better school and it would most likely keep me out of trouble. My mom arranged for the testing and I knocked it out the park.

P.S. 159 had a lot of history. Built in 1907 by prominent East New York developer Isaac Pitkin, the brick, four-story, box shaped building wreaked of tradition and antiquity. I started second grade in 159's Exceptionally Talented (E.T.) program. Immediately, I noticed my teachers seemed more serious and my classmates more disciplined, engaged, and eager to learn. It felt amazing to sit amongst other swift learners. Finally my intellectual hunger was fed. I started learning Spanish, which I always felt guilty about not knowing, considering my Panamanian heritage. I even performed in a bilingual play with my classmates - "Un Día De Paseo." Being in the E.T. program, my classmates and I were mostly insulated from the "regular" kids, except during lunch. In the cafeteria I noticed kids seemed to whisper and snicker behind my back. "Raheem don't sit with him… he's one of those E.T. niggas!"

After school, Jonelle would pick me up for the four block walk to Grandma Gloria's house on the corner of Euclid and Belmont. I'd watch the "regular" kids pile into their parent's Nissan Maximas blaring "Smooth Operator" or "So Wat Cha Sayin." Maximas were like Bentleys back then. Often the kids would pull off while hurling the word "nerd" as an insult from the backseat. I couldn't understand why being smart was so despised.

***

"When people ask you who your favorite rapper is make sure to tell them Slick Rick, aight Meek? Slick Rick is the nicest out!" Uncle Dwayne would try to drill into my head. To appease him I'd nod in approval, knowing KRS-One was obviously the best, but I was elated to have any Hip Hop conversation with my elders. Hip Hop connected us across generations through music, vernacular, fashion, and even hair. High top fades came into style around 1989/1990. There was a strong Afrocentric vibe going on in Hip Hop around that time. Hand sewn African medallions hung from every kids' neck. I'd see guys walking around with designs and sometimes colors dyed into their intricately sculpted haircuts. Dudes wore their high tops like the proud head dress of Egyptian Pharaohs. I had to get one. The caesars and regular fades I'd get at Bautista's Barbershop with my dad just didn't cut it any more.

Dwayne said he had a friend named Zack up the street on Sutter who was "nice with the clippers." His clientele included EPMD, Big Daddy Kane and Special Ed. I was sold. I remember the walk down Euclid Avenue towards Zack's crib like it was yesterday. In between idolizing Slick Rick and bragging about the latest dancehall sensations, Dwayne would tell me, "Nobody will pay you like you pay yourself, remember that Meek. You gotta have your own hustle like Zack." We finally arrived at Zack's crib and lining the walls of the dimly lit brownstone were hand drawn three-dimensional prototypes of high top fades. I felt like I was in a Hip Hop art gallery. After gawking at each sketch in awe, I was finally led to the barber chair. To my amazement, Zack, one of the most revered barbers in Brooklyn, cut hair out of his bedroom. Post-haircut Polaroids autographed by Hip Hop's most popular rappers adorned Zack's mirror.

"So what do you want?" he shot to me and my uncle.

"Just do something dope," I responded.

"Okay. I've been wanting to try this idea called the high-low," Zack explained.

I nodded my head in approval. While Zack sized up my little skull, he conversed with Dwayne about Cypress Hills' most notorious thug, King Tut. "Yo that nigga robbed the Kingdom Hall!" Zack exclaimed.

"The Jehovah Witness joint?" Dwayne asked.

"Yes, he been wildin for a minute. Matter fact, let's stop talking bout that nigga… I don't even want the roaches saying I said some shit about Tut," Zack laughed.

In no time he was spinning me around to the mirror to look at my one-of-a-kind cut. The high low ended up being a mid range flat top, rounded on the edges. Zack threw in a half moon part for good measure. The haircut exceeded my expectations. Class photos were the next day and set against the blue and pink laser background, my arrogant grin emerged from the pride I had in my hair.

After taking the freshest elementary school pic ever, my parents told me we'd be leaving Brooklyn for The Bronx. We were moving on up, to a deluxe apartment in the sky… of Co-op City. My mom's division with Towers Perrin relocated from Midtown to Westchester, twenty miles north. Commuting from East New York was a two hour debacle. As well, my dad had already worked at the Bronx VA for years. Moving to Co-op City made the most sense in minimizing my parents' commute. Hearing them describe living in a highrise next to the Hutchinson River made me teem with excitement. I was finally going to get my own room and not have to share a bunk with Sabree - *too hype!*

I Am A Black Man 36

Coney Island 1988

CHAPTER THREE

SECTION 5

There's a war goin' on outside no man is safe from
You could run, but you can't hide forever.
- Prodigy (Mobb Deep) "Survival of the Fittest"

We moved into Apartment 6F at 2420 Hunter Avenue in the winter of 1989. A few inches of snow covered the ground. My father leaned over his right shoulder to parallel park the Grand Prix in a tight spot while "Fight The Power" played. I remember looking up at the twenty-six-story red brick building in awe. To the left was a long twenty-four-story brown brick building, to the right there was an identical brown brick building. Within walking distance I could see countless other gigantic red, brown, and tan brick buildings. But this wasn't like the projects where Momma lived. These buildings were more stylish. The lobby of the building was clean, with spotless, buffed floors. There was no pee in the elevator to tiptoe around. In fact, the elevator smelled pleasant like the ones where my mom worked in Midtown. When I stepped off the elevator onto the sixth floor fluorescent lighting and yet another clean hallway emerged. As I followed my dad to our new abode, I heard the door from 6C creak open behind me. "Hi, we're your neighbors," revealing three skittish, middle-aged women, all sisters. Seconds later their door closed and the locking sounds of three separate deadbolts echoed through the hall. Shocked, I reeled, *They're white? Wow, we've made it out the hood.*

That thought was even further solidified once my dad unlocked the front door to reveal our new pad. My mom had already beat us there and was in the kitchen cooking. She kissed us all and wore a smile from ear to ear. "Christmas in Hollis" was playing on WBLS near the stove. Impressed with the wooden floors and spaciousness of the three-bedroom apartment I couldn't contain my excitement, "Where's my room?! Where's my room?!" I ran down the hallway past the two bathrooms to see my new digs. Upon entering, a large window overlooking the New England Thruway caught my attention. A significant upgrade from the back alley I grew accustomed to scanning in East New York, my days of watching for the VCR burglar were behind me. My new life would be great.

A few days later my dad would depart on his new intra-Bronx commute only to discover our car missing. It was not parked in a tow away zone, someone had stolen it. We couldn't believe it. The Grand Prix was a huge source of pride for our family. We left behind the chaos of East New York only to be robbed of our dignity in Co-op City. The police eventually found the car vandalized and in poor condition, a complete loss. Heartbroken but refusing to remain without a vehicle, my father saved up to buy lemon after lemon in the following months. First, there was a white 1985 Delta 88 coupe that lasted about a year, followed by a sky blue 1984 Buick LeSabre, and a navy 1991 Cadillac DeVille.

Life in Co-op City turned out to be more of an adjustment than we all expected. The Hutchinson River Parkway created a physical boundary between our nine building portion of Co-op City and the other twenty-six buildings comprising the world's largest cooperative complex. We lived in Section 5, Co-op City's black sheep. People would sing praises about Co-op City until you told them you lived in Section 5. Section 5's reputation for being thuggish lingered throughout The Bronx. Co-op City's outcasts and lower middle class residents were exiled there, so as not to disturb the good working class folks living in the other four sections.

We soon had affirmations the Section 5 folklore might be accurate. "Fifth City," scrawled in graffiti and permanent markers, appeared in stairwells, on street signs, and park benches, despite the general cleanliness of the community. The Caucasian family below us in 5F were lunatics. Often, sleep was disrupted by Fat Pat cursing out her husband at the top of her lungs. Many times it sounded like the WWF's Royal Rumble taking place under my feet. Sometimes I could decipher the voices in arguments between their drugged out teenagers Missy and Mikey. Too often my room would shake from the sheer brutality of their physical conflicts. The funny thing is Fat Pat considered herself Hunter Avenue's overseer. Bearing an eery resemblance to the Teenage Mutant Ninja Turtles' nemesis Krang, Fat Pat faithfully occupied one of the red wooden benches in front of our building. She would size up every passerby to gossip and talk shit about everybody in the neighborhood.

In contrast to the hell Fat Pat and her family raised below my feet, just above my head in 7F was the incredible Crouch family. I loved going upstairs to the Crouch's, they were good people. Headed by WWII vet and community leader, George Crouch, the Crouch's were pleasant, well educated, and compassionate. George Crouch was a strong advocate for community building, so he would often invite my family upstairs for soul food and politics. Gail, the matriarch, was bright, beautiful, and twenty years younger than Mr. Crouch. Her demeanor resembled the light-skinned Aunt Viv from TV's Fresh Prince of Bel-Air. Their daughter Tanya was tall, shaped like a coke bottle, and drop-dead gorgeous. She dated Greg Nice from Nice N' Smooth. Tanya's little brother, Eddie, a heavy-set, jovial, Michael Jackson fanatic, was one grade my senior in school. While our parents chatted over Connecticut sweet corn and pigs feet, Eddie and I bonded over Nintendo, music, and sports. I felt lucky to know another Black kid who loved baseball.

I admired how Eddie's dad, Mr. Crouch, had personal relationships with our local politicians. Prior to meeting Mr. Crouch, politics weren't a mainstay of my interests. Like most kids in New York, I was only familiar with the faces of Ronald Reagan and Ed Koch. Outside of them, I could recall raising my hand in Ms. Irizarry's first grade class when she asked, "Who thinks Michael Dukakis will win the Presidential election against George Bush?" That was the extent of my political engagement until Mr. Crouch shared how connected he was to our local Assemblymen and others. Mr. Crouch held sway in the community. He had enough political clout to get Eddie enrolled in Co-op City's top rated elementary school, P.S. 153 in Section 1. I was on my own at Section 5's P.S. 160.

By pure coincidence, my new second grade teacher at P.S. 160 would also be a Crouch, with no relation to my upstairs neighbors. Ms. Crouch was a petite, White woman in her late twenties with frazzled, blonde hair. Off the strength of her name I figured she had to be a good person - she was a Crouch. It didn't take long for me to realize she was nothing like the Crouch's that lived above me. She was short tempered and spent whole class periods yelling at the Black and Latino boys in the room. Due to mid year relocation, I was placed back in regular ed, as my new school district declined to acknowledge my gifted and talented designation. Ms. Crouch's class was the polar opposite of the nurturing school environment I had just left in Brooklyn. Emotionally abusive is the only way to describe going to school with her at the helm. I struggled to understand why Ms. Crouch taught at all, since it was so obvious she hated us as much as she hated the job. In East New York my report cards were perfect, yet somehow the twenty mile move turned me into a student nuisance overnight. Red "N's" for "Needs Improvement" filled the boxes next to "Shows Self-Control" and the other behavioral categories on the first report card I received in Ms. Crouch's class. "What the hell is going on at school Meek?!" my mother exclaimed. I was just as baffled as she was. To my recollection I never posed a disciplinary problem in Ms. Crouch's classroom. She always had a shitty attitude and lumped all the Black boys into one disorderly group of thugs. The only people who could excuse Ms. Crouch's performance were school to prison pipeline proponents.

    Alvin, a wiry, green-eyed, light-skinned kid from Down South, was also a target of Ms. Crouch's prejudice. Well mannered and intentioned, he favored Cuba Gooding Jr. in Boyz In The Hood. He had a perfect white smile, a six pack (yes, in second grade), and a pure Georgia accent. Bold kids made fun of his southern drawl. That never worked out well for them; Alvin fought like a rooster in a cockfight when pressured. One time, Alvin came to my rescue, right as I was to be pummeled by an invariably angry, bushy-haired kid named Jamahl. The only thing I knew about the kid was his dad wasn't in the picture and he stayed with his grandma, Ms. Dolly. For no apparent reason Jamahl hated my guts, and seeing my intelligence as a weakness, picked on me relentlessly. He set an appointment to whoop my ass after school one afternoon. When the door for dismissal flung open, he wasted no time tripping me over his outstretched leg and slamming me down to the concrete. Kids swarmed as we tussled. Having never been in a fight, I found myself disoriented and out of my element. As Jamahl cocked back to draw potency for an overhand right, out of nowhere Alvin intercepted him with a straight left hand to the jaw. Jamahl reeled from the blow, but Alvin continued to slug him, pushing him back a few feet with each punch. Holding my bloody, scraped elbow, I stood up to watch Alvin and Jamahl rumble to the opposite end of the schoolyard. Embarrassed, I was relieved to have the school's attention off of me. But I knew the right thing to do was repay Alvin by helping him kick Jamahl's ass. Before I could summons the energy to race across the schoolyard, the police intervened. Thank God. The most I could have done was embarrass myself further. I repaid Alvin with loyal friendship over the course of the school year, leaving Jamahl to scowl from a safe distance. At the end of the semester, Alvin's mother moved the family back to Georgia, where she felt it was safer for her boys. We stayed in touch and on a family roadtrip to visit my mom's friend Jackie in Alpharetta, we even had a brief opportunity to reconnect. Alvin was happier in the south and wished me luck in dealing with New York's chaos.

Before Alvin left, I also befriended classmate Luis Nieves, a half Puerto Rican, half Mexican kid who lived on the fourth floor of my building. Everyone called him Louie. In the mornings before the doors opened to let us in school, Louie would show off his arm by beaming kids' rear ends with hand balls during furious rounds of "Booties Up." Occasionally, I would fail to catch a ball as it careened off the limestone façade of P.S. 160. Once a ball was fumbled, the objective called for sprinting as fast as you could to a chalk inscribed penalty box and tapping it while proclaiming "Booties!" At any point in this process, another player could recover your rebound and launch the ball at your body. If hit by another player prior to tapping the penalty box and shouting "Booties," the hit player would have to bend forward, hands touching the wall, to receive a penalty pelting from each player in the game. Anticipating the sting Louie would leave as he wound up to hurl precision fastballs was abuse enough; but then one had to suffer the impact. I admired Louie's rocket arm and figured he'd be a great person to talk baseball with. I was right. Louie had aspirations to be a Hall of Fame pitcher and played organized baseball for Co-op City Little League. Perfect - I wanted to be down. The season didn't start until the spring though.

When I wasn't facing the wrath of Ms. Crouch or dodging handballs in the schoolyard, I was fixated on Tiffany Mercado. Her golden brown skin, chinky eyes, and perfect smile were overwhelming. She was the most beautiful girl I had ever seen. I would watch her from my peripherals as she squinted to read the chalkboard. Tiffany seemed significantly more mature than the rest of us second graders and kept to herself most of the time. Her mysteriousness intrigued me. I also found it intimidating and therefore difficult to let her know how hard I was crushing. She was the kind of second grader that got the fourth graders' attention. I didn't have a shot, so I kept my distance. Coincidentally, we would end up in the same class until 4th grade, and the same school until 8th grade.

In the midst of admiring Tiffany one morning a voice mocked, "You ain't never gonna get that!" and trailed off in laughter. I turned around to see a brown-skinned, unibrowed kid in coke bottle glasses grinning at me a few seats behind. His name was Darryl Roberts, a certified class clown. He had two younger sisters and lived in building 31, bordering the train tracks on Erskine Place. Hopped up on Sour Power, Darryl rarely found productive uses for his sugar highs. Right when the class needed comic relief from Ms. Crouch's doldrums, Darryl would step in like a court jester. He was the king of "Yo Mama" jokes and I admired his use of humor to neutralize threats. I incorporated this tactic into my arsenal and we became friends.

The following year, Darryl ended up in my class again. We were fortunate to draw Ms. Crawford's 3rd grade class; she was the complete opposite of Ms. Crouch. Ms. Crawford was Black, gorgeous, patient, and caring. Her dimples and raspy, yet sweet, intelligent voice hypnotized me. "N's" in "Needs Self Control" were replaced by "E's," for excellent, under Ms. Crawford. What a difference a teacher makes in a child's development. Had I enrolled in another class with a teacher like Ms. Crouch, there's a good chance I may have checked out of school altogether mentally. Nonetheless, the universe gave me Ms. Crawford; I fell back in love with school again.

Darryl and I ended up going to Iglesia Evangelica's after school program in the Einstein Loop Community Center, where mischief ensued. The after school program operated in the same room Iglesia Evangelica rented for its Methodist church services. Naturally, most of the kids and staff were Latino. Darryl and I were two of merely a handful of Black students there. Elsewhere in the community center YAK, a predominantly Black after school program, claimed most of our other classmates. After due diligence, my mother decided the Christian based program would be better for my development. Outside of the dry services we endured at Brooklyn's St. Lydia's from time to time, I had a shaky religious foundation. Iglesia Evangelica promised to promote basic Biblical principles in the most subtle ways possible. Instead of secular books, we read children's Bible stories. Unlike YAK, rap was banned at Iglesia Evangelica in favor of Spanish gospel music. Since we weren't fluent in Spanish, Darryl and I tuned out the music, teaming up instead to tell jokes and reenact In Living Color. Other times we would form a cipher and freestyle, taking turns on the beatbox. Darryl believed we could be the next Kid N' Play and get rich one day rapping for sellout crowds.

He always had a get rich quick scheme. When third grade rolled around, Darryl, being the enterprising Negro he was, became the Sour Power plug. The tart sugar coated tubes were a hot commodity in Section 5. The only place that sold them was a deli in Einstein Loop directly across the street from P.S. 160. One morning Darryl defied school rules, which demanded we remain in the schoolyard once dropped off by parents, and snuck out in pursuit of Sour Power. The deli sold each flavored strand for ten cents. Darryl would flip them for twenty-five cents in class. I watched as he slipped undetected past 160 personnel and out the gated schoolyard. I turned my attention back to the intense two-hand touch football game at hand. A cocky Puerto Rican kid named Isaiah Martinez, better known as Munchie, was drawing up a play for me in his palm with his index finger. Suddenly I heard a loud boom and the whole schoolyard ran towards the fence. My stomach dropped when I saw the commotion. A short yellow school bus hit Darryl as he raced across the street for Sour Power. Louie and my new homie, Naeem Kingston, described how Darryl flew twenty feet in the air before hitting the pavement. Instinctively, Darryl sprung up and made it to safety on the sidewalk before passing out. An ambulance came within minutes and I clung to the fence staring at Darryl's lifeless body. That was the first time I prayed for anything other than food, toys, Tiffany Mercado or Ms. Crawford to fall in love with me. Darryl opened his eyes as the paramedics loaded him onto a stretcher. Besides a massive knot on his forehead, Darryl sustained no life threatening injuries. God was real.

    As much as Darryl thanked his lucky stars for not dying in the bus accident, I'm sure he doubted God's existence the following day when he got roasted at school. P.S. 160's students were unrelenting, "This nigga got hit by the short bus!" as fingers pointed and hysterical laughter ensued. Still, as brutal as the kids were, they were no match for Mrs. Taylor, the Assistant Principal's, verbal assault that morning. She was a hulking, dark-skinned disciplinarian with piercing eyes. I always believed she could have been James Brown's sister. After parents dropped their kids off in the schoolyard, she would make totalitarian threats through her white megaphone.

    Like Morgan Freeman in *Lean on Me* she'd shout, "Slow down! Get away from that fence! Everyone line up to go in the building… NOW!" Mrs. Taylor would have made an excellent drill sergeant. That morning, as Mrs. Taylor guided third graders up the staircase to our second floor classrooms, she broke protocol and stopped everyone at the first landing. "I want everyone to stop and look at this foolish Negro right here," pointing at Darryl. "As you are all aware, this clown disregarded all of my rules, snuck out the schoolyard, and got hit by the little school bus… for some Goddamn Sour Power!" As much as everyone wanted to laugh we were all too scared to crack a smile. And then Mrs. Taylor continued, "My job is to keep you all alive when you're on this property. The news is saying you ain't supposed to live to see twenty-one out here. I'm trying to protect you from bullets, drugs, and killers, but you want to go kill yourself for some Goddamn candy? I got half a mind to strangle you my damn self… cause you're so stupid… you don't think. Let that big ass knot on your head be a reminder to use your brain!" I'll never forget those words and I'm sure Darryl never forgot either. More than anything, the accident damaged his ego. Darryl became a little more reclusive. While he dealt with the emotional consequences of his actions, I hung out with Naeem more.

    Naeem was rail thin like me. His dark gums matched the pigment of his skin in sharp contrast to his bright white teeth. We both loved A Tribe Called Quest, so I'd jokingly refer to him as Naeema Applebum, unaware Applebum referred to a woman's derriere. Naeem loved Air Jordans because that's all his high school brother wore. He kept his pairs of Air Jordan VI's and VII's immaculately groomed with a toothbrush. I wore what my parents could afford, Etonics, New Balance, and occasionally Nike. Naeem forced me to step my sneaker game up. The frequency with which our favorite rappers and athletes rocked Jordans, Bo Jacksons, and Barkleys hit my radar. These trends trickled down into the P.S. 160 schoolyard causing non-adopters to be clowned decades before "What are those?!" was trending.

Naeem's older brother, Troy, always carried a Walkman and wore headphones around his neck. Him and his crew of Truman High School students wore fatigue jackets and jungle hats daily. It's as if they were preparing for war. But Naeem's mom was very well educated and socially conscious. She preached about us being alert in New York City's war zone. She enjoyed having me and his brother's friends over because it meant we were safe. "Ya need to understand you're an endangered species," she would profess to our sighs and eye rolls.

I'll never forget the night I realized *there really was* a war going on outside. It was June 7, 1992. Troy and his crew were sitting outside a bench behind my building late, around two A.M. It was so late that the typical noise from passing city buses and people blasting music from their apartments was absent. As a result, the snickers and jokes being told on the bench were amplified in the night's silence. From my sixth floor apartment, the crew's voices were almost discernible. My bedroom faced the front of my building, yet I could still hear their banter from the bench behind the building. I finally drifted off to sleep before two thundering gun shots snapped me out of slumber. Across the hall, the light in my parents' bedroom sprang on and they rushed to the kitchen. I followed behind them to see what was going on. Through the trees, we could see a teenager with his arms spread wide along the top of the bench. His head tilted back as if he was gazing at the moon. His eyes were still open. In the center of his forehead was a quarter sized black hole. My mother was frantic, "Don don't let him see that. Meek get away from the window!" I stepped back from the window, but it was too late, the memory of murder could not be forgotten.

Word on the street indicated the killing was retaliation by kids from The Valley for conflicts that frequently arose between them and Section 5 kids at Truman High School. The eight lanes of the New

England Thruway were the only thing separating The Valley From Co-op City. One hundred feet of space in distance, yet worlds apart in perspective. Gary Gonzalez, the kid that got killed, was the best friend of Naeem's brother Troy. The rest of the crew narrowly escaped death, and any of them could have met the same fate had the bullet traveled a few inches to the left or right. Gary was a year older and was apparently telling the rest of the crew how exciting college was when it went down. Fellow writer and Section 5 alum, Miles Marshall Lewis, detailed Gary's murder on page thirty-seven of 2004's *Scars of the Soul Are Why Kids Wear Bandages When They Don't Have Bruises*:

> "Gary Gonzalez, a former Truman High School acquaintance, sat trading college stories at two-thirty A.M. with four friends on benches in the back of his building at Hunter Avenue on June 7, 1992, when a roving crew of fifteen to twenty from the Valley approached. Nineteen-year-old Gonzalez spoke of transferring from the New York Institute of Technology to the City College of New York and switching his major to architecture as the thick posse fired gunshots outside a nearby Red Lobster, and again at a passing bus entering Killer Curve. Listening to his homeboy Joe Resto compare living in New Jersey with his former residence in Section Five, Gary Gonzalez was suddenly shot in the head by a bullet that ripped through the shirt of another friend. The bullet that entered 'was in a sensitive area and could not be removed' at Jacobi Medical Center, according to the local *Co-op City Times*. Detective George Wood of the Forty-fifth Precinct determined the incident was a 'senseless, random shooting - no words were exchanged.' I remember Gary Gonzalez as a pretty boy whose attention from females sparked envy in his peers, the very picture of the kid who 'never did nothing to

nobody.' I remember him as a pitcher, shortstop, and co-captain of the Mustangs high school baseball team; in fact, he shared the number seven with Leonard Nelson, another tragically killed classmate, crushed to death on December 28, 1991 in a stampede at the infamous City College celebrity basketball game in which Sean Combs and rapper Heavy D were held partially responsible by Judge Louis Benza for the deaths of nine and injuries of twenty-nine. Certainly Gary Gonzalez, as innocent in his own way as baby Kharel Slade, did not deserve to die. My homeboy from high school was guilty only of a childhood in Co-op City." [1]

For Naeem's mom, this was the final straw. She resolved to flee the war zone and moved her boys to San Jose, California. I never saw Naeem again.

In Naeem's absence I resolved to playing baseball with Louie and Eddie as much as possible. Darryl had a noodle arm, so he was exempt from the circle. Whether it was throwing on the greenway behind our building, or batting practice with tennis balls in the P.S. 160 schoolyard, we played baseball every day. Our fathers got in on the action too. In anticipation of my first season with Co-op City Little League, my dad would take me outside to practice over the shoulder catches and work on ground ball mechanics. Along with Louie's dad, he volunteered to coach my first team - the Townhouse Restaurant Wildcats. The first time I put on the grey and white uniform I felt invincible. I was a centerfielder and I felt like I was born to play the position. Catching sessions with my dad made me feel like Willie Mays reincarnated.

Saturday mornings couldn't come quick enough. The fields would open early in the morning, around seven A.M. Eagle eyed

---
[1] Lewis *Scars of the Soul*

parents filled the stands. The mouthwatering scents of pastelillos emanated from the faithful Puerto Rican food truck. Though it was Saturday, this was Co-op City's version of Friday Night Lights.

Often, I was the lead off batter, while Louie batted clean up. I dreamed of drilling homers into the Hutchinson River beyond the outfield's chain linked fence, two-hundred-fifty feet from home plate. Regrettably, I never hit a ball out of Co-op City Field, but I was still pretty good nonetheless. Along with Louie, I made the All-Star team virtually every year I played. Since Eddie was a grade above us, we never ended up on the same team. That didn't break our bond though; baseball was the backbone of our friendship. We would bike a few miles to the Turtle Cove Batting Cage on City Island whenever time allowed. I loved baseball so much that I convinced my mom to let me take my third grade class photo in my Little League uniform. Most of the other kids wore their flyest fits and thought I was weird, but Ms. Crawford admired my Braves jersey; I smiled from ear to ear in my school photo that year.

By fourth grade I considered I might have a career in baseball if my skills continued to progress at their established rate. Either that or I'd be a writer. Knowing how bored I would get while the other students struggled to keep up in class, Mrs. Jones, my fourth grade teacher, would force me to write stories to stay productive, leading to The Demetrinator series. I wrote about adventures to dark worlds ruled by the evil Robo-Dean, a moniker devised to chastise fellow classmate, Chanel Dean, who frequently highlighted my skinniness. The tales were one part *Darkwing Duck*, one part Slick Rick's "Children's Story," and one part *Robocop*. Mrs. Jones would allow me to read them in class on Friday afternoons and I loved having a captive audience that hung on my every word and laughed at my juvenile humor. Like Mrs. Crawford, I could tell that Mrs. Jones believed in me. I hoped to impress her enough to meet her goddaughter Shanice, singer of the hit single "I Love Your Smile." I didn't feel slighted when I settled for an autographed picture though, I knew Mrs. Jones tried. Mrs. Jones recognized my potential and collaborated with my mother to have me tested for entry into the "Exceptionally Gifted" program at Pablo Casals' Intermediate School 181. Like I had in Brooklyn a few years prior, I killed the test. I was excited to head to classes that actually challenged my intellect, but I knew it meant missing Darryl, Louie, and the rest of my friends' daily hijinks.

CHAPTER 4

MEEK THA FREAK

Original rude boy, never am I coy
You can be a shorty in my ill convoy
Not to come across as a thug or a hood
But hon, you got the goods, like Madelyne Woods
By the way, my name's Malik
The Five-Foot Freak
-Phife Dawg (A Tribe Called Quest) "Electric Relaxation"

Although I knew I earned a spot in the gifted program, I was unaware of the criteria used to distribute students between Co-op City's two middle schools, M.S. 180 and I.S. 181. When I entered Ms. Bialo's "Exceptionally Gifted (E.G.)" fifth grade class I was one of two Section 5 kids in a room of thirty-three. Curiously, the other students matriculated from either P.S. 153, Co-op City's higher ranked elementary school, or P.S. 83, a school twenty minutes away surrounded by nice, brick, two-story homes. The higher degree of racial diversity was noticeable as well. More than half of the "Exceptionally Gifted" class was White, Middle Eastern, and Asian. Our ambition and reputation for being scholars united us, nonetheless. All the brainiacs, geeks, and high achievers east of the Bronx Zoo found insulation from subpar teachers, delinquents, and shitty curriculum here. It wasn't until decades later when I learned about education tracking in *Waiting for Superman* that I realized how that happened. We were on the fast track while the public school system had given up on my basic track peers. If it wasn't for Mrs. Jones, my prospects for success would have been limited.

Being new to the gifted program, I naturally gravitated towards people with similar interests - Hip Hop, baseball, and video games. It wasn't hard to find people like me in Ms. Bialo's fifth grade class. A short brown-skinned kid, Akil Myers, and the Gower twins, James and Jameel, all fit the bill. Akil's parents were from Barbados and his small stature made him a great second baseman. The Gower twins, known for their signature braided tails protruding from the base of their scalps, were perennial All-Stars. Their dad was one of the more respected coaches at Co-op City Little League. During lunch we took turns creating beats on tables and freestyling.

Although he wasn't a Hip Hop head, I also befriended a tall, awkward, copper-toned Puerto Rican kid named Nelson Lopez. Nelson didn't live in Co-op City, but rather in a safe enclave on Allerton Avenue. He came over from P.S. 83 and lived in a two-story home with his little brother and parents. Nelson was the first person I knew with the internet. His America Online dial up service was magic to me. We'd surf chat rooms with his short, fat, Italian friend Nick, who went to Catholic School and often told off color jokes. Nick was a dead ringer for the obnoxious New York transplant in Project X. Most of the time the three of us found unity through our chronic video game addiction. Nelson had subscriptions to magazines like *Nintendo Power* and we'd convene to master Metroid and Street Fighter II with his preferred music of the Red Hot Chili Peppers or Nirvana playing in the background. When we tired of video games, we laughed at Beavis & Butt-Head until we got sore throats. Nick was into Hip Hop, but he viewed it from a spoiled White boy's perspective, and that made me somewhat uncomfortable. I'd cringe inside when he recited every "nigga" Wu-Tang uttered. I never voiced my displeasure because frankly I didn't want to make things awkward. But hanging out with Nelson's faithful pal Nick often made me question whether I was a sellout. Nelson and Nick were nothing like my Black and Latino friends in Co-op City. They sported Billabong instead of Karl Kani and talked White. To maintain harmony, I kept my Ebonics to a minimum. Though it was sometimes uncomfortable, I maintained the friendship because of Nelson's unwavering loyalty.

Nelson's mother, Millie, worked for the school system and his dad was a bus driver. They were a hardworking middle class family with aspirations of greatness. I never felt I deserved the kindness Nelson and his family showed me. Nelson's mom would sometimes pick me up on the weekends and bring me, Nelson, and Nick to suburban arcades just north of The Bronx. Other times they would arrange for me to join them Upstate for rafting down pristine portions of the Hudson River. I loved the Lopez' dearly, but felt conflicted when obligated to choose between weekends with them, Nick, and alternative music, and weekends with my other friends, family and Hip Hop.

Sometimes I just wanted to dive into Black Moon or Onyx with someone who could truly relish in their gun clapping and misogyny. Someone like Frankie, a delinquent, fair-skinned Dominican kid, who lived on the twentieth floor of my building. Frankie rode the cheese bus (that's how we distinguished between school buses and mass transit) with me from Section 5 to I.S. 181 every morning. He was the kid Tony, our foul mouthed bus driver, would always catch spitting on cars from the bus window. Upon arrival at school we would go our separate ways as Frankie would disappear into his Special Ed class and I would hike the extra flight of stairs to my E.G. homeroom. When we would reconvene on the cheese bus, Frankie always had mad shit to talk about any and everybody. He was wildly unpredictable and seemed intimidating despite his diminutive frame. Maybe it was his disfigured thumbs that curved away from his hands at forty-five degree angles, or perhaps it was the fact everyone knew he was in Special Ed, that gave Frankie street cred. When push came to shove, Frankie avoided fisticuffs by any means. He dodged bodily harm by convincing opponents he wasn't in the mood to rumble that day. Jigga had Frankie in mind when he spit, "You know the type: loud as a motorbike, but wouldn't bust a grape in a fruit fight." Because we lived in the same building, Eddie, Louie, and I were the select few who knew Frankie had a sweet mom, and an extremely polite little brother, Sonnell. His father lived in Santo Domingo and he never talked about him. Frankie's mom, a nurse, looked to us to keep Frankie out of trouble, a task easier said than done. He sucked at baseball and pretty much anything that required hand eye coordination. He even sucked at video games because his thumb deformity made tapping buttons difficult. As a result, Frankie entertained himself with hooliganism.

One time Frankie successfully dared me to kick Fat Pat's door. To prove my bravery, I embraced the challenge. We entered the sixth floor staircase and tip-toed down to the fifth floor landing. Cold feet caused me to hesitate, but Frankie, being the great hood motivator he was, convinced me not to be a "bitch ass nigga" and follow through with the plan. I darted out the staircase, kicking Fat Pat's door with all the fury I suppressed on the sleepless nights faced at the hands of her dysfunctional family, and continued running down the staircase on the opposite side of the hallway. Never breaking stride or looking back, I met Frankie in the lobby where he greeted me with, "Yo, Meek, you a crazy motherfucker! I ain't think you was really gonna do it!"

Before we could go outside to plan our next caper, the elevator door opened and a fuming Fat Pat rushed off to confront us, "You think you're gonna get away with kicking my door you little bastard? I will have your little ass thrown in jail Frankie! I know it was you!" For the first time in… well… ever, Frankie wasn't the culprit though.

Arrogantly, he smiled and calmly responded, "Actually it wasn't me."

Fat Pat, sensing the sincerity in Frankie's voice, turned to me and said, "I know it wasn't you. You's a good kid. Stop hanging around with this asshole," and barged her way outside to inform the community about the crime that was perpetrated against her. Petrified of Fat Pat's volatility, I didn't regain my heartbeat until she made it all the way out the lobby.

"Frankie you better not tell anybody about this," I said.

"Of course not Meek, you know I got your back," Frankie promised.

Everything seemed to be alright until the next morning when Fat Pat came ringing my doorbell like a mad woman. Fast asleep, it rattled everyone in the household, including my parents. My mother rushed to the door pissed, yelling "Who the hell is ringing the damn bell like this?!" She swung the door open to see Fat Pat fuming with her arms crossed. "Can I help you? Why are you ringing my damn doorbell like this?" my mom exclaimed.

"Your son kicked my door yesterday and left a dent!" Fat Pat vented.

"I know my son didn't do that. How dare you bring your crazy ass up here accusing my son of something like that? I don't know what kind of mental problems y'all have downstairs, but don't come in my face with that bullshit!" my mother returned.

"Frankie told me everything. I know it was your son!" Fat Pat shouted.

Utter disbelief made my heart sink. I couldn't believe Frankie sold me out. That was the last thing I expected. "Did you kick her door Meek?" my mom asked with Fat Pat looking on from the doorway.

I shook my head, "No, I don't know what she's talking about." My mom slammed the door in Fat Pat's face.

That day as we headed out to Brooklyn to visit Greg, his wife Yvette, and my little cousins Justin, and Isaiah, at their new public housing unit in Brownsville, I felt extremely remorseful. I beat myself up all the way there. *Why was I stupid enough to kick her door?* I was concerned I had started a war between Fat Pat's lunatic family and my own. The perpetual chaos that could result from the situation made me nervous. A can of worms was opened. Worst of all, I had to live with the lie I told my mom, forever. She talked shit to my dad about the incident all the way to Brooklyn. Trust between me and Frankie was lost and our friendship was likely over.

The next day I rode the elevator up to Frankie's crib to ask him why he ratted me out. "My bad Meek. Fat Pat ran up on my moms in front of the building telling her I kicked the door. My moms came up here and told me to swear on the Bible that I didn't kick the door, so you know I had to Meek. I don't play with that God shit so I told her the truth." *This dickhead.* Frankie turned on his Nintendo and attempted to deflect my attention to Super Mario 3. I found this curious, as my Super Mario 3 cartridge had gone missing in an unsolved mystery months ago. Even though Super Nintendo commanded my immediate attention, my first generation Nintendo and games remained in play position, ready to be revisited when boredom struck. It was apparent Frankie had swiped my game at some point. Between this new revelation and snitching on me, I was through.

After that, I found excuses not to hang out with Frankie whenever he called or rang my bell. Frankie was a bad person. I was a good person; or *was* I? After all, I had just created a messy, tense situation for my family. I started praying to God nightly for forgiveness. Asking for my sins to be wiped away and believing they would brought enough solace for me to ask God for a shot with Tiffany Mercado. Worth a try I figured. As time went on, I grew concerned that I didn't know enough about how this whole God and religion thing worked though. My family didn't go to church every Sunday and visits to St. Lydia's in East New York were rare. I remember asking my dad, "What kind of Christians are we?"

Confused, he responded, "What do you mean?"

"Are we Baptists, Episcopalians, or Methodists?" I inquired.

Recalling all of his experiences going to church with Momma, my dad revealed, "We're Baptists."

I knew Eddie faithfully attended Co-op City Baptist Church in the basement of Einstein Loop's Community Center. He asked if I wanted to go with him a few times, but I chose Sunday slumber over service. Finally, I was compelled to acquire the Biblical knowledge that was apparently the key to morality and fulfillment in life. Going to Hell for being too lazy to learn the secrets of Christianity seemed negligent. Considering every rapper thanked Him on stage and wore His pendants around their necks, it made no sense not to investigate the efficacy of Jesus. Therefore, Bible study and service with Eddie every Sunday became routine. My mother and grandparents were proud. Grandma Gloria even told me I might make a good preacher one day.

The ladies that taught Bible study were church elders. At first, they found my naiveté and curiosity of The Word amusing. After I began to acquire knowledge and thoroughly question them about specific passages, I'm sure I drove them crazy. "You'll have to ask Reverend Williams about that Demetrius. I've answered it as best as I could for you dear," Sister Thomas would say. During the brief transition period between Bible Study and church service I would approach Reverend Williams. I took pride in trying to stump him, watching the wrinkles on his balding forehead, along with his eyebrows, and eyelids rise upwards as he considered a response. Impressively, he always seemed to have an explanation. Though Reverend Williams' responses didn't always answer my questions completely, I would rely on Proverbs 3:5-6 to eliminate lingering doubt: "Trust in the LORD with all your heart and lean not on your own understanding; in all your ways submit to Him, and He will make your paths straight."

Every Sunday after Bible study, I sat through the mundane service waiting for the juicy part to pop off. The majority of the congregation was elderly, or at least as old as Eddie's dad, Mr. Crouch, who would join us at church and frequently nod off as the service dragged on. The praise and worship team consisted of old crusty dusties singing off key. Sometimes they were comical. Often, I wished I could fast forward to Reverend Williams' sermon. That's where the fireworks were. I instantly woke up a few notches when Reverend Williams would ask everyone to look down into our programs and recite the verses he selected for the church that week. Seeking the secrets to limitless wisdom, I was wide eyed. Reverend Williams' command of the room captivated me. The call and response prompted by "Does the church hear me??? Say Amen!" electrified my soul. The range of furious emotions Williams would evoke from the congregation with his ascending tone and extravagant gesticulations affirmed the power of the tongue; I wanted to have that power. Even still, as Reverend Williams unraveled and decoded King James' English, I would attentively search for holes in his logic and assertions. Most of the time I could find no flaws, Reverend Williams was on point. But there were always burning questions that intrigued me enough to continue searching for legitimate answers in the Good Book. *How could evolution and the creation story coincide? Is everybody who does not accept Christ going to Hell? How does that make sense? And how can we be sure Christianity is the way to get to Heaven while all other religions have it all wrong?* If I continued to study I figured, I would find the answers to these questions.

While I pursued wisdom in church, I looked for love at school. Tiffany Mercado continued to get finer every year, so by sixth grade she was already dating high school guys. She was so far out of my league I didn't consider stepping to her on the boyfriend tip. Instead, I crushed on a thick girl named Khadijah, who coincidently looked like Queen Latifah (who played Khadijah James on the sitcom Living Single). She was a grade above me and only saw me as "the cute little nigga that rides the 28 with me to school." I thought by graduating to a bus pass from the cheese bus, I'd gained some clout; but no, not with Khadijah.

Luckily there was Monique, a thick Puerto Rican chick who adored me. She was also from Section 5. I loved her clear skin, thick, pink lips, and tig ol' bitties, which swallowed me during hugs. I'm convinced Monique was the "butter pecan Rican" Meth rapped about on Raekwon's "Ice Cream." A year my senior, she was one of the baddest chicks at 181. For reasons that defy comprehension, Monique would encourage me to kiss, grope, and massage her whenever we crossed paths. I was grateful for this physical touch, it made me feel like *the* man. Due to our age and height disparity, I knew she couldn't consider me to be a potential boyfriend, yet she playfully encouraged my flirtation and infatuation.

I remember running into her in the hall one morning during a chance bathroom break. She stopped me in front of the lockers to give me one of her typical three minute hugs; the kind that typically led to plenty of inappropriate groping. My classmate, Duane Dawson, also on a bathroom break, spotted us mid-embrace. His jaw dropped when he made eye contact with me, my hands gripping Monique's buns. In disbelief, he covered his mouth and proceeded to head to the bathroom, silently drifting by, so as not to cock block or alarm Monique. When I finally returned to class, he put his hand on my shoulder and said "I can't just call you Meek anymore. For now on it's Meek The Freak Who Did Stuff With Monique!" The class went wild, the nickname went viral, and weeks later shortened to "Meek Tha Freak."

    Feeling emboldened by my new monicker, I figured I might as well try to lock Monique down. Three motivational mirror talks later I built up the courage to ask her out. Going for the gusto, as we rode the 28 around Killer Curve from Section 5 towards Bay Plaza, I was so nervous my heart sank into my stomach.

    "Hey, do you wanna go out with me?" I mumbled.

    "What? What? Aw sweetie I'm flattered.... but no, you know we're just friends right?" she divulged.

    "Yeah, yeah, I know… I just thought..." Before I could finish my sentence she thrusted me towards her for a typical hug. Suddenly I was ok with settling for this option - with Monique. But I still wanted a girlfriend I could waste evenings with on the phone, hold hands, and brag about to my friends. The same afternoon I ran into Frankie on the bus ride home.

    "Yo Meek where you been? Why you been playing me?" he questioned.

    Finding an excuse, I redirected the angst and said, "I've just been focusing on baseball. Plus I asked Monique out, and she said no."

    Frankie genuinely felt bad for me. "Yo that's tough Meek. Just remember you're a good dude. If I was a girl I'd go out with you."

    I turned to Frankie and said "Nigga, What?!" The whole rear of the bus started laughing hysterically.

    "I ain't mean it like that… you know what I meant son!"

The next day I left determined to find a girl who would be proud to be my girlfriend. I went down my short list of candidates and determined there was one girl who was cute, in the same grade, and most of all approachable: Michelle Bailey. Michelle was a brown-skinned tomboy with long curly hair. Single strapped overalls and all, she favored Chili from TLC. Michelle was also in the sixth grade at 181, albeit in a "regular" class. She'd ride her bike with me and the fellas from Section 5 to Pelham Bay Park and play paddleball with us on the handball courts in the summer. Despite her good looks, I was never really attracted to her, she was one of the guys. But I figured a cute girlfriend was better than no girlfriend at all. Luckily, Michelle felt the same way about me. Walking into the rear entrance of Building 26 one afternoon I popped the question,

"Hey, you wanna be my girlfriend?"

"Umm, yeah, I guess so," Michelle cooly responded.

Great, I had somebody to hold hands with on the way to and from school. Michelle had more in mind though. One afternoon as we strolled into the rear lobby, Michelle asked, "Have you ever kissed somebody before?" I told her about me pressing my lips against Monique's. "No, I mean like using your tongue?" Stumped, I didn't know where to begin.

"Nah, I haven't tried that yet," I revealed.

"Well don't you want to tongue kiss me?" Michelle questioned.

"Okay, I don't know what I'm doing though," I responded.

"Really? Meek Tha Freak?!" Michelle laughed, "I'll show you, come here."

I went with the flow as she pulled me in, cocked her head to the side, and opened her mouth. Not knowing what to do, I used my tongue to lick the inside of her cheek. *This is really weird and kind of nasty. Why do people like this again?* Afterwards, Michelle comforted me saying we would practice until we got it right. But we never did, kissing Michelle never felt right. There was no spark that ignited a deeper emotional or physical connection. It just seemed like a chore and I began to hate having to kiss Michelle. When I told her I wanted to go back to being friends after a couple weeks of swapping spit, she was left aghast. The awkwardness that ensued when we later crossed paths culminated in a bunch of silent waves and head nods. Our friendship died, never to be recovered.

Still, nothing would deter me from finding the perfect woman to hold hands with through the halls of middle school. I scanned my classroom for winners, and there were several. None stood out more than Lauren Martinez, however. Lauren was a core member of what I considered my E.G. crew at 181. While the entire class grew to be tight nit, united by our common distinction as "nerds" by the general student population, a small segment of us formed an even tighter circle. We ate lunch together and sometimes met up on the weekends. That cluster consisted of Isis Semaj, Mariama Jerrell, Desiree Moore, Deirdre Massop, Akil Myers, The Gower Twins, Kodi Shay, myself, and Lauren. Although Lauren was probably half a foot taller than me and most of the boys in my class, she had a perfect smile, vibrant personality, and she was brilliant. Most of all, she loved Hip Hop as much as I did. Lauren turned me onto Digable Planets and I envisioned her as a younger Ladybug Mecca. I trusted Lauren's musical expertise so much that I even took her advice on giving the Smashing Pumpkins a try; she was right, they were dope too.

One day I realized Lauren might be the girlfriend I was looking for. What Reverend Williams meant when he said "Godly aura" fit Lauren's description more so than anyone else I knew. But, because we were such close friends, I hesitated to suggest a relationship. I knew it would be extremely awkward for me and our

E.G. crew if Lauren declined upon me asking her out. So I sat on my impulses… until I couldn't anymore. During Ms. DeBenedictis' English lecture, I reached into my Jansport to rip a sheet of looseleaf from my composition notebook. I wrote a simple note, something along the lines of "Do you want to be my girlfriend?" with a check box for "Yes" or "No." As the note slid from Akil, to Isis, to Kodi, my chest pounded. Mariama nudged Lauren, who turned to her bewildered. Out the corner of my eye I could see Lauren mouth "What is it?" as Mariama discretely slipped her the note under her desk. Lauren looked down at the note and beamed with amusement. I tried to play it cool while the note trekked back down the underground student railroad. Unfolding the paper below my desk, I was excited to see she checked "Yes," and included a smiley face under the box for good measure!

Lauren and I spent hours on the phone after school in the ensuing months. The yapping was so excessive my parents installed another line so I wouldn't tie up the phone all night. 379-CULO sounded like a phone sex line and was always good for a laugh between the few friends that had my number. Lauren and I would talk about *everything* from Wu-Tang to aliens. Even when we had nothing to talk about, we held the phone to our ears in silence until we fell asleep. Lauren commuted to 181 all the way from University Heights on the West Side of The Bronx, so the phone was essential in keeping our relationship going.

We must have spent a few thousand hours on the phone before we went on our first date. After a vigorous debate between Outbreak and Batman Forever, we settled on the caped crusader. My dad and Uncle Greg were so excited they both drove me to West Fordham Road to finally meet Lauren's parents and chaperone our first date. I had no idea what to expect as we pulled up to the three-story, brick walk up, typical of Bronx architecture outside of

Co-op City. Though I appeared harmless as a rail-thin, babyfaced, thirteen-year-old, Lauren's dad, a stern man of few words, didn't seem too thrilled to meet his baby girl's first boyfriend. He only cared to know where we were going and how soon I'd have her back. On the contrary, her mother embraced me with a suffocating hug and the same smile Lauren had obviously inherited. Her older brother Eddie shook my hand firmly, while her younger brothers, Adrian and Stephen, snickered like giddy schoolchildren waiting for their sister to catch cooties. After a few awkward minutes of me being on church behavior, we headed down to my dad's powder-blue Cutlass. Dad and Greg were both pleasantly surprised when Lauren, a tall, post-pubescent Puerto Rican girl climbed into the backseat with me. They looked at each other, then looked at me. I neglected to inform them Lauren was Puerto Rican. Unintentional, it just happened to be a detail that never came up. Blacks dating Puerto Ricans and Dominicans was such a common occurrence in The Bronx I didn't consider seeing a Latina interracial dating. I had just as many Black friends as I had Hispanic friends, so I didn't believe there was anything taboo about me and Lauren's relationship. Besides, my mom was Panamanian and her side of the family *still* spoke Spanish. "Chip! Chip! Chip! For now on I'm not calling you Meek anymore. You a chip off the old block!" Greg exclaimed. Embarrassed, I smiled at Greg hoping he wouldn't make Lauren uncomfortable with further banter. I held her hand to reassure her everything was cool. Unbothered by my dad and uncle's immaturity, she smiled. When we finally got to the Bay Plaza movie theater, my dad insisted on giving me an extra twenty dollars for popcorn and soda. I took the money then waved them off and told them I would call from a payphone for pickup at the movie's conclusion.

    Batman Forever was rated PG-13, and I was still knocking on puberty's door. As Lauren and I slowly corralled our way through the velvet stanchions, I mentally rehearsed asking for two tickets with confidence. With as much bass as I could muster, I made eye contact with the clerk and muttered, "Two tickets please." She looked at me, then looked at Lauren towering six inches above me and printed the tickets. I dug a crisp twenty dollar bill out of my pocket attempting to complete the transaction when Lauren stopped me.

"I can pay for myself," she revealed.

Dumbfounded, I insisted on performing my gentlemanly duty of paying for the film. For the first time, I saw Lauren get agitated. Her cheeks turned bright red, and she refused to let me pay for both tickets. Finally, I conceded and watched Lauren slide her money under the metal divot. Internally, I debated whether Lauren had challenged my manhood, or whether I had offended her with my traditionalism. Nonetheless, it was up the escalator to see Bruce Wayne whoop some ass. In the back of my mind, I knew the movie theater was where most teens went to let their hormones rage under the cover of darkness. For months I plotted how I would approach Lauren for our first French kiss. Though licking the inside of Michelle Bailey's cheeks had given me some experience, I had no confidence in my kissing skills. *Would kissing Lauren be as weird as kissing Michelle? What if I'm just bad at kissing and it makes Lauren hate me?* Doubts of my kissing competency kept me from attempting any tongue action prior to our date. To settle my nerves, I used the extra cash my dad gave me to buy candy and popcorn from the concession stand. Unlike the ticket counter fiasco, Lauren allowed me to treat her this time. I felt a little more manly.

Nervousness returned as we headed into the theater to watch the previews. My head pointed straight towards the screen as I cradled the popcorn bucket in my left hand and used my other hand to lock fingers with Lauren. Sensing the inevitable was near, Lauren proactively placed my arm around her shoulder once the opening credits started to roll. She rested her head on the upper part of my chest and smiled to make me feel comfortable. I finally relaxed. Batman Forever quickly got our hearts racing with action. Fans since In Living Color, we had high expectations for Jim Carrey's Riddler, and hung on his every word. With half my mind focused on tonsil hockey and the other half focused on Gotham City, I waited patiently for the right opportunity to seal the deal. But it never came. Joel Schumacher ruined everything with his corny ass rendition of Batman. The script was cheesy, the acting was horrible, and the disruptive crowd expressed displeasure at every turn. Popcorn and loud boos were hurled at the screen. I consider going in for the kill once the credits rolled, but the theater was so rowdy it would have just been awkward. So we headed for the exit and a payphone to call my dad. On the ride back to University Heights I shamed myself for being a coward.

The following Monday, word of our first date got around school. Inquiring minds wanted to know the nitty-gritty details.

"It was cool. We had a good time," I told my boys when they asked.

"Did y'all kiss? Y'all didn't mess around in the theater?" they pressed.

"Nah we just chilled. It wasn't that serious," I responded.

Later that afternoon at baseball practice, my teammate Ernest was more blunt. "Yo y'all been dating for like a year, did you suck her titties yet?" he pried.

"What? That's none of your business man," I replied.

"Nigga, I just don't understand why y'all together if you ain't trying to get freaky with her," he laughed, his chipped tooth showing. "If that was my girl I'd be all over them big ass titties. You better hope niggas don't take your girl Meek."

I laughed it off, as if I was unbothered. "Wu-Tang Clan Ain't Nuthing to Fuck With" blasted off someone's terrace onto the greenway, but for some reason Method Man's "You're All I Need To Get By" came to mind. Lauren loved the Razor Sharp Remix. I determined Ernest was right, I needed to man up and start doing more mature things with Lauren. It just felt awkward because Lauren was such a good girl and I didn't want to violate her trust or innocence. Plus I didn't want to go to hell or be the reason Lauren went to hell. Bible study taught me premarital sex was a sin. I even asked for clarity on the topic and found out lustful thoughts or even *thinking* about sex were sins. At the same time, I didn't want to lose Lauren's attention. Lots of kids at school were having sex, or at least talking about it. I wasn't ready to go that far, but something had to give. So, I decided the next day after school would be the day I pushed for us to begin a physical relationship.

The school clock was on meth that day as I struggled to figure out how to approach Lauren for our first makeout session. First period turned into second and third period quicker than Usain Bolt off the block. By the time eighth period rolled around I had still drawn a blank. Upon dismissal I walked with Lauren towards the bus stop a block away; this was customary. I'd wait with her for the 26 or 28 to come before crossing the street to catch it in the opposite direction. On this particular walk, Lauren could sense I was nervous.

"Is everything alright?" she quizzed.

"Yeah, yeah... I'm cool," I responded, trying to stay composed as I lied.

"C'mon, you think I don't know you?" she hit back.

Instead of responding with words, something triggered me to seize the opportunity for a kiss. In my haste, I forgot to open my mouth wide enough so our teeth wouldn't gnash against each other. Our incisors clanged like billy clubs on jailhouse bars. Our tongues finally made minor contact and within seconds it was over. Talk about awkward, I was pretty embarrassed by how bad the kiss went. But we were both relieved to have it behind us. Lauren blushed and hopped on the 26, I watched her move into the center of the bus through the windows. Mission accomplished.

Lauren and I kissed a handful of times afterwards, but things never progressed beyond first base. We were best friends, and it was just too awkward. After a while I questioned why we were even in a relationship. My teenage hormones would have loved a chance to get to second or third base with most of the girls at school, but I just couldn't imagine ever violating Lauren like that. I decided it was time to break up, but I didn't want to hurt Lauren's feelings or make things weird for us at school. Lauren took the hint when our phone time diminished in the evenings. During recess one day, our mutual friend, Isis, handed me a note. Lauren had written me a lengthy letter explaining how much she valued our time together, but it was clear we were better off as friends. My heart sunk, *She broke up with me?!* Although I contemplated how to break the news to Lauren for weeks, I never imagined she would be the one to drop the axe. My pride hurt, I vowed never to be on the receiving end of break up news in the future. Once I put my ego aside, Lauren and I resumed our close friendship. We kept in touch when she enrolled at Fieldston, a private school on her side of The Bronx, for eighth grade.

I had my sights set on leaving public school for a more challenging and safer private school environment too. Excluding Mr. Cassidy's eighth grade social studies class, I never had to study for tests in public school, the work was simple for me. Although the kids in my "Exceptionally Gifted" program were among the brightest minds in The Bronx, I wanted to match wits with the best in the world. Furthermore, I was sick of hiding my report cards from the boneheads who took pride in how many classes they cut or failed every semester.

One way or another I learned of a summer program at Fordham Prep, which promised to test my mettle. The six week program was designed to see if students had what it took to keep up with a fast paced secondary school curriculum. At the end of the course, one or two of the twelve students would be selected to skip the eighth grade and enroll in Fordham Prep as a high schooler. My mouth foamed at the challenge. Since my mom was all for keeping me busy and off the streets when school was out, she gave me the green light to attend the program.

The first day I got off the BX12 and walked onto Fordham's sprawling campus, I knew I belonged there. I had ridden past the campus countless times en route to the streetwear stores on Fordham Road. Never had I noticed the exquisite nineteenth century architecture hidden behind the layers of carefully manicured foliage that Fordham provided. The campus was truly an urban oasis, a concealed gem of intellectualism hidden in plain sight of The Bronx' perpetual chaos. I gave props to the Jesuits for sculpting such a marvel. Upon entering the gates, I instantly went from being in the majority to a minority. Almost every one was White... at a school in The Bronx! I was unbothered though, I had something to prove - that I belonged there all along.

The instructors inundated me and the other eleven guys with loads of work. For the first time I had to study, and I enjoyed it. More than testing our aptitude, the instructors tested our character to see if we were mature enough to make the leap to high school. They gave us the chance to seize leadership opportunities like caring for the class' pet crawfish, devising team building exercises, and identifying community service opportunities. I volunteered my services wherever possible and crushed the curriculum. By the time the admission packet arrived, I was confident I'd been selected to be a Ram. The only thing left to do was figure out how to brag to my friends that I'd be skipping the eighth grade and moving on to greener pastures.

Surprisingly, my mother torpedoed the opportunity. She reasoned I needed another year to physically mature before entering high school. Though I was small, I knew it had more to do with money. Even with financial aid, Fordham Prep would have been a hefty expense for my family.

Around the same time, the relationship between my parents had become increasingly strained. My father was rarely home, and when he was, he was extremely withdrawn. Beyond popping his head out the bedroom to say, "Oh what's up Meek?" when I got home from school, he didn't want to be bothered. Throughout my childhood he always seemed to be more preoccupied with other interests, and we rarely spoke of things outside of sports or music, but now he had become a complete stranger.

My parents made their best effort not to argue around me and my sister, but being the night owl I am, I eavesdropped on a few heated discussions. "I waited up all night to make love to my husband, and where were you Don? Out in the fucking streets getting high with your friends? Is that where you really want to be? Answer me Don!" I could never hear my father's responses, if there were any. Personality-wise my parents were polar opposites. My mother has always been detail oriented, disciplined, and assertive. On the other hand, my father was more reserved and free-willed; he seemed to go with the flow and take shortsighted risks. He was also a philanderer. An extremely handsome man, women flirted with my dad all the time, right in front of me. I was smart enough to know it was impossible for him to turn down *every* advance he received. So I was not surprised when it appeared my parents' marriage was headed for the inevitable. As their relationship crumbled and deteriorated right before my eyes, I decided I didn't want to be around for the fallout.

Once eighth grade rolled around, I learned of another option that would not only test my intellect, but allow me to escape the inevitable collapse of my family: boarding school. Most of my friends thought I was insane for wanting to forego my high school years in the city, but I saw freedom in the boarding school experience. Living in a dorm away from home, free to determine when I came and went sounded a lot like college, except four years earlier. *Who could pass on an opportunity to have a college experience at fourteen?* Research revealed the best schools in America were all boarding schools in the Northeast. Millionaires and billionaires sent their kids there. Fascinated, I shared the idea with my mom and she requested catalogues. She was also tipped off about a nonprofit called A Better Chance, which sought to place inner city youth in boarding schools. Eager to secure my place, I applied to schools independently, while waiting for A Better Chance to accept me into its program. Whether A Better Chance accepted me I would find a way to boarding school. I applied to the best of the best: Andover, St. Paul's, Groton, Lawrenceville, Trinity-Pawling, Choate, and Taft. Cost prohibitive application fees were all that stopped me from applying to more. My mother stayed up late after long days at work to help me perfect my essays, as she often had throughout my school years. We were in this together.

Some of the fondest memories I have are from the weekend school visits my mom, sister, and I took in our white '93 Bonneville through New England's fall foliage. Finding random college radio stations that played uncensored, exclusive Hip Hop was exciting as we crossed state lines. Escaping New York City to inhale fresh air was refreshing. Every campus we visited was absolutely gorgeous; the converse of the drab, prison-like, concrete and asphalt inner city schools I had attended for a decade. Boarding school campuses even diminished my perception of Fordham Prep. St. Paul's, situated in the pristine hills of New Hampshire, was awe inspiring on approach. Groton, hidden away in the backcountry of Massachusetts, had a unique, circular campus layout. I particularly remember being awed by Andover's architecture and regal atmosphere. Not to mention, there was a Pizza Hut tucked away in the basement of one of its buildings! I made sure to leave a lasting impression on the Black administrator, a dark, bald fellow, who interviewed me and told me about the lifelong opportunities I would have should I decide to enroll at the nation's top ranked preparatory school. Andover was what I imagined Harvard would be like, I was sold!

Until I visited Taft. I'll never forget pulling up to Headmaster's Circle for my tour there. Under two feet of fresh snow, the campus was a winter wonderland. My mom and I sat patiently in the posh waiting room for my tour guide, Noel Peña, to appear. By chance, Lance Odden, Taft's Headmaster, stopped in the waiting area to chat with the receptionist. "And who do we have here?" he queried. I recognized Mr. Odden's bald head, piercing blue eyes, and regal demeanor from Taft's brochure. At the other schools I toured the Headmaster was an inaccessible mystery figure, too busy to chat with random student prospects. Meeting Mr. Odden within minutes of arriving at Taft made an immediate impression.

"You're going to love it here Demetrius. Who is your tour guide?" Mr. Odden asked. Before I could answer, the exceptionally polite receptionist revealed we were waiting on Noel. Mr. Odden extended his hand to me, looked me in the eye, and told me, "Noel will take good care of you. See you soon." I grabbed his hand and processed the weight of his reassurance. Shortly after, Noel showed up. I'm not sure what I was expecting, but I was surprised to be greeted by a muscular, Latino jock with a New York accent thicker than my own. The birkenstocks at the base of his sweatpants signaled boarding school assimilation.

"Y'all ready? Let's roll," he signaled.

Upon leaving the admissions office, scores of gorgeous blondes and brunettes flanked Noel. "They lovin' the kid out here," he divulged. With a few thousand push ups and the pubescent growth spurt my father promised, I pictured myself filling Noel's sandals the following year. My mom asked Noel the difficult questions, like how challenging it was to balance schoolwork with sports, and how prepared he felt for the SATs. I asked if there was a Pizza Hut on campus. "Nah, but we have a restaurant called The Jig. It's dope, I'll take you there now" he disclosed. We abruptly cut across the campus, past the frozen pond where an impromptu co-ed game of hockey was taking place, and into The Oscarson Jigger Shop. Everyone was extremely happy to see Noel. "Yo Marty, let me get a bacon, egg, and cheese real quick," Noel shouted. "Matter fact, let me just come back there and make it myself," he recanted. I was awed when Noel got behind the griddle, putting in work with a metal spatula. "Yo D, go check out the other room while I hook this up," he instructed. I opened the door to an adjoining room where I found a couple of Black students lounging on small leather cubes laughing about first period biology. They asked if I was touring the campus, I nodded my head. My mom asked if they liked Taft and they nodded theirs. Through the glass walls of the room I could see other students engaged in a furious game of ping pong, and beyond them another set shooting pool. Suddenly Andover's Pizza Hut seemed lame.

After another twenty minutes or so of touring, Noel dropped me off at the Dean of Admissions, Mr. Maher's office for my interview. Mr. Maher had a cool, indifferent demeanor. He laid back in his leather office chair, hands behind his head, feet propped up on his desk. He may have even been chewing gum. Maher asked, "So what do you think of Taft so far?"

Reminding myself of my determination to be accepted, (with a scholarship no less), I stared in his eyes and offered, "It's great. It exceeded my expectations."

"Good. I already see you're a smart guy from your grades here," pointing to the manilla folder on his desk, "What's your favorite subject in school?"

What a layup. "I really like all subjects, but science is my favorite if I had to pick just one."

Mr. Maher pointed his index finger behind his head to bring my attention to the school's current science building a few hundred feet beyond his window, "If you end up coming here that thing won't be here much longer. We're building a brand new, top notch science building. It'll be ready by your sophomore year. That's if you were to be accepted here, of course."

I responded, "Well that's definitely something to consider."

"So what is your least favorite subject Demetrius?" Maher inquired. I gave careful consideration to this question because I knew it might be a setup.

After a brief pause, I responded, "I like every subject I come across. I love to learn more than anything else."

Mr. Maher looked at me with a cut-the-bullshit scowl and said, "So you're telling me you're the perfect student and you love everything you come across? Cause that's what it's starting to sound like. Now seriously, I know there is at least one subject you care for less than the others. What is it?"

I hadn't prepared myself for this type of pushback, so I concluded I might as well be honest: "If I have to pick one subject I guess I'd have to say history. I don't find history to be a fun subject. I find it to be really boring actually."

Mr. Maher united his left hand fingertips with his right hand fingertips, forming a hand pyramid in front of his chin. "Interesting, what's your favorite sport?" he pressed.

"Baseball. It's a sport that requires a lot of thinking. It's not like contact sports, you know?"

Maher paused to absorb the information, then revealed The Taft School baseball team was being coached by Joe Brogna, the father of New York Mets slugger, Rico Brogna.

"That's great. I've played Little League since I was eight-years-old. It would be fun to play at Taft."

Mr. Maher nodded his head in approval and said, "Okay. Okay. What questions do you have for me Demetrius?"

Having been interviewed at five other boarding schools, I mastered the strongest questions to ask any interviewer. I reached into my mental rolodex and pulled out: "How do you know when a candidate is an optimal fit for your institution?"

Genuine intrigue flooded Maher's face as he responded, "Great question. I look for somebody that's honest with themselves, first of all. Second, I look for someone who doesn't mind handling pressure. What else would you like to know?"

I figured I'd turn the tables on him by asking, "What's *your* favorite subject and sport?"

Maher lit up once again and shot back, "Well, besides acting as the Dean of Students, I also teach upper-mid history, and coach the Men's Hockey team."

Jesus Christ, you gotta be kidding me! I acknowledged his response with a sullen head nod.

Mr. Maher promptly disclosed, "I believe our time is up now Demetrius. I certainly enjoyed our discussion. You'll be receiving a letter from me on our decision in the coming months."

I reunited with my mom in the waiting room and we headed out to the Bonneville. "So how did it go Meek?" she asked as soon as we got beyond earshot.

"I don't know if I gave the right answers during the interview," I revealed. Sensing my disappointment my mother smiled and rubbed the back of my head with her left hand. We drove back to The Bronx weighing the pros and cons of each of the schools we had visited over the past two weekends. I couldn't help but to feel I most likely squandered my opportunity to get into Taft due to my poor interview.

CHAPTER FIVE

BECOMING A BLACK MAN IN BOARDING SCHOOL

> I wanted to walk just like him (remember?)
> Wanted to talk just like him (word)
> Often momma said I look too much
> And I thought just like him (and I'd get happy)...
> Do you even remember the tender boy
> You turned into a cold young man
> With one goal and one plan
> -Jay-Z "Where Have You Been?"

The following months dragged on and on as I waited for acceptance letters to roll in. Considering how well the majority of my school visits went, I knew I had to have gotten in *somewhere*. Our mailbox in the lobby continued to disappoint, however. After a while, the mailman, my former sensei at Co-op City Kung Fu, would stop me with a head shake on approach. He was usually filling the boxes when I walked in from school every afternoon.

While the suspense drove me crazy, my parents' relationship disintegrated further. I stopped being sure of when I would see my dad. Every once in awhile I'd come home from school and he'd peek out the bathroom with a toothbrush in his mouth, his demeanor subdued. I never asked questions, rather I respected my father's choice of solitude.

One week, after an extended absence, my father appeared only to reveal he had been at a drug detox clinic in Westchester. As he tried to explain going AWOL for the past week, I pushed past him and went into my room to cry. The tears flowed not because I was disappointed that my father had a drug problem, but because I wasn't sure whether to believe him. Over the last few years he had grown increasingly distant and unreliable. He stopped being an assistant baseball coach after my first season. To make matters worse, he would promise to show up at games and sometimes not appear. I made excuses for why he stood me up: double shifts at the VA, the car wasn't working, etc. Always promising to make it up to me, he seldom compensated for his absence. I feigned indifference while burying the disappointment in the trenches of my heart.

In my father's absence, Mr. Crouch, Eddie's dad, became my mentor. Going upstairs to talk politics with him I enjoyed. A stalwart Democrat, Mr. Crouch encouraged me to aspire to political office. Recognizing my intelligence and ambition, he genuinely enjoyed hearing my interpretation of current events. Mr. Crouch treated me and my sister like his own children; he included us on family visits to the Crouch timeshare on Virginia Beach and piled us into the car with Eddie for amusement park tours in Pennsylvania and New Jersey. Many times I wished my dad was as engaged as Mr. Crouch in encouraging my development into an upstanding citizen. But I also knew at more than thirty years my father's senior, Mr. Crouch was more mature, experienced, and adept at raising a family. I forgave my father's transgressions and concentrated my efforts on being better than him in every way imaginable; I knew it was *my* responsibility to carry my family into good fortune.

Boarding school seemed like the best step towards meeting those means. Surrounded by posters of Lamborghinis and other sports cars in my Co-op City bedroom, prosperity was my destiny. To remain motivated, I pasted a headshot into the driver's seat of a red Dodge Viper on the wall next to my bed. On the ceiling, I taped an electric blue Diablo next to a graffiti tag my delinquent classmate, Alex Coghan, taught me to draw in Ms. Notice's art class. The last thing I would see at night and first thing I would see in the morning was my name next to wealth. From an early age I felt it was my birth duty to improve the plight of my family. I was cognizant of my gifts. My mother confirmed them when she convinced my father to invest in a full World Book Encyclopedia set. Prior to the internet, encyclopedias were the primary resource for myriad fields of information. Hours were spent thumbing through each alphabetized volume, carving out mental real estate for the most random facts about the planet we inhabit.

World Book taught me the difference between tortoises and turtles, information I used to prove my academic dominance in my household. Convinced the words were mere synonyms, my father dismissed me when I questioned him on the differences. I seized the opportunity to flex my intellectual superiority, quipping, "That's wrong. Tortoises live on land and turtles live in water."

With a side smirk my dad returned, "Meek, they're the same thing."

I refused to back down. "No, you're wrong. World Book says they're very different."

My father grew visibly agitated, so my mom stepped in to defuse the situation before it escalated into something more heated. This was the confirmation I sought; I hadn't yet exceeded my father's strength, but I was indeed smarter than him. Hence, I rationalized it was incumbent upon me to achieve what my father couldn't.

When the acceptance letters finally rolled in, I basked in confirmation of my brilliance. All six schools accepted me. Though I fumbled the interview, I even got into Taft, my number one pick. Still, the decision of which school to attend was not easy. Andover, with its on site Pizza Hut, had a reputation which preceded itself. For a week, I gave careful consideration to whether Taft was actually a better choice. Ultimately, I settled on Taft for numerous reasons. Beyond the two hundred and twenty-six acres of sprawling hills, the gorgeous pond, eighteen hole golf course, The Jig, and numerous other amenities, Taft was breaking ground on a state of the art science building.

After Lauren and I picked Batman Forever over Outbreak, I read Robin Cook's best seller believing it would reveal what I missed in the film. Outside of encyclopedias and assigned classroom reading, *Outbreak* was the first book I read for pleasure. Intrigued, I devoured it in three days. Virology was fascinating! Soon I followed up with readings of *The Hot Zone* by Richard Preston and *The Coming Plague* by Laurie Garrett. Then it clicked: I wanted to save the world from diseases as a level four virologist. Taft's Ivy Kwok Wu Science Center promised to host the most advanced high school chemistry labs in New England, the perfect place to embark on my path towards virology.

Sweetening the deal, a Joe Brogna coached baseball team was hard to resist. All those years of Little League might pay off under Coach Brogna's tutelage. Puberty could potentially transform me into a Major League slugger. Andover's baseball coach didn't have a son in the league.

Even still, beyond the new science building and baseball prospects, Taft genuinely felt like home. No, it wasn't anything like Co-op City. But with just five hundred students, and at half the size of Andover, *everyone* on campus knew each other. Sure, there were only a sprinkle of Black and Brown faces, but it seemed impossible for me not to fit into the family. Regardless, in the unlikely event I had problems fitting into the Taft community, the school was a hop, skip, and a jump from The Bronx - a mere ninety minute drive. If for any reason my mom's Bonneville was out of commission, I could even take the Metro North train to Waterbury and catch a bus from there to Watertown. Andover was no less than a four hour drive, a long way to be if I ever got homesick. Taft was the most logical option.

Based on my parents' income, Taft offered to cover eighty-five percent of my tuition. The remaining six grand would have to be paid out of pocket by mother and father, who were never on the same page financially, nor at the time emotionally. I knew I would put my family in a bind by insisting to go away, but I gambled on being smart enough to pay them back with interest down the line. My mother made the same bet. She vowed to do whatever necessary to facilitate my boarding school opportunity, no matter if my father balked at the cost. And like that, it was settled - I would be a Big Red Rhino in the fall.

As I fulfilled my final semester requirements at 181, my father virtually disappeared. Suspicious evening calls from a woman wanting to know whether he was home came at random. This resulted in my mother calling the phone company to make our line private. By June, my parents' separation was obvious. Though we missed my dad, my sister and I didn't ask many questions about his whereabouts. Instinct informed us not to inflict further trauma by questioning whether he had walked out on us.

Right when it became obvious we could no longer skirt our family's dissolution, my father showed up at the apartment requesting for me and my sister to join him on the bench behind the building - the same bench where Gary Gonzalez met his demise. Sabree and I were eager to get an update on what was going on.

My father started out with, "What have you guys always wanted?"

Dumbfounded, I scratched my head while my sister shouted, "A pony!"

He gave his signature baritone chuckle and said, "No, it's not a pony. What about you Meek?"

I had no clue what he could be talking about. Confused, I finally offered, "A puppy?"

Again, my father chuckled before revealing, "Noooo. Remember y'all said you wanted a little brother a long time ago?" Still confused, my sister and I nodded. "Well now you have a little brother. His name is Dontae."

Our jaws hit the floor. I knew my parents had grown apart over the past couple of years, but hadn't fathomed they grew *this* far apart. Despite his extended absence, my father having a baby with another woman wasn't on my radar of possible scenarios.

Feigning excitement I asked, "How old is he?"

Avoiding the intimacy of eye contact, he looked down towards Gary's enduring blood stains and disclosed, "He was born a couple weeks ago on June 21st. I'll bring y'all over to meet him soon. That will answer the rest of your questions."

Despite the multitude of thoughts flooding our minds, we refrained from asking any follow-ups. Over the years we grew accustomed to suppressing our feelings and voices. We found security in silence.

In time, we finally met Dontae and his mother Corinne, my father's mistress. To our surprise they also lived in Co-op City, close to the Little League fields. In fact, their building overlooked the greenway my team practiced on three times a week. At any given moment, my father could have looked out the window to see our tiny bodies lobbing baseballs in the distance. I found myself in disbelief my dad was so close the whole time he was away from us. I also felt every bit my mother's betrayer for entertaining his extramarital blunder. Torn between loyalty to my mother's emotional well being and seeking my dad's validation, I hoped to remain as neutral as possible in the ensuing fallout. So I got in the car the time my father showed up in an ugly, orange, Nissan Sentra. Based on the hooptie, economic advancement couldn't have been his motive for leaving my mother. Nonetheless, I sought to understand his rationale. As we pulled up to the thirty-five story, tan tower buildings of Benchley Place, I had no idea what to expect. I surmised my father's new partner had to be gorgeous, considering how often women flirted with him in public; he could have his pick of the most attractive Sistas in New York.

After a long elevator ride upstairs, a pale, petite, White woman, with a gold incisor, greeted us at the door. Based on my pop's Playboy collection, which served as a box spring to him and my mother's waterbed, I knew he was fond of looking at White women in private. From an early age, I always found Playboy corny and questioned my dad's interest in maintaining a subscription; the women weren't thick enough for my interest. But in that instance everything became clear - my father had an undiagnosed case of Jungle Fever.

While trying to cut through the awkwardness of meeting my Dad's new significant other, I couldn't help but to notice Corinne didn't *sound* White. Yet beyond the gold tooth, Corinne's features revealed no hint of color. Sensing our confusion she volunteered, "I'm half Italian and half Puerto Rican." Louie had told that lie countless times when trying to kick game to White girls at Orchard Beach. Corinne's fluent Ebonics led me to believe she was telling the truth, however; my father's Jungle Fever wasn't full fledged. A brief tour of Corinne's apartment revealed scenic aerial views of The Bronx that surpassed even those of Momma's window. Finally, my sister and I were led to the bedroom where an infant Dontae lay asleep in his crib. He looked White too. I could tease out the Blackness in his lips though. He also had the signature lengthy eyelashes my sister and I inherited from my dad. We took turns holding him for pics on our disposable camera.

My sister seemed more excited than I was to meet Dontae. Walking the line between allegiance to my mother and loyalty to my father, I chose the path of indifference. To protect her from the shame and embarrassment she must have felt when given the news of my father's indiscretions, I never brought up Dontae's name in my mother's presence. I didn't want to reopen the agonizing emotional wound I assumed she carried. Remarkably, my mother kept her composure despite the obvious pain she had to be dealing with. From years of suppressing my emotions, I didn't know how to be her comforter, so I didn't try. I left for boarding school hoping my departure would uncomplicate the chaos generated by my dad's Jungle Fever. One less burden to bare, I figured my mother could concentrate on healing with the assurance I was safe from physical and emotional harm in Connecticut.

My parents remained civil enough for the ride up to Watertown to move me into my freshman dorm. I think they expected me to cry as I relinquished their final embrace. Instead I remained stoic, not shedding a tear as I watched them get into the Bonneville parked in Main Circle. As they slowly pulled off, I smiled and waved trying to reassure them I would be just fine. Proving my capabilities without parental supervision imbued me with excitement.

Taft gave me the isolation and freedom I sought since imagining a life away from home under the kitchen table in Brooklyn. School administrators granted my preference of a single room, one of only two such units in the lower-mid (freshman) dorm, HDT4. (HDT stood for Horace Dutton Taft, President William Howard Taft's brother, and our school's founder. Ironically, Horace moved his school from its original location at Pelham Manor, just a mile north of Co-op City, to the Watertown site in 1893). Not having to share space with anyone was a relief.

Still, HDT's unwalled communal showers proved it difficult, if not impossible, to hide even the most intimate details from fellow freshmen. Moments alone were scarce, especially after bonding with friends who would become closer than family. There were four other Black guys on HDT4. Venroy, Marc, and Harold were from New York like me. Mshangwe, (pronounced Oom-shong-way), a bandwagon Bulls fan from Newark, weathered a perpetual onslaught of "Dirty Jersey" jokes. Closest in size to me, he was also a runt. During the summer leading up to our first semester at Taft, I met Mshangwe at an A Better Chance orientation in Montclair, New Jersey. (Soon after I received my acceptance letter from Taft, A Better Chance notified me of my acceptance into their program as well. Though my mother and I had done most of the groundwork, it made sense to join A Better Chance as a supplemental resource to my boarding school experience). Mshangwe, and his older brother, Onaje, also a Taft student, were both given African names by parents sympathetic to the Black Power Movement of the seventies.

Venroy was a Jamaican immigrant who lived in The Bronx, not too far from Co-op City. Although he was a year younger than me, having started school early in Jamaica, Venroy could have easily passed for a college graduate with his stature and facial hair. His penchant for loudly arguing people into submission foretold his following in his father's footsteps as an attorney.

Marc, a basketball junkie from Brooklyn, was taller than Venroy, yet more wiry. He always bore an air of mystery and a perpetual chip on his shoulder. Marc regretted his consequential familiarity with the sweet, rancid smell of crack and knew far more than the average fourteen-year-old about sex.

Compared to the rest of us, Harold, from Queens, was a Herculean Huxtable. Known as "Hoss," he was a Prep for Prep kid who played tennis and aspired to be the next Stuart Scott. Awkward and reserved around some of Taft's other Black students, Hoss made friends with White students easier than the rest of our crew. They found comfort in his non confrontational demeanor and admired his physique.

I entered Taft a diminutive five-foot-three, weighing just seventy-seven pounds. The physical differences between me my peers were never more apparent than they were during my freshman year of high school. Puberty had not yet gifted me bass, height, or weight (I'm still waiting for facial hair). To catch up, I resolved to stacking my tray with plates upon plates of food in the dining hall. I even forced myself to drink four to five glasses of milk with every meal.

Despite our physical differences, Venroy, Marc, Harold, Mshangwe, and I found unity in our skin color and shared love of Hip Hop. In a satirical nod to the cheesiness of South Central's O.G. Bobby Johnson, we deemed ourselves the Deuce Crew. When we weren't raiding the rooms of unsuspecting lower-mids with homie socks, we'd spend hours in Venroy and Marc's room dissecting bars from Jeru The Damaja, Wu-Tang, and Nas. Mshangwe put me on to Brick City's Redman, who became my favorite emcee. Soon, our love for Hip Hop would open dialogues between us and our classmates. The amount of rap consumed by privileged White kids came as a surprise. Had it not been for wealthy Southerner John McCardell, I may have never caught on to the brilliance of Outkast and the Dungeon Family; people weren't checking for them on the East Coast like that in '96. Brad, a spoiled Jew from California, (who didn't make it through freshman year), would bring DJ Quik CDs to my room, and vouch for the quality of the chronic mentioned. I couldn't relate to Phish and the Dave Matthews Band, favorites of the White elite, so I was grateful for Hip Hop's convenient ice breaker.

At the time of my enrollment, Taft had exactly two Black faculty members: Mennette DuBose San-Lee and Lenny Tucker, both Taft alumni. Mr. Tucker, or LT as he was commonly known, was fresh out of undergrad at Princeton when he assumed his roles as a history teacher and junior varsity football coach. He was younger, more outspoken, and more Hip Hop than Mrs. DuBose San-Lee, so most of the Black students, male and female, flocked to him as an advisor. LT was so overwhelmed with requests to serve as student's' faculty advisor that by the time I met him he was no longer taking on mentees. Nonetheless, whether formal or informal, LT served as a counselor, consultant, and confidant to Taft's sparse Black and Latino population. He moderated countless debates, arguments, and discussions amongst the campus' Hip Hop enthusiasts, in his apartment. LT was our big brother, the glue that kept Taft's minority population from splintering into pockets of culture shocked, homesick, melanated adolescents. There were no Black churches in Watertown, so we found fellowship, comfort, and faith we could overcome boarding school's challenges at LT's place.

Despite the sanctuary I often found in LT's apartment, I considered a few members of the congregation devils. Sophomores Jamahl and Shaun were dickheads. Jamahl, a Harlem native, exuded the typical Uptown arrogance known to infuriate all other homo sapiens outside of the "wild hundreds." Shaun was a cocky Cape Verdean kid from Dorchester with a perpetual chip on his shoulder. In tandem, Jamaal and Shaun demanded to be the center of attention in all discussions. They were the propagators of vicious jokes that many times extended beyond humor and ventured into bullying.

From the jump I was targeted, due to Shana Simmons setting expectations I would be Taft's new, hysterical court jester. I met

Shana at the same A Better Chance orientation where I met Mshangwe over the summer. She was also from The Bronx and gorgeous. Since she already had one year of boarding school under her belt, she served as a peer counselor at the A Better Chance summit. Shana adopted me as her little brother after I made her laugh all weekend. I would have preferred to be her suitor, but I figured our proximity in the Taft bubble would provide at least three years for me to grow handsomer and convert her later. If only I had known the infinite gravity of the friend zone before high school…

In any event, the Black, Latino, and Native American community at Taft was a family. We even had a support group called NAALSA (pronounced Nahl Suh, an acronym for Native American Afro Latino Student Alliance). When we didn't have assigned seating at Taft's twice weekly, formal "sit down" dinners, we all sat at the same table - raisins in a bowl of milk. Betwixt classes, we'd look for each other at The Jig to battle in pool and ping pong. Every evening during the forty-five minute break between study hall and dorm lockdown, we'd convene at "The Scene" to gossip, roast, and court each other. Every group at Taft had its own "scene," or a designated place to meet with close friends or individuals with whom one sought social recognition. There was an Asian "scene," a geek/day student "scene," a lower-mid, mid, upper-mid, and senior "scene." Our "scene" claimed the wooden furniture in the corner of the hallway that connected Main Hall to the dance studio, Black Box theatre, and computer lab.

"The Scene" was the last place we'd get to bond with fellow freshmen Kimberly Noel, Karla Timmons, Margaret Wilkerson, Tiffany James, Janelle Matthews, Nicole Dessibourg, and Tulani Gonzalez before retiring to our gender specific dorms. Kim was the studious athlete of the crew, while Tiff was often the loud-mouthed comic relief. Janelle was a chunky, baby-faced, bookworm, who frequently walked around reading cheesy, supermarket romance novels. Pale, Peruvian blooded Nicole could have passed for White had she not been in a relationship with Deuce Crew member Harold when we arrived on campus. Brown-skinned Margaret was as strong-willed, as she was mysterious.

I couldn't help but to fall in lust with Tulani's thickness, until both the guys and girls teased me enough about our obvious size disparities. Until I let my pride ruin the connection, we were briefly an item.

Except for New Orleans native Karla Timmons, almost all of these young ladies of color hailed from the Tri-State Area. Obviously that led to endless jokes about Karla's countriness. Out of ignorance, I joined in on the fun, believing the East Coast to be the arbiter of everything hip. I would eventually discover the merits of crawfish, bounce music, No Limit, and Cash Money through friendship with Karla. She opened my mind to Southern ideals that would later shatter my New York-centric belief system.

People often pointed out the uncanny resemblance sophomore Kayode Leonard and I bore to each other. With our matching skin tone, head shape, and facial structure, I could have easily been his little brother. In many instances he treated me like one, helping me cultivate my Hip Hop palate. When I initially resisted Bone Thugs-n-Harmony's double time flow, Kayode, an unusually open minded Harlemite, encouraged me not to dismiss them. He put their catalogue in my hand and pushed me to go listen. I ended up studying to their music through college. In exchange, I shared with Kayode the genius of my Roots collection. *Things Fall Apart* made him respect my ear for music. Back then it was impossible to buy *every* album that came out. There was simply too much good music coming out of Hip Hop during the tail end of the Golden Era. At fifteen dollars a pop, it would have been unrealistic to purchase each project, so I was grateful for Kayode filling in the gaps.

Beyond Hip Hop and skin tone as connection qualifiers, for the first time I befriended White guys I genuinely adored as much as my other friends. David Wisner, the son of U.S. Ambassador to India, Frank Wisner, fit into the Deuce Crew seamlessly. Dave had already travelled around the world, interacting with diverse populations, before joining us for freshman year on HDT4. He listened to ska and snuck parody porn into the common room for the floor to enjoy. Dave's rebellion against snobiety naturally drew us together. While Taft's aristocrats threw secret off campus ragers, (many of which Black students were not privy to until we heard the stories days later), Dave would have us as guests at his parents' wooded weekend home in Brewster. Many times, Dave's love for us seemed inexplicable; he could have easily rubbed shoulders with the millionaires and children of other political figures populating our school. Yet he was grounded enough to spend hours playing James Bond with us on Nintendo 64. Since his grandfather, Frank Gardiner Wisner, set the precedent as the CIA's Director of Plans under President Dwight Eisenhower, we predicted Dave would eventually move into the family business. How the rebel would get there hanging out with a bunch of Black guys was up for debate, however.

Shawn McCormack, a White day-student, was also down with the clique. Like Blacks, Latinos, and Native Americans, day-students stood out like sore thumbs in boarding school. Being able to go home every day made them outsiders to the general student population. Day-students didn't get to bond after hours when dorm room antics were prevalent. Facing fierce competition for the few day-student allotments available, they were also typically brainiacs. For instance, one day-student, a Chinese orphan by the name of Paul Zhang, wrote a two-hundred page paper on the mechanics of quantum teleportation. (Yes, really… and I've been fascinated by the topic ever since). In any event, Shawn was no nerd; he fell along the cool spectrum of the day-student acceptance curve. Like Dave, Shawn opened his home to us in the Waterbury suburb of Wolcott. His parents' backyard featured the first hot tub I experienced. Many weekends, we turned Shawn's pool into the set of "Juicy," or at least it felt that way to a bunch of broke kids from New York. Adding to his value, Shawn would be the first to own a car, an ugly, sunburned 1983 Buick Skyhawk. The "u" and "k" had fallen off the car's logo so we jokingly referred to it as "The Bic." For all we cared "The Bic" could have looked like Fred Flintstone's whip and it wouldn't have mattered, it provided much needed respite from Taft's academic pressure cooker.

Coming from public school, classes at Taft were intense. For the first time, I found myself intellectually challenged in every subject. Initially it was exhilarating; I could feel my brain cells multiplying. I wasn't looked down upon as a nerd, it was liberating. Saturday morning classes didn't even bother me, I was a sponge looking to soak up all the knowledge New York City hid. Most of all, I could gage whether I was really smart, or whether it had just appeared that way in a flawed school system. Proving I belonged at Taft motivated me to study, something I rarely had to do in my previous setting. So, instead of clowning around during study hall hours in the evening, I remained focused. Even after I sacrificed my single room to accommodate an uncomfortable gay student, I refused to allow my roommate Mshangwe, or anyone else distract me. Despite my efforts, missing the honor roll by fractions of a point left me frustrated. While I didn't struggle as much as other students of color, not being the cream of the crop was disheartening. I resented my privileged classmates for their considerable head start in most subjects, particularly math and science, though my strong writing shined in history and English. Ironically, history, the subject I told Mr. Maher I least liked during my Taft interview, became my favorite course.

Outside of the academic battle, peer pressure overpowered my resistance to playing football. Prior to attending Taft, I never considered the possibility of putting on shoulder pads. Sure, growing up in Section 5 I played padless tackle football on the grass behind my building. However, I never developed a love for the sport or its violence. I was too frail and concerned with keeping my limbs intact to show further interest. When the rest of the Deuce Crew unanimously agreed to join the JV football team I became the odd man out. LT coached the team, so it was the natural choice above soccer and cross country for my friends. Only fresh off the boat immigrants played soccer in New York, and none of us had any idea cross country was even a sport (*so you run to… just… run?*). As small as he was, even Mshangwe wasn't afraid to play football. Therefore, I was out of excuses for declining to join the ranks of ruffians.

I looked like a caricature of myself in towering pads that rose above my neck to connect with the base of my helmet. Any peripheral gaze required the full movement of my torso. Pee wee league football players would have recognized me as a teammate in my getup. My mother laughed hysterically when she received the locker room pic I sent. I knew it was funny before I applied the postage. The purpose of leaving New York was to preserve my livelihood. Clad in armor, I had reasonable assurance I wouldn't get hurt.

At my first practice, Taj Frazier, a tall, Flavor Flav Black, sophomore from suburban Montclair, New Jersey called me out in nutcracker. Fearing emasculation, I was unwilling to back down from the challenge. David slew Goliath, so maybe with irrational confidence Meek could take down Taj, though he favored Samson. Taj had somehow successfully assimilated to Taft's prep culture, while simultaneously reveling in his Blackness. He had dreads and clout in the NAALSA community, all the while dating a White girl in his class. To this day I can't figure out whether Taj thought it'd be funny to launch a seventy-seven pound weakling fifteen feet into the air, or whether he was trying to preserve his respect within the Black circle by flattening a kid from The Bronx. Regardless, he laid me out. All I remember is laying helmet to helmet with Taj as LT dropped the pigskin onto my chest. Before I could gain my footing and attempt to plow through Taj's tackle, I was airborne - long enough to observe a flock of Canadian geese heading south against a backdrop of fluffy cumulus clouds. I finally hit the ground, landing in the same position from which I started, the back of my helmet kissing the grass. The whole team found it hysterical. With scrambled eyesight I could see Taj enter the frame of my facemask to extend a hand to help me up. He grinned, "Welcome to the football team." I was right to assume football was just a veiled excuse for barbarism and toxic masculinity. But it was too late - quitting the team would mean I was soft; no Black guy from New York could be *soft*.

  I stayed on the team, earning a spot at split end. Though I never fell in love with the sport, it grew on me, until I fractured my right pinky against the helmet of an opponent on a reception. The previous year, I fractured the same finger on a line drive hit back to the mound in the 181 schoolyard. The finger was so disfigured it would have been impossible to continue without risking further damage. So, I sat out the remainder of the season and set out to prove I could handle the physical punishment the following fall. That didn't go according to plan, as the subsequent year I graduated from breaking my right pinky, to shattering my growth plate and fracturing both my fibula and tibia at the base of my right leg. A dopey freshman, Teddy McCarthy, heard LT's whistle, but refused to give up my leg as I dragged him following a round of nutcracker. Teddy rolled unnecessarily onto my ankle, audibly snapping my bones. The pain was excruciating. Still, it was not as bad as the unexpected torture my physician inflicted as he asked me to hold my breath and count to three, before resetting my leg without warning. For two months I would walk with crutches before progressing to a walking boot. Football career cut short, I never got my unwanted shot at the NFL.

But I did get another shot at proving I wasn't soft. Believing the JV basketball coaches didn't give me a fair shot at making the team due to my height, I entertained Venroy's suggestion of joining the wrestling team. Prior to Taft, my only knowledge of wrestling was the WWF. Even as a teenager, I held onto a childhood dream of flying off the top rope and landing a crushing elbow to somebody's cranium. While high school wrestling was nothing of the sort, I figured it was the closest I would ever get to my Black Hulk Hogan fantasy. Besides, it was time I learned to defend myself. In addition, LT helped coach the team, having competed himself in the heavyweight division just six years prior. I knew he'd look out for me. Finally, Venroy closed me on earning a Varsity letter during my freshman year. Taft desperately needed a contender at 103 pounds, the entry level weight class. Fourteen-year-olds weighing 103 pounds and interested in wearing a unitard were rare. Unable to fill the spot, many schools forfeited their first match at every meet. For obvious reasons, head wrestling coach, Mr. Wynn, preferred not to lose. Wynn knew simply having a 103 pounder guaranteed Taft points at most meets. At long last my puniness conferred some advantage!

At my first weigh in, Coach Wynn and the team stood dumbfounded as the weight on the scale's balance beam continued to creep leftwards. The team's captain, brawny 156 pounder, Ben Gross, quipped, "Dude, my cock weighs more than you!" Giving a sarcastic grin, I pretended to be unaffected by the laughs and taunts. Inside, I cursed myself for being stuck with an inadequate chassis. The minimum threshold for competing at 103 was eighty-three pounds. Ranking in the lower first percentile of adolescents, I was seven pounds too light for even the entry level weight division. But to quit would indicate I was soft and, remember: no Black guy from New York could be soft.

    Wrestling made it impossible to avoid how much I hated my body. While most of the team bonded behind the struggle of trying to cut weight, I was the exception, trying to bulk up. They ran the indoor track in rubber sweatsuits, while I watched from above, curling girly dumbbells in the weight room. They starved themselves, complaining the whole time about how much they missed food, while LT ordered pizzas and encouraged me to consume whole pies in his apartment. They chewed packs of ultra sour Quench gum, spitting pesky water weight into styrofoam cups. I had ten minutes to take a gallon of water to the head, just to hit eighty-three pounds at my first competition. I made it off the scale just in time to throw it back up. I spent the rest of the season inhaling anything with calories, often making myself sick to my stomach. Physically, it felt like I was playing an insurmountable game of catch up with my peers. I hated everything about being scrawny. I looked like a praying mantis in my skintight singlet. Worst of all, people had no qualms about vocalizing how hilarious, ridiculous, and/or unattractive my bonyness was to them. Most people have the common decency not to voice unflattering things to the face of an overweight person. Yet, as an underweight person, I invited everyone's open criticism and judgment. Years of constantly being reminded about how skinny I was made me extremely insecure. I knew the prettiest girls weren't attracted to guys that weighed less than them. Other dudes highlighted and capitalized on my muscle deficiencies, making me feel like less than a man many times.

They even encouraged my friend, Shawn McCormack, to compete for my 103 spot midway through the season. Shawn was a couple pounds over, but followed the rest of the team's regimen to make weight after a couple of weeks. With a brief head start on skillset, I was able to dispatch of Shawn the first few times he challenged me for my Varsity position. In the last stretch of the season, his twenty pound weight advantage proved to be too much to overcome and he pinned me, taking my roster spot before a major tournament. Devastated, I retreated to the hallway outside the wrestling room and stared through the windows to the hockey rink below in disappointment. The ramifications of my defeat stormed my mind: I'd be the subject of more jokes when my friends no longer saw me introduced to "Welcome to the Jungle," with the Varsity squad at meets. I couldn't understand why God had slighted me so.

The only thing that kept me optimistic was the approaching baseball season. Baseball was my number one sport - the sport in which I *knew* I was skilled to compete. I felt I excelled in tryouts as Mshangwe, who tried out with me, even voiced, "Yo, you mad nice in baseball son!" Unfortunately, the coaches saw it different. Not making the JV baseball team my freshman year was heartbreaking. Never given a reason for the snub, I attributed the slight to anatomical bias. The coaches saw my athletic potential, but my lack of physical prowess *had* to be the reason I was told to "try again next year." Co-op City Little League had made me an excellent outfielder. Getting cut from JV baseball made no sense.

Rage and disappointment translated into swinging titanium sticks at the heads and chests of my peers in lacrosse. Just six months prior, I was vaguely aware the sport even existed. Another new experience, lacrosse was one of the few sports that offered an entry level "thirds" team, below Varsity and JV, for freshmen. Mshangwe didn't make the baseball team either, so he joined me and Dave in playing North America's oldest sport. Lacrosse was surprisingly easy to pick up. Hand-eye coordination I gained from years of baseball translated well into the sport. As well, the physical five on five matchups reminded me more of Bronx street basketball than brutish football. Yet, I was still aware lacrosse was "White boy shit." My coach, Mr. Lansdale, was the prototypical White guy: inexplicably chipper, rhythmless, and commandeering. Inner city kids dribbled basketballs, tossed baseballs, and caught footballs; they didn't cradle lacrosse balls. On "They Don't Love You No More," Jay Z would later rap, "Wrong sport, boy, you know you're as soft as a lacrosse team."

Even Major League Lacrosse star Jerry Ragonese admitted "lacrosse is labeled as a sport for the 'privileged white youth' who often are looked at as 'soft' individuals, and has, in the past, been personified by tall, skinny boys with a familiar Baltimore-style haircut wearing pastel colored pants as they drive their parents Range Rovers to practice."

Eddie, Louie, and Darryl would laugh me out the room if I told them I picked up lacrosse, I figured. Lacrosse was soft... no Black guy from New York could be *soft*.

While I was grateful for the new experiences boarding school afforded, assimilating and losing my former identity was a frightening prospect. I didn't go to Taft to become some White talking, khaki clad prepster; I went to fulfill Sonny's *A Bronx Tale* vision for C - to fuse street knowledge with formal education and become unstoppable.

Being turned down by Meredith Morris was a wake up call. She was my first White girl crush. Black and Latino chicks at Taft were slim pickings, so the common boarding school send off "you better not come home with no White girl," was easier said than done. After concluding I was too skinny to step to Kim, and any of the other NAALSA chicks, my attention turned elsewhere. Between reading paragraphs of Oedipus Rex in English, I couldn't keep my eyes off Meredith. She had curves like a Black girl. She smiled brightly every time we spoke and seemed to be extremely interested in everything I had to say. Perhaps it was just her personality, but my conclusion was she *had* to be feeling me.

Mshangwe got sick of me talking about Meredith late night in our dorm room. He encouraged me to pursue her despite our obvious differences in race and class. The only problem was I didn't know how to kick game to a White girl, I had no experience from which to draw. In The Bronx, it took irrational confidence, machismo, and a lightning quick mouthpiece to "bag a chick." In contrast, aggressive pursuit seemed to do the opposite for White girls. So I thought, and thought, and thought some more about the most delicate approach to take with Meredith. The best I could come up with was what worked for me with Lauren in sixth grade - a handwritten note with checkboxes for yes or no. Lame, I know; it would be years before I learned the virtues of open ended questions and competent communication. But I didn't have the cojones to look Meredith in the eye and ask her to be my girlfriend. Perhaps *that's* the reason she turned me down. From two seats away, I watched her blonde bob tilt downwards as she read my note. When her eyes and mouth grew wide in disbelief, I knew I made a mistake. She slowly shook her head and silently mouthed, "I'm sorry" behind the backs of our unsuspecting classmates. Maybe my note was unbelievably lame. Maybe I mistook her friendliness for adoration. Maybe she didn't find me attractive at all. Maybe I wasn't rich enough. Maybe I was too small. Maybe I was too Black. Whatever the case, I knew it was my last time having my ego shattered by a White girl.

***

Requests for height and weight, followed by prayers for my mother and sister's safety were sent to God for intervention every night. A blanket prayer to enhance the lives of all my friends and family was factored in, before concluding with a plea for forgiveness of my daily sins. My religious conscience reminded me God was watching my every movement, my every thought. I knew God had a plan for me and I was special. I just needed to be obedient to what God wanted, and in turn, He would grant the things I wanted. But it was hard not to lust for Kim, or Jazmin, or Shana, or any girl with curves and a pulse. I needed Jesus to save me from the Devil's puberty. Luckily, Mshangwe loved Jesus with more conviction than I did. I'd come back to the room to catch him nodding his head along to Gospel music. While I'd walk a mile to town to spend my last fifteen dollars on a Method Man or Redman LP, Mshangwe would reserve his funds for Gospel albums on trips back to Newark. His church experience was different than mine. Co-op City Baptist Church wasn't a "holy rollie" congregation where Gospel singing was a theatrical showcase. Praise and worship consisted of elderly women singing like screeching cats. So, I met Mshangwe's Gospel music with great skepticism. *Could people really love Jesus that much?*

Whatever the case, it seemed to keep Mshangwe sane when feeling naive, misunderstood, and unwanted. At times he and Venroy, both a year younger than the rest of the Deuce Crew, could not mask their seeming immaturity. More physically developed, Venroy was able to withstand jokes about his massive cranium and Jamaican quirkiness though. On the other hand, Mshangwe came across as a Momma's Boy, with skin not thick enough to take a joke. He developed a reputation for being an asshole, an identity he co opted once he realized people would see him that way regardless of his true intentions. Before it became popular online Mshangwe fashioned himself a troll. "Asshole Gwe" was born and would grow to become a disagreeable nuisance. Often, others would approach me with "Yo, you better talk to your boy Gwe before I…" People couldn't understand how I tolerated his behavior, which admittedly, I found to be frustrating myself. However, I could see the good in Mshangwe. When exhausted from playing Devil's advocate, he would retire to our room to find comfort in Kirk Franklin's "Melodies From Heaven." I admired his relationship with God; it seemed to make his bond with his parents and siblings more fulfilling. I wished *my* relationship to *my* family was as warm and close. Unmotivated to call home regularly or pen all the letters I promised to my sister, I couldn't figure out my apathy towards my family. Expressing the love I felt became more awkward as time progressed. Acedia replaced affection as my father grew distant and the family disintegrated. Perhaps I was too spiritually immature to love at my full potential, I considered.

Taft wasn't a religious institution, though there was an appointed chaplain to serve any spiritual needs, questions, or requests anyone on campus might have. But he was White and didn't appear to view God through the Black lens that made sense to me. He seemed clueless to the different function God served in the lives of oppressed people. We needed God to liberate, not just sit in the sky and receive thanks. I ran into the same problem after walking a couple blocks from campus to attend First Congregational Church. The sanctuary was vintage eighteenth-century and smacked of Whiteness. Erected in 1739, I could imagine the ghosts of congregants past praying for favor from White Jesus while my ancestors begged God to abolish slavery. The service was painfully mundane, while the praise and worship portion lacked any emotion whatsoever. Suddenly, I missed the off key singers at my home church; at least those old Black ladies in Section 5 tried. White church was awful. I couldn't understand what they got out of it, let alone what I would ever get out of it. So I added White church underneath White girls on the list of things I would probably never try again.

***

That summer I went home with more questions than answers to the enigmas I hoped boarding school would solve. Would I ever catch up to my peers physically? Spiritually? Intellectually? Economically? Each individual task seemed insurmountable. Unwilling to cooperate with my desires, weight and height were held up by my genes. God was either ignoring me or slow to intervene in my requests. I failed to gain a greater understanding of God or the Bible's place in my life. In the uphill battle against classmates afforded world class education since birth, motivation required spiritual strength - strength I often lacked. How was I ever going to be rich?

To compensate for my lack of muscle, money, and wisdom, I resolved to outwork everybody. I found a job through the city's Summer Youth program. High school students from every borough fought for the few hundred slots Summer Youth offered for employment. Once accepted into the program, a better than minimum wage job awaited *somewhere*. Due to my continued interest in science, I saw my enthusiasm rewarded with placement in the cold basement pharmacy of Beth Abraham Hospital. Labeling plastic prescription bottles and delivering them to geriatric patients were my duties. In the quiet, pale, yellow dungeon I abhorred the monotony of printing and applying stickers to pill containers. The pharmacists were the most boring people I ever met. I kept my Discman with me, relying on Hip Hop to keep a pulse. The real action occurred when I got to walk around the hospital delivering meds in brown paper bags to seniors. Some of them were delighted to have someone new to talk to, however brief our encounter. Others were senile and bat shit crazy. Unpredictable and likely to fly off the handle at a moment's notice, they were exciting and I looked forward to seeing them. There was even one old White lady with a bad case of Tourette's Syndrome who would shout, "You're a nigger! You're a nigger," as I sat her bag of meds next to her bed. Admittedly, the first few times I heard a White person scream "nigger" in my face with so much conviction I was alarmed. Summoning the power to stifle a knee-jerk response of congruent venomous rage was no easy task. Though she was off her rocker, I felt a small piece of her brain subscribed to this way of thought, for why would her mind randomly select that particular phrase for word vomit?

Finding resilience in learning to accept her mental illness, I'd smile widely and retort, "I have money though!"

It was true… I had a few dollars to spend on CDs, food, and clothes. It didn't take long for some of the girls around the way to notice. Jacquay, a well developed, redbone, Truman High School chick, tried to have sex with me in the Building 26 staircase. I wasn't ready. I was shocked at how fast things progressed from us flirting outside, to her unzipping her shorts in the stairwell. Just a few weeks earlier I couldn't get a chick to look my way, let alone take her clothes off. But here I was being offered my first piece of poontang. Not knowing where to begin or how to operate a condom, I was too scared to be turned on.

She pressed, "I thought you was Meek Tha Freak, what's wrong?"

Coyly, I asked, "Don't you think we should get to know each other a little better?"

Incredulous, her eyes and mouth grew wide. She pulled up her pants and stormed down the steps pissed. I figured it was only a matter of time before word spread I was wack, lame, or gay.

Eddie, Louie, and Darryl got the biggest laugh out of it. Apparently, while I was away at boarding school, they all gained new, untold experiences in the female department. I felt naive. I felt like an outsider. I felt like my parents, particularly my father, had kept me sheltered from the realities of human interaction and purpose. The birds and the bees talk never happened. I felt betrayed. At fifteen, while everyone else was becoming men, I still had the mindset of a boy.

Tank, my mom's new boyfriend, hipped me to the game though. A five-foot-eight corrections captain, he was a dead ringer for rapper Rick Ross (their shared occupation a total coincidence). He lived a few floors up and enjoyed taking me and the guys for rides in his black 745. At first I couldn't understand what my mom, a tall, gorgeous woman saw in Tank, a short, bald, and inexplicably arrogant, fat dude. It didn't take long to see he was charming and fun to be around. When he wasn't coaching me and the fellas on keeping rubbers and not laying down with women we "wouldn't want to be with in case an accident happened," he'd take us to the firing range to test our aim with his service pistol. It made me feel like a man. Just in case I had to "kick in the door wavin the four-four" I was prepared. In return, Eddie, Louie, Darryl, and I performed free construction work for Tank's new real estate ventures. It was the first time I had ever worked with my hands. Like shooting guns, it also made me feel like a man.

Tank recognized my love for dogs and seized on it to win my favor. Co-op City forbade canine ownership and I missed my days in Brooklyn with Sheba. When his good friend, Sal, the Italian, Section 5 Pizza Shop owner got divorced, Tank convinced Sal to entrust him with his German rottweiler, Nitro. I loved Nitro. At 165 pounds and standing almost six feet on his hind legs, Nitro looked menacing. He was a giant, drooling teddy bear though. I'd sneak him up and down the staircase to avoid being caught violating Co-op City's no pet policy.

Once Tank finally opened his first rental property, my mom, sister, and I would drive over to Castle Hill to walk, feed, and spend time with Nitro in his new backyard digs. Soon, Cheecago, a pot bellied, brindle pitbull, joined the family to keep Nitro company. Sabree came up with the name in support of Sammy Sosa's steroid fueled campaign to break Major League Baseball's home run record. And just like that, our family dynamic changed. Tank kept us ensnared with our pooch appreciation.

So much changed over the course of the summer I failed to recognize my rapid growth spurt. It wasn't until I got back on campus at Taft that I became aware of the six inches I gained in height. Tiffany James, who had also blossomed over the summer, brought it to my attention.

"Yo, get out of here... you got mad tall!" she pointed out jokingly.

I responded with bewilderment, "I did?"

Her disbelief heightened, "Yo, your voice got mad deep too! Look at you growing up!"

Back then, we wore our clothes so baggy it was easy for an increase in height and weight to go unnoticed, the same clothes still fit. I was too busy putting in work with my summer job and Tank to realize I had shot up to five-foot-nine. Still rail thin, I also saw triple digits on the scale for the first time. No more would I have to chug a gallon of water to qualify for wrestling's 103 weight class. In fact, I would move up a division to 112 pounds. No longer worried about stunting my growth, I hit the weight room convinced this was the year coaches would put some respect on my name.

The crew formerly known as Deuce grew in size and number sophomore year. (We had to drop the Deuce moniker at the administration's request, due to the grossly misperceived threat we posed with our Homie socks on HDT4). Michael Martinez, a coveted Puerto Rican baseball prospect from Harlem, joined the fold. Mike, a boarding school veteran, having been away from home at Boston's Fessenden since the seventh grade, was initially reluctant to seek acceptance from Taft's strange new campus community. He found comfort in being a loner. Mike cared about chasing his Major League Baseball dream first, and making friends second. Naturally, over time, our mutual love for baseball led us to become confidants. Over Bone Thugs-N-Harmony we'd chat about everything under the sun. Mike was Taft's AC Slater. Chicks would inquire about Mike's availability through me. Girls, Black, White, and otherwise threw coochie at him. Via association, I figured some would eventually fall my way, but that wasn't a major motivating factor in making Mike's acquaintance. Ultimately, my friendship with Mike led to his acceptance by the rest of the fellas.

Before Marshwan Lynch popularized the phrase "Beast Mode," we used it to jokingly acknowledge the collective state of frustration we had with Taft's women. Hormones raging, we often wished the sistas would be more liberal with hooking up. At five-hundred students, the Taft community was already small; the Black and Latino population was an even further microcosm. Competition for the attention of such few females was considerable. Being friends made it even more interesting. We had to accept the fact most of the chicks we fooled around with would eventually end up in the arms of a comrade. At one point or another it happened to all of us, a consequence of the crew being in perpetual "Beast Mode." Replete with bull horn hand signal, the Beast Mode Squad evolved from the Deuce Crew.

While the Beast Mode Squad got chose, the most action I got was laughs from Ms. Roberts during my nightly dance routine. Ms.

Roberts was the full figured English teacher that lived across the hall from me in an HDT 3 faculty apartment. She had cakes like Michelle Obama. One night, during roll call, Ms. Robert's accidentally walked in on me fresh out of an evening shower. Toweled from the waist down, I knew the incident was awkward for both of us, so I broke the tension with an impromptu pop lock. From that day forward, whenever Ms. Roberts was on duty she could expect me to be waiting, music at the ready, for live entertainment when she opened me and Mshangwe's door. I knew shaking my bones was hilarious; I could have competed for the crown in Richard Bey's Mr. Puniverse competition. My skinniness was too obvious to hide, so I figured *why try?* I was finally becoming comfortable in my skin.

Still, there weren't any chicks on campus throwing themselves at me. Even with the additions of Khayriyyah Muhammad, Ciara Rakestraw, Carla Gracia, and Tarik Asmerom, there just weren't any viable love interests. So I took my search off campus. My boy, Andre Charles, who grew up across the street from me on Hunter Avenue, also made it to boarding school. He ended up at Westminster, about an hour north of Taft. He gave me the scoop on a flirty, bright-skin girl named Chandra. I had met her previously through a Prep For Prep mixer I attended in Manhattan. The Black and Latino boarding school circle was so small, we were all less than a degree of separation away from each other in some way. Andre told me Chandra was single as a dollar bill, so I dropped her a letter reintroducing myself. Soon, we communicated daily over email, fresh technology at the time. Every evening, I ran to the computer lab to first check HipHopSite.com, then login to my Hotmail account to view her latest reply. It beat spending money on phone cards and waiting to use one of the two payphones in the dorm.

Eventually I would make arrangements for Chandra to accompany me to the annual Formal. Since we didn't have an official prom, The Formal was a pretty big deal. Decked out in a tuxedo, top hat, and cane, I convinced my friends to defy Taft protocol and commission our limo to a pitstop in Simsbury, Connecticut. They gave me props when Chandra stepped into the limo looking like a million bucks. I don't remember much about The Formal besides the customary closing song and White Privilege national anthem, "Brown Eyed Girl." My mind was fixed on sneaking Chandra up to my room and possibly getting lucky. I still wasn't ready to go all the way, but I figured I'd approach the border of manhood to see if it led me to new territory. Like ninjas, we were swift, yet light-footed as we traveled down the corridor of HDT 3. Getting caught by Ms. Roberts would have resulted in an embarrassing disciplinary violation, so I was extra cautious. Once inside the room, my heart pounded like a Taiko drum. Chandra was relaxed and ready to engage, but paranoia prevented me from enjoying the experience. We relocated to the dark, dusty, key coded bike room in the basement, only to interrupt another couple mid action. I apologized and took my date around the corner to the well lit laundry room, where we fooled around awkwardly for a few moments. Afterwards, I escorted Chandra to the girls' dorm, where I arranged for her to overnight with our mutual friend Tiffany James.

    The next morning, at breakfast in the dining hall, I noticed Chandra was extremely distant. She barely acknowledged my presence. I figured she was disappointed that we had not done more and/or that I was too much of a coward to provide her with a comfortable environment for us "explore" the night before. Curiously, dickhead upperclassmen Jamahl and Shaun seemed to be most amused by the obvious cold shoulder I was receiving. They snickered, stared, and smiled at me across the table. Gut instinct told me something was wrong… and it was. Right after I sent Chandra back to Westminster with my Spanish teacher, who just happened to be heading that direction for mountain biking, Jamahl pulled me to the side. With his rotten front toothed smile he said, "Thanks for bringing her out here man... we had fun last night!" I was crushed. I went upstairs to the common room to debate my next move. Pummeling Jamahl seemed like the only logical option. Luckily, Mike was there watching TV and allowed me to vent. "Why you mad at him instead of her? She's the one that played you like a sucker," Mike calmly delivered.

He was right. Prior to that, I never considered women could be as trifling and untrustworthy as men. Chandra changed how I viewed females forever; never again would I let a chick play me for a fool.

That summer I went home with a chip on my shoulder. Even with making and excelling on the JV baseball team, I felt I had more to prove to the world, more to prove to myself. Sixteen-year-olds were men in most parts. Adult decisions like joining the military, dropping out of school, and driving were in play. With no interest in the first two, I got my learner's permit and convinced my mother to let me drive the Bonneville home from Pathmark on our grocery runs. Back then, she drove with a lead foot. Like most New York drivers, she was impatient, aggressive, and defensive behind the wheel. In fact, one time at the lead up to the Williamsburg Bridge, she even got out the car to go ham on a blonde that cut us off. My sister and I had to restrain her from going upside the lady's head with "The Club."

Despite suffering from road rage, my mother figured she was a capable driving instructor. And she was surely capable... capable of driving me insane with her micromanagement and irritability from the passenger seat. My dad was more patient, allowing me to drive back and forth on I-95 to arbitrary points in New Rochelle. It was the little time we got to spend together over breaks from school. Just beyond the city limits, New Rochelle allowed people to test for full fledged licenses at sixteen. Most inner city New Yorkers don't drive, deferring to the Subway and mass transit system to get by instead. With a license and access to wheels I knew I'd be the man. See, back then, if you had *A* car you were the BX version of Baby (word to Kanye!). Women wouldn't be able to resist a guy with transportation. Nothing said manhood like having your pick of women… women to have sex with.

    I wanted to lose my virginity more than Patrick Ewing wanted a ring. It didn't much matter who the chick was, Beast Mode was activated. The only one off limits was Lauren, the last remaining girl I trusted. Preserved in memory was the innocence of our middle school romance. Despite distance, we had remained friends through the years. I refused to subject her to my carnal desires. Everyone else was in play though. I had three goals that summer: get mobile, get paid, get laid. While I was working on getting my license, Summer Youth got my paper right with a great resumé builder - an internship in the Global Asset Management division at Chase. Working across the street from my mom on 47th and 6th, summertime N.Y. was a lustfest. Sundress season was enough to make any man's eyes pop out of his head. Commuting on the subway gave me and my mom opportunities to catch up on the time boarding school stole from us, but it also cramped my style. I couldn't holler at chicks in front of my mom. So that left me the weekend to recruit a young lady for my plan.

    By chance, I bumped into Shanté behind Building 26. She was only in Section 5 to visit a cousin. I reeled her in with something slick that made her smile. The same shade of light brown, we hit it off quickly. The only problem was… she was seventeen, a year older than me. High school chicks seldom date younger guys. Initially, Shanté took exception to my boyish features, but I assured her I was just a babyfaced seventeen-year-old. I even flashed my learner's permit for 0.3 seconds to "prove" I was of age. Healthy and well proportioned, I knew I had to get Shanté up to 6F before my mom and sister returned from Tank's mother's house. My game was tight, I said all the right things and Shanté agreed to come upstairs. We made out on the purple living room sofa, where I struggled to unhinge her D cup bra from under her t-shirt. After some assistance, I grabbed her hand to lead her back to my bedroom, but she was reluctant. Snatching her hand back to flick her box braid extensions, she dropped "Umm, I just met you… I'm not ready for all that yet." *Of course... the universe wants me to die a virgin.* Disappointed, I apologized to Shanté for any perceived disrespect. "You're lucky I like you," she shot back.

    Speaking to Shanté on the phone, I realized I didn't like her at all. Beyond physical attraction, we had little in common. Nothing she said was intellectually stimulating and she had no plans for her future. Shanté was just out to survive. I was out to thrive. But that didn't stop me from wanting to lose my v-card, and she was my warmest lead. So the next time I had the house to myself, I invited her over to do the deed. Sensing I had no idea what I was doing, she asked if I had prior experience. I told another lie and produced a condom to confirm my know-how. Fearing my mother's unexpected return, she kept on most of her clothes, even her panties. By the time I realized I was having sex it was over. Mission accomplished. Relieved, I patted myself on the back and welcomed myself into the man club. Nowhere in my calculation was Shanté's instant emotional attachment. She wanted to talk on the phone even more and take the bus to Section 5 at every waking opportunity. Annoyed, I became increasingly distant. And such was my arrival into manhood.

***

I returned to Watertown more confident than ever. No longer did it matter if Taft girls were prude or uninterested, I had options back home. But as fate would have it, the ninety mile trek back to The Bronx in search of affection became unnecessary. Tiffany Bryan was apart of the new contingent of Black and Latino freshmen. Over the summer I wrote a rap titled "I Never Met a Girl Named Tiffany I Didn't Like," and she proved my theory infallible. Her smile was perfect and radiant, she had the kind of teeth that a person with braces could only dream about, yet never gain. Her golden, buttermilk skin could have made her kin to Tisha Campbell. Two grade levels younger, Tiff entered Taft with a fully developed body and a sense of maturity foreign to most lower-mids. A Brooklyn Jamaican, the natural assumption was she would end up with fellow yardie Venroy. But Venroy fixated on another freshman, Cherese, a cute dark-skinned girl from The Bronx. That left room for me and Tiff to become close friends. Brought together by daddy issues, we both filled each other's emotional void. Tiff's dad lived in Toronto and they barely interacted. His seeming indifference towards her existence carved a deep wound into her soul. She saw something in me that helped to ease the pain. I cared about her accomplishments. I made her laugh. I hugged her. I kissed her. I comforted her. I loved her. The love I had for Tiff was orders of magnitude more intense than what I felt with Lauren in middle school. The difference was: I didn't just love Tiffany, I was *in* love with her. I wanted to heal her and allow her to heal me.

In the evenings, we'd meet in the basement of main building to talk at length about everything imaginable. Off campus we were just as inseparable. During holiday breaks, I would catch the bus to Pelham Bay Park, then take two different trains to her mother's crib in Fort Greene. Her mom, Claudia, and her older brother, Tajeme, embraced me with caution. Eventually, they saw I made Tiff happy and accepted me as a fixture in her life. Gelling with them made me and Tiff's bond feel even more righteous. Years before his senseless murder, Tajeme would happily buy tickets for us to accompany him to Reggae Fest on Randall's Island. With puppy love blinders, I fashioned it impossible for better potential in-laws to exist. I was head over heels for Tiff and our compatibility made the prospects of marriage very real. Referencing school history, a number of Taft relationships led to subsequent nuptials down the line (at least they did for wealthy White folks limited in potential suitors of equal socioeconomic standing). Envisioning forever with Tiff didn't seem far fetched.

    Of course I was naive. I wished I could eliminate Tiff's pain, but I couldn't. The absence of her father created a black hole with gravity too intense for her resentment to escape. Succumbing to insuppressible bouts of depression, Tiff's pessimism was sometimes overwhelming. My attempts to coax her out of abjection were frequently futile and frustrating. I started to feel like I was being pulled underwater by the person I was struggling to keep afloat. Not prepared to deal with my own repressed feelings, I was reluctant to shoulder Tiff's suffocating burden on a daily basis. Despite how much I loved her, I had to let her go for peace of mind. The emotional turbulence was ruining our first class flight to matrimony. I knew I was being selfish, but like any stewardess would tell you, you have to place the oxygen mask on yourself before you attempt to save your seatmate. So after a year, I bailed and broke Tiff's heart. In my freedom, I explored romances with transfer students Sharifah Mtingwa and Bridget Asekunowo. After becoming emotionally unavailable, I broke their hearts too… and circled back to Tiff - our love forever enduring.

    During my stint as Don Juan, I never lost track of my first true love, Hip Hop. After a customary rub of Honest Abe's brass nose in Lincoln Lobby, I would ascend five floors to The Tower in the attic of CPT, to consume as much music as possible. Few guys elected to occupy one of the two large rooms in The Tower because it meant walking an additional flight of stairs after classes and practice. However, The Tower held a very noble secret - it was the only place high enough on campus to receive Hot 97's transmission. Out of all the Hip Hop heads on campus, Mshangwe and I were the only in position to witness Funkmaster Flex drop bombs on new tracks nightly. I'll never forget the bewilderment and excitement I felt the night he debuted Eminem's "My Name Is." Never had I heard anything like it. I turned my ear towards the speaker, *did he just say what I think I heard?* In that way, The Tower intensified my interest in the diverse sounds and emcees the East Coast lacked. Before it was acceptable for New York dudes to consume "ignorant" Southern music, The Tower's seclusion gave me the privacy to secretly listen to Cash Money and No Limit sans judgement. Marc and Harold would have certainly shamed me for even considering "trash" like that.

By senior year, Mshangwe and I were tired of making the five story climb to The Tower, so we settled on a large room on CPT4 with the gen pop. The Notorious B.I.G's scowl haunted me from a framed picture hanging on the wall adjacent to my bed. Looking at the photo always brought me back to the reality of Black nihilism outside the Taft bubble. Ultimately, it would also serve as an icebreaker between me and reticent dorm parent Mr. Hall. Strikingly articulate yet reclusive, Mr. Hall joined the English department my junior year. Any addition of Black faculty was highly welcomed by the melanated Taft community, so Mr. Hall's arrival on campus was cause for excitement. Joined by his gorgeous wife and former HBCU cheerleader Mrs. Hall, the young newlyweds kept a low profile, only popping out of their faculty apartment when absolutely necessary. Living on campus seemed to be a chore for them, and understandably so - what twenty something couple wants to live amongst dorm room debauchery during their foundational years? Most students found the Halls to be well-mannered, but distant. Taft seemed to be merely a pitstop in their careers, as Mr. Hall pursued his PhD from Harvard and Mrs. Hall completed graduate work at nearby Yale. Although I never had him as a teacher, Mr. Hall held a reputation for being a tough grader, stirring resentment in the students whose papers were left bloody with gobs of red ink. As someone who took pleasure in writing I admired his passion for English. Just by having a casual conversation with him, a person would learn a slew of potential SAT words. Mr. Hall could have ran laps around Michael Eric Dyson.

 I'll never forget him stopping in my room one afternoon after hearing me blast Common's *Like Water For Chocolate* in passing. After knocking, he peaked in and started bopping his head, "That brother's saying something right there D." *Oh shit, Mr. Hall likes Hip Hop?*

 I agreed "Yeah Common is dope, I was waiting for this album to drop all month. I just got back from town with it," referencing the two mile trek from Watertown's only record store on Main Street. Mr. Hall stood in the middle of my room soaking in the rest of the album and visibly enjoying it. From there he would stop in frequently to ask me what I was rocking to. *"Things Fall Apart...* this is jammin' Mr. Hall". Quickly, we bonded over Hip Hop and became friends.

 One day, Mr. Hall asked if I'd like to ride with him to Yale for a Hip Hop summit hosted by The Source. Common and dream hampton were headlining a panel discussion. "Are you kidding me? Yes, let's go!" I was stoked. Mr. Hall advised I should bring along my new Common album in case we got close enough to get it autographed. *Great idea.* During the forty-five minute drive to New Haven, I got to know Mr. Hall pretty well. Since 2000 was an election year, and the first year I'd be eligible to vote, we engaged in a political discussion. "Do you see how stupid this guy George Bush is? There's no way anybody with a brain is gonna vote for him," I laughed.

"Well… to tell you the truth my wife is warming me up to him."

Whaaaaat?! This Negro can't be serious.

"Really? Why on Earth would y'all even consider that?"

Mr. Hall then revealed how his conservative Christian beliefs led him and his wife to believe Bush was the candidate with the best moral compass. Dumbfounded, I couldn't believe Black people anywhere could rationalize supporting such a dimwit, let alone Mr. Hall, a Hip Hop fan and the smartest Black guy I'd ever met. Struggling to reconcile how we could both appreciate Common while having such divergent views on politics, I left the topic alone and brought the focus back to music. In subsequent months, I would ride back and forth to Yale with Mrs. Hall to interview AIDS researchers for my Senior Project on the risk of viral threats to humanity's existence. She would crank up Rush Limbaugh and try to convert me, unsuccessfully.

In any event, the Hip Hop summit ended up being extremely intimate and dope. Less than fifty people filled the room for the event. After fielding questions on Hip Hop's role in awakening the consciousness of the Black community, the panel disassembled and people lined up to meet the panelists individually. With *Like Water For Chocolate* in hand, I waited patiently with Mr. Hall to ask for an autograph. When we got to the front of the line, Common greeted Mr. Hall with unexpected excitement. "How you been Mark? What's good?"

What the hell? Mr. Hall knows Common?!

My whole mind was blown. They conversed for a sec then Mr. Hall told him how big of a fan I was and asked him if he could sign my CD. Starstruck for the first time, I barely mumbled a response when Common asked me my name. He signed the disc "To Meek with much love... Common," and asked if me and Mr. Hall would like to join him for lunch. Keeping my composure, I agreed and off we went to an Ethiopian restaurant a few blocks from campus. Common was dating Erykah Badu at the time so he was on a vegan kick and wore a big ass dashiki with some weird pants. I sat quietly in awe, as he and Mr. Hall caught up over injera and red lentil stew.

On the ride back to Watertown, Mr. Hall revealed he had known Common for years. Not one to toot his own horn, Mr. Hall failed to disclose he was secretly one of the nation's preeminent Hip Hop scholars, having contributed significant literary works and presentations as a teaching fellow at Harvard prior to his stint at Taft. There was no LinkedIn or web accessible Curriculum Vitae at the time, so there was no way to know this beforehand. It was like finding out Clark Kent was Superman all along. In that regard, Mr. Hall was the most humble and unassuming person I had ever met. I respected his humility, discipline, and most all, his faith. After Taft, he would go on to complete his doctorate at Harvard, publish a plethora of works related to Hip Hop and African American literature, and serve as a professor at a major university in the Midwest. I could only hope I would be as intelligent, as gifted a writer, and as dedicated to pushing the barriers of Hip Hop as Mark Hall when I grew up.

***

Senior year would be life changing for obvious reasons. It was time to take the SATs, apply to schools, and figure out where to spend the next four years of our lives. After several freezing autumns, winters, and springs at Taft, I decided I no longer wanted to go to college in the Northeast. Small town New England had to be the most unfun place in America for a Black man. Still, I hedged my bets and applied to Northeast schools Cornell, MIT, Upenn, and Johns Hopkins, in addition to southern schools FAMU, Emory, and Vanderbilt, because they were great universities with impeccable science and engineering departments. My father always spoke of how he missed his shot at completing an engineering degree at Cornell. He earned admission into a two-by-two program at Bronx Community College, which required he complete his first two years at BCC, before transferring to Cornell to complete his bachelor's degree. Instead of finishing out the program he joined the Navy. Becoming an engineer to fulfill my father's dream was an interesting prospect. However, I still wanted to fight diseases. Biomedical engineering offered what I thought to be a compromise. I might develop some device, mechanism, or treatment to ward off life threatening illnesses.

Upon visiting the Northeast schools in search of motives to remain up north, I found few compelling reasons to stay on the East Coast. They were all frigid, uppity, and unfun. I could see why students jumped hundreds of feet to their deaths from the suspended walkways at Cornell. MIT students were socially awkward. Johns Hopkins had an ugly campus, and a few of its Black students even pleaded with me not to commit four torturous years to the institution. UPenn was a lot nicer, but I found myself indifferent to joining the ranks of the Quakers.

Once I finally got around to visiting Emory, I realized I was onto something by considering the South. Atlanta was emerging as the new Black Mecca, and it wasn't just the the climate that was warmer there, people seemed to be more pleasant, less stressed, and lively. The southern Hip Hop scene had taken off with Atlanta at the forefront. Lil Jon, the Ying Yang Twins, and Ludacris headed the crunk movement, injecting new energy into rap music. I loved Wu-Tang and Beanie Sigel, but I was ready to party and dance with women. And the women Down South: way thicker and less stank than the girls up North. There were gorgeous women at Emory; amazons who knew how to twerk and were studying to become doctors. Sistas outnumbered Brothas four to one, I was told. Considering this *and* the fact Emory offered a microbiology program which could lead to work at the CDC, the school moved to the top of my list.

Vanderbilt was smart though. Realizing how easy it was to have misconceptions about Black college life in country music's capital, they paid for me to attend their aptly titled Black Student Recruitment Weekend. The red carpet was rolled out. A nonstop schedule of social events was on the agenda. Upon arrival at Nashville International Airport a chartered bus awaited. With my narrow East Coast perception of Tennessee, I was happy to see people weren't still riding horse and buggy. As the bus filled up with more and more Black faces, excitement kicked in. I had already decided I would go to Emory if accepted, so at the very least, I would have a good weekend partying with folks like me. That's what I felt I missed out on most by going to Taft - interaction with hundreds of people just like myself. Yet, here I was on a bus filled with brown faces flown in from all over the country to check out Vanderbilt.

To my immediate left, the only remaining vacant seat hugged the aisle. Just as the driver was about to pull off, a light-skinned dude in a fitted cap knocked on the motorcoach's glass door requesting entrance. He sat down next to me and it became immediately clear he was from the East Coast too. With exceptionally thick eyebrows and a familiar accent, he introduced himself as Clarion Johnson from Washington, DC.

"You know I'm not coming to this country ass school right? I'm just here because they paid for me to visit," he chuckled.

I laughed out loud, "Yo, I was thinking the same thing! We might as well have fun though."

A pact to stick together and make the most of the three day visit was forged.

At registration, I learned Issa Deas, a buff, bald, baritone, brown-skinned, Boricua Bronxite would be my host for the weekend. I assumed Vanderbilt matched us based on hometown. *Clever.* Coincidentally, it turned out Issa was a close friend of my middle school sweetheart, Lauren's family. I couldn't believe how small the world was. *Could this be a sign?* Certainly seemed like it. But before I got ahead of myself, I observed that Issa was taking a hands off approach towards actively recruiting me to campus. Besides giving me a key to his room so I could come and go as I please, he remained neutral in suggesting I join him as a Commodore. He left it up to me to make my own determination. *What did I need to keep my eyes peeled for?*

For starters, I wanted to know how cool the Alphas were on campus. A few months earlier, Mshangwe, Venroy, and I spent Columbus Day weekend visiting Mshangwe's older brother, Onaje, at Boston University. Having graduated from Taft two years prior, Onaje had just crossed the burning sands of A Phi A, and convinced us to witness Boston's biggest Black Greek event. We had no idea what we were in for, but we knew it had to be more stimulating than playing ping pong in The Jig.

It would be our first taste of college life. Upon arrival, Onaje swung us by the frat house to meet his bruhs. They were all brilliant guys who seemingly liked to kick it. "We party hard… we stay up late.. but most of all we graduate," one of them, a rum drinking Bajan, affirmed. Descending into the basement of the the two-story house, a painted mural of Dr. Martin Luther King, adorned the wall. King pledged this same Sigma Chapter of Alpha Phi Alpha in 1952.

Impressive. Soon we would come to learn about other prominent Alphamen, further piquing our curiosity in the organization. These guys had their act together.

The atmosphere in Boston was electric that weekend. Students packed the streets, before funneling into a huge convention center to watch the Divine Nine battle for prize money and bragging rights. Never had we seen so many students of color fill an arena for a non-sporting event. The Greek tribalism, call and response, hand signals, colors, and signature steps captivated us. Hearing the crowd roar as their favorite fraternity and sorority members stomped, clapped, and shouted in unison was thrilling.

And then the Alphas hit the stage. Executed with military precision, their flawless step routine brought down the house! Venroy and I looked at each other with muted smirks confirming the obvious: *this was some shit we had to be down with.* Afterwards, Onaje helped sneak us into the step show afterparty. None of us were eighteen, and I even looked too young to pass for my current age of seventeen. Onaje told us to follow his lead as he and "the good bruhs" skipped the massive line, bypassed security, and cockily walked into the sweltering gymnasium. "Whatever you do, don't break anybody's line while they're strolling" Onaje advised sternly. *What the hell is strolling?* We soon found out as the salty, second place Sigmas attempted to avenge their step show loss by marching through the dancefloor in coordinated motion. In no time, Onaje and the Alphas similarly began to dance, chant, and penetrate the crowd. Behind them were the prissy AKAs, divas of Delta Sigma Theta, barking Ques, and shimmying Kappas. Mshangwe, Venroy, and I ended up trapped in the middle of the dancefloor with other unsuspecting students, as the Greeks encircled us and took over the party. The spectacle caused me and Venroy to look at each other again - *this was DEFINITELY some shit we needed to be down with!*

The next morning we pressed Onaje, "How did you know you were supposed to be an Alpha?"

Delighted by the inquiry he revealed, "Being an Alpha is in your heart. You don't become an Alpha, you're born an Alpha."

Pledging Alpha Phi Alpha was a no brainer for me. I was ambitious, scholarly, and passionate about uplifting the Black community. Plus, I wanted to kick it - hard. Vanderbilt's Alphas didn't disappoint in reinforcing my perception during Black Student Weekend. Rumors abounded that the Alphas ran the yard as soon as I stepped foot on campus. Freshman, Rashaka Caldwell, confirmed those sentiments when me and Clarion ran into him at registration. "The Alphas got it, hands down. My boy Bichar is on line with them right now. I think he's gonna probate during the step show. Keep that on the hush hush though." *Dope.* Like the step show in Boston, the whole weekend centered around the impending Greek spectacle. The Alphas were shaping up to be cool. Vanderbilt was becoming more and more attractive.

Speaking of attractive, there was plenty of eye candy to go around. Nia Toomer, a bad yellow-bone from New York, and Kim Brooks, a brown-skinned Southern belle, stopped me dead in my tracks. "Wait til you see Lauren Duncan," Rashaka confidently smiled. *Wow, Vanderbilt got honeys like this?!*

Besides the stallions already enrolled, there were also winners amongst the prospects. The baddest one, Nydia Streets, a half Black/half Chinese bombshell from Chino, California, took an immediate liking to me... *Me?? Me!!!!* We met on the dancefloor of the posh University Club on night one. From repeatedly embarrassing myself during the few and far between boarding school parties, I was aware I couldn't dance a lick. But I still had New York City game. Nydia ate it up. She had the sweetest voice, demeanor, and smile. Episodes of A Different World convinced me I'd be Dwayne Wayne and here was my fine ass Blasian, Kinu. We became inseparable. The upperclassmen took notice and gave me props. Lo and behold, I made a name for myself before receiving an acceptance letter.

After macking the finest prospect, the freshmen dudes wanted to meet me. Rashaka introduced me to Kevin Harnsberry and Andrew Nichols. Along with Clarion, I spent the rest of the weekend squeezing into Kevin's teal Honda Accord to roll around campus. Blasting the Big Tymers and Three Six Mafia, while riding on chrome twenty inch rims, we felt inspired. The African American dream was ours for the taking. Jovial spirits ruled the weekend. By the time the step show went down at the Vanderbilt Rec Center, I felt embraced by the Black community. Five percent of Vandy's six thousand undergraduates were Black. Coming from a lily White boarding school with less than thirty melanated students, I was thrilled by the prospect of three hundred Black and Brown faces surrounding me; it was a thousand percent increase. Little did I know the Black community was even larger than I realized. I hadn't factored in the neighboring HBCUs of Tennessee State University, Fisk, and Meharry. Walking into the gym was like entering a chocolate Shangri-La. There were people like me as far as the eye could see - all smiling. Hundreds of beautiful women outnumbered the lucky Brothas who managed to make it to this point. Many of the students were from Nashville's Historically Black institutions. A good portion of them were Greek. I admired how their unity wasn't confined to the walls of their campuses.

And then the Alphas hit the stage. A contingent of sharp looking Brothas in formal suits marched out to handle business. Vanderbilt's Kappa Theta chapter comprised the majority of the group, with Fisk's Alpha Chi bruhs providing assistance. And man were they on point! The crowd "oood" and "ahhhd" as they commanded the stage with forceful precision. Anticipating the secret probate Rashaka promised, I was on the edge of my seat. But instead of coming out and being introduced to the crowd, Bichar and his line brother Robert Boxie continued to build suspense for their unveiling by running through the audience in tattered black robes with gargoyle masks. Like the rest of the spectators, the mysterious code of secrecy intrigued me. Then without a hitch, our attention was brought back to the stage. The icing on the cake was the men in black and olde gold building a trilevel human pyramid that swayed back and forth, before offering a few gratuitous pelvic thrusts to Jodeci's "Freakin You." Game, set, match... the scores of awed students jumping out of their seats declared the obvious winners of the Spring 2000 Black Student Weekend Step Show. I couldn't wait to share the stage.

Following the step show, everyone flowed over to the afterparty in the loft space atop Memorial Gym's garage. Like the party I went to in Boston a few months prior, the Greeks set it out. Down South strolling was known as "party hopping," and for good reason - these people elevated, stepped, and chanted with more fervor than ever before witnessed. Still, the party was only mildly interrupted, as unbothered undergrads grinded to "Whistle While You Twurk." It was exactly what I envisioned partying in the South would be, and then some. As I mustered up as much rhythm as I could to freak down Nydia on the dancefloor, I was overcome by how much fun the intermingling of Vandy, Fisk, and TSU students was producing. *This is how college should be!*

It became clear attending Vanderbilt would give me the best of both worlds, as I'd be going to a PWI without necessarily missing out on the HBCU experience. Having visited FAMU a few weeks earlier, I was seeking more from a university facility wise. As one of the reasons I chose Taft, my interest had always been in using cutting edge technology in the most advanced classrooms. Vanderbilt, and the predominantly White institutions to which I applied, could afford state-of-the-art facilities due to the huge wealth disparity they held over HBCUs. I had to come to grips with the fact I valued technology slightly more than the cool Hillman experience. But, by going to Vanderbilt it appeared I might be able to have my cake and eat it too. That's if Vanderbilt accepted me with an excellent financial aid package; there was no way my parents could afford the 50K annual tuition they were asking.

If accepted, Nydia promised she would also attend Vanderbilt to put our romantic intentions to the test. Once I got back to Taft, I spent every evening calling her across the country from the dorm payphone. A college experience with her seemed grand. While it would have made an incredible love story, I knew better than to hinge my life's decision on a girl. Recent experience hinted they were just too unpredictable. But I figured even if Nydia reneged, there'd be plenty of beautiful women to greet me once I touched down in Nashville. So I waited intently for the letters and financial aid packages to roll in. I had faith that my strong GPA and 1280 on the SATs (back when the scale maxed at 1600) would qualify me for acceptance into most of the schools to which I applied. And they did. Cornell and Johns Hopkins gave me the best offers, virtual free rides to attend their institutions. Despite everything waiting for me at Vandy, *could I really turn that down?* My family and I would be free from the debt that weighed us down like yacht anchors. Plus I'd only be a few hours away from home.

Surprisingly, I had a much more difficult decision than I expected when the big envelope from Vanderbilt finally reached my mailbox. Vandy's package was good, not great. Scholarships and financial aid only accounted for eighty percent of the room & board, food, books, and tuition. That left a ten thousand dollar shortfall. By going to Vanderbilt I would be selfishly forcing my parents to cough upwards of eight hundred dollars a month in salary. But could I live with myself knowing I left warm weather, Southern hospitality, twerk fests, a hybrid PWI/HBCU experience, and Nydia's fine ass on the table? Movies and tv shows taught me college was supposed to be fun - the last opportunity to wild out before the dullness and responsibility of adulthood took hold. After isolating myself in the remote confines of rural New England, and competing with the world's most brilliant minds six days a week for the past four years, I was ready for fun. Something had to give. *Why not just take out a few student loans?* Problem solved!

Naturally, Nydia and her family faced similar dilemmas in making her college decision. Though I braced for the possibility, I was still shocked when Nydia told me she would be declining Vanderbilt's offer. Her parents preferred that she go to school on the East Coast, somewhere closer to West Point, where her brother was enrolled. While I'd be fleeing The Bronx for Southern comfort, Nydia would leave the palm trees of Cali to attend Fordham - *in The Damn Bronx!* Oh the irony...

Still, by graduation time at Taft, I was confident I made the right decision to descend below the Mason-Dixon line. However, I wasn't as prepared for the emotional impact separating from The Beast Mode Squad would have on us all. We became closer than family. After four years of living together, eating together, conversing together, competing together, arguing together, not to mention frustrating, suffocating, and supporting each other, graduation was a heart wrenching event. Post graduation we couldn't even look at each other without tearing up. Cuban cigar smoke filled the air as we gathered on the soccer field behind Centennial Dorm. Venroy was the most distraught; the rippled football and wrestling captain bawled uncontrollably. Knowing he wouldn't be around for my timely head jokes made me sad too. *How was I going to cope without Head Flintstone, Heddie Murphy, Headrick Douglass???* (Venroy, I love you bro… you didn't think I was gonna leave that detail untold, did you?!). I knew I'd miss Venroy's laughter, Mike's common sense advice, Harold's Hip Hop commentary, Mshangwe's honesty, Marc's indifference, Shawn's generosity, and Dave's wisdom. The pounding Cohiba headache we suffered right after graduation served as a physical indicator of the pain we were set to endure being apart.

The Marshall Mathers LP was the soundtrack to our final hurrah, as we criss crossed the Northeast for senior parties at the extravagant estates of our wealthy classmates. From a vineyard in Sag Harbor to a sprawling property in suburban New Jersey, the Class of 2000 partied til the break of dawn for two weeks straight. And *we* were finally invited. It became clear why these off campus parties were so exclusive. There was plenty of binge drinking, weed smoking, and presumably, other illicit drug use. Though I had mostly abstained throughout high school for fear of developing an uncontrollable habit, I was finally prepared to indulge. I can attribute my very first hangover to drinking gin under a tent on someone's elaborate property. While it wasn't my first time trying marijuana, I also smoked my first bowl under that tent. (Previously, I had puffed a blunt or two after I allowed Darryl, Section 5's Smokey, to sell me on weed's wondrous properties). Overall, senior parties served as the penultimate revelation of what hid behind the curtain of White Privilege.

The Beast Mode Squad (Left to Right Top Row: Mshangwe Crawford, Mike Blomberg, Me, David Wisner, Venroy July, Marc Greggs. Bottom Row: Harold Francis and Shawn McCormack. Not Pictured: Michael Martinez)

CHAPTER SIX

BLACK GUY AT A PWI

Lord it's obvious we got a relationship
Talkin' to each other every night and day
Although you're superior over me
We talk to each other in a friendship way
Then outta nowhere you tell me to break
Outta the country and into more country
Past Dyersburg and Ripley
Where the ghost of childhood haunts me
Walk the roads my forefathers walked
Climb the trees my forefathers hung from
Ask those trees for all their wisdom
They tell me my ears are so young (Home)
Go back, from whence you came (Home)
My family tree, my family name (Home)
For some strange reason it had to be (Home)
He guided me to Tennessee (Home)
-Speech (Arrested Development) "Tennessee"

After lending his most powerful ship to the Union Navy during the Civil War, Cornelius Vanderbilt endowed Bishop Holland N. McTyeire with one million dollars to open Central University in Tennessee. In a nutshell, "he spent a million of money in sending a vessel against the Southerners to show his views then, and he wanted to give the money after the war was over to show them that the men of the North were ready to extend the olive branch."² Later, the school took on its donor's namesake. Before his death, Vanderbilt never visited the university named in his honor, he had too much business that needed his *real* attention; a privilege only Whites could reasonably attain. Black people were an afterthought in the whole equation. In fact, "Vanderbilt, it should be noted, did not help freed slaves, now hungry for education, land and work. He saw the South through the summer visitors he mingled with at Saratoga Springs, N.Y.—the white elite."³ White Privilege. White Privilege. White Privilege. Yet, here I was on campus, eager to shake the ivory towers White Privilege erected, while extending my own olive branch to the Black South for the douchey elitism Black Northerners exuded.

Life at Vanderbilt started out the same way it had at Taft: with a single room my freshman year. Rarely was my room in Kissam Quad empty though, for I always kept company. Though I eventually acquired a country twang, my New York accent initially conferred a competitive advantage in courting ladies. It stood out amidst the sea of Southern drawl. I was shocked by the attention I received in Rand, the dining hall, from other Black students that just wanted to hear me talk.

"Say toilet again… watch this guys."

Amused by these requests, I'd respond shaking my head with incredulous New York attitude, "Tawlet… tawlet… what's so funny?!" The whole dining hall would erupt.

"What's this?!"

"A lollipop."

More laughter.

"What am I drinking?!"

"Soda."

---

² TJ Stiles: The Commodore's Civil War.
³ TJ Stiles: The Commodore's Civil War.

Loud fits of giggling.

"What do I have on my feet?!"

"Sneakers."

By this point there'd literally be people rolling around on the floor laughing their asses off. Unaware lollipops were suckers, soda was coke or pop, and sneakers were tennis shoes in the South, I was often left scratching my head. *Why the hell would Jordan's be tennis shoes when the man clearly played basketball?*

I didn't mind being the butt of a few jokes considering I found the overt countryness of some of my classmates to be downright comical. My first work study job assignment placed me at the admissions office with LaKerri Mack, a Pittsview, Alabama native. She was as tickled by my New Yorkness as I was by her 'Bama drawl. When she told me she was getting her "hair *did*" with her first paycheck I died laughing! Not realizing what she said was out of the ordinary, LaKerri laughed at me laughing at her. Once I brought to her attention why I found getting her "hair did" so funny, we laughed some more. In fact, we laughed about it for our entire stint at Vandy!

Making friends in my new environment wasn't difficult, but I missed the type of bonds I formed in boarding school. Clarion, who also saw the light and enrolled at Vandy, was around, but kept a suspicious distance. As the first semester unfolded, he curiously became close with girls I liked, who would later grow an inexplicable disdain for my presence. I could never tell whether the animosity stemmed from Clarion hating, or my guest appearances on VUTV's "Collard Greens and Cornbread." I'd cut up with sexist jokes on camera whenever I found Adrian Hill and Jelani Teamer filming Vandy's version of the Howard Stern show. Surely, my jokes weren't meant to be taken seriously, I was merely a budding college clown. I mean, *why would the same girls who chanted the lyrics to Ludacris' "Ho" be offended by me searching for the campus hoasis?*

It wasn't until I needed a haircut that I came across another guy I felt I could really trust. Before Google and Yelp, the best way to find a good barbershop was through word of mouth. Two weeks into school, I ran into another dude as perplexed as I was about where to get his hair cut. At Taft, I grew accustomed to cutting my own hair, as well as the rest of the Beast Mode Squad, since there wasn't a single Black barber in Watertown, Connecticut. There were just too many Black students and locals in the city of Nashville for it not to be a Black barbershop there though. College required a crispy, professional cut, and my goal was to stay a cut above the rest. When I checked with upperclassmen I met during Black Student Weekend, they all claimed to get dorm room cuts from football players or other random guys. Not willing to sacrifice my hairline to an amateur, I resolved to finding a barber off campus. It just so happened that Sebastine Ujereh Jr., another of the handful of Black engineering students in the class of 2004, was in the same predicament.

"Hey, do you know where to get a haircut?" Sebastine asked as we crossed paths below the bell tower of Kirkland Hall.

"I've been trying to figure out the same thing. We should just go to the hood. There's gotta be a barbershop there."

Sebastine, always cautious, thought about it for a moment before concluding, "Let's do it."

Knowing nothing about the Metro bus system, we resolved to catching a cab, with a Black driver - *they would have to know where a barbershop was... or at least the hood.* Expecting a few cabs to racially profile and pass us by like the taxis in New York, I was shocked when the first cab we signaled on West End Avenue stopped and encouraged us to hop in. "Hi Sir, please take us to a barbershop." It never occurred to us that we probably sounded as silly as Prince Hakeem and Semi when they first arrived in Queens.

The cab driver looked over his right shoulder and smugly responded, "Which barbershop?"

Sebastine inquired, "Are there any good ones close to here?"

"I don't know, I cut my own hair."

SMH. *Of course.*

"Can you just take us to the hood so we can find one?" I asked.

"You mean by Fisk? Yeah, sure."

After circling the neighborhood bordering W.E.B. DuBois' alma mater for twenty minutes, we finally spotted a swirling red, white, and blue barber's pole suspended from the awning of a shop across the street from Jo Johnston Projects. Relieved, we walked in and immediately felt everyone's eyeballs scan us from head to toe with true "Who are *these* niggas?" dubiety.

"Yall boys just started at Fisk, huh?"

"Nah, we go to Vandy."

Their eyes grew exceptionally wide like they'd seen a flying pig.

"What brought yall over this way?"

"Man we just needed a cut."

The two barbers with people in their chair exchanged a suspicious glance, while the third and closest to the front window made note of his immediate availability. "I can cut you right now" the youngest of the barbers suggested. We looked around at the seated line of gentlemen who were patiently waiting on the two middle aged barbers to finish with their clients. Then we looked at each other, communicating with our eyeballs what we knew must be true - *the third barber obviously sucked*. Turning down his proposition would have been extremely rude and awkward considering we were newcomers though. Since the whole thing was my idea, I figured I'd take one for the team and be the first guinea pig. Reluctantly, I sat down in the vacant chair, praying to the hair gods for salvation of my hairline. Sebastine, watched intently hoping one of the other barbers would free up before my haircut concluded.

"What you want me to do to it?" the eager barber asked.

"Just give me a fade, low on the sides, but keep the waves on top."

"Oh an Ivy League?" he asked for confirmation.

"Nah, a fade," I restated, making sure he heard me well.

Detecting the apparent cultural difference, he asked, "Man, where y'all from?"

"I'm from New York - The Bronx."

"Oh yeah, I figured. I can hear it," he said before turning to Sebastine.

"Mine's a little more complicated," Sebastine chimed. "I've been all over from New Jersey, to Senegal, to Zimbabwe, to Indianapolis. My parents are missionaries. My dad is Nigerian and my mom is from New Orleans."

"Well goddamn, boy you from everywhere!" the barbers laughed hysterically.

For that brief moment I felt the universal brotherhood that pervades Black barbershops. The moment was brief because soon after I would wince at the pain of steel blades carving razor thin lacerations around the perimeter of my head.

Not trying to sound like a punk, I disclosed, "Yo your clippers are kinda sharp man."

"Yeah, I know. But they cut better. Wait til I'm finished."

The torturous ordeal couldn't be over soon enough. My whole head stung from all the nicks and cuts I suffered during my twenty minutes in his chair. Then... then... as final protocol, he doused me with alcohol from a spray bottle. Instantly I knew how it felt to get KO'd by Dhalsim's Yoga Flame. Beaming from ear to ear, he walked around me with a hand mirror reflecting all angles into the large shop mirror in front of my chair. My hairline had taken the worst beating of its life. I wasn't sure it'd ever recover.

Disheartened, I mumbled, "How much do I owe you?"

"Fifteen dollars."

Fifteen dollars? For this shit?!

My father always taught me to tip my barber, so with the customary gratuity of twenty percent, I ended up spending eighteen dollars on the worst haircut of my life. With the shop still as full as when we arrived, Sebastine suffered the same fate - a scalp on fire and eighteen dollars poorer. The bad haircuts left us without enough money for a cab back to campus. So we were forced to relish in our misery on the two mile trek back to Vandy.

Along the way I got to know Sebastine pretty well. Though he'd spent his high school years in Africa, he was a consummate Hip Hop consumer. Of course, gaining access to all the hottest American music while living in Zimbabwe was a challenge. Sebastine had significant gaps in his rap library. I promised to let him hold Mos Def's *Black on Both Sides* when we got back to Kissam, provided we made it over the other side of the tracks in Nashville's scorching heat.

About a mile into our voyage we looked up to observe hundreds of pigeons lining the power lines on both sides of the street on 21st Avenue. I gave Sebastine the heads up, "man, we better walk fast. I'm not trying to get shitted on by these birds." He found my paranoia to be laugh out loud hilarious! "Okay, I've seen more than my fair share of pigeons in New York. Walk slow if you want to." I started speed walking my ass off. Sebastine continued to stroll leisurely and taunt me the further I increased in distance. Out of nowhere the pigeons decided to punish Sebastine for his hubris, arising from their perch to block out the sun as they swarmed. Suddenly, splats of incoming pigeon poop could be heard smacking vengefully against the pavement. I turned around to see Sebastine hauling ass in full sprint down the middle of the street. By the time he reached me he was fully covered in grainy, white bird droppings. It was my turn to laugh! And I did for a minute. But I couldn't let Sebastine walk back to campus looking like a pigeon port-o-potty. So I took off my blue, short-sleeved, tiger mural, Phat Farm button-up and gave it to him to wear. I had a wife-beater underneath, so it was the least I could do. We became brothers that day.

Soon, the duo of Meek and Sebas would become brothers to several others. Brookes Gore was a stocky, copper-skinned, hairy, Blasian dude from DC. Like us, he was a huge Hip Hop head. Residing *from* the Mason-Dixon line, he was as equally knowledgeable about East Coast rap as he was about the Southern variety. He even loved West Coast music and appreciated Snoop as much as I did. Brookes, who sounded a lot like Raekwon when we got drunk and freestyled, was a brilliant guy. He had the highest SAT score out of everybody we knew, loved to analyze lyrics, and rigorously debate any and everything from contrarian perspectives. As someone who was half Black/half Asian, half Christian/half Buddhist, half Northerner/half Southerner, I welcomed Brookes' insight on most subjects.

Between Brookes being a graduate of DC's illustrious Sidwell Friends, and Clarion being a product of the capital's St. Albans, we were plugged into the Washington prep school alumni circle. That's how we became acquainted with the ever abrasive, Kim Ford. Most of the girls on campus (and many of the guys) were intimidated by Kim's quick tongue. To the contrary, I was drawn to her wit, rebelliousness, and dedication to getting tore up. Plus, she was an AKA, and *everybody* knew the AKAs shared historical ties to the Alphas, as the first of all Black Greeks. Since that stepshow weekend in Boston, I was eager to immerse myself in Greek life. Somehow I figured being close to Kim would bring me closer to being an Alpha. At the very least it would bring me closer to the fine ladies of Alpha Kappa Alpha.

Sensing our interest in becoming Greek, Kim convinced her chapter to resurrect a long defunct auxiliary group - MIAKAs (Men Interested in AKAs). Auxiliary groups were not officially sanctioned by Greek organizations. In fact, many local chapters were given orders from their national governing bodies to cease and desist any operations pertaining to auxiliary groups. Nevertheless, Black freshmen often found themselves joining the ranks of the Alpha Angels, Omega Pearls, Sigma Doves, Kappa Sweethearts, Delta Beauxs, Zeta Knights, and MIAKAs. I had no idea MIAKAs on other campuses were typically gay men who longed to be AKAs; I just knew *I* was a man interested in AKAs as the title suggested. Besides that, it would give me the ability to party hop as a first semester freshman, instead of having to wait until second semester for Alpha intake. I imagined the dance floor stopping to admire me and my crew's steps. Becoming a MIAKA was a no brainer. Sebastine, Brookes, and Clarion came to the same conclusion. When Jarrod Woodley, a burly dude from Little Rock heard about our intentions, he was down too. Jarrod fashioned himself a mogul in the making and always spoke of great ambitions. The final member was Ronald Hatcher, Vanderbilt's blue-Black, punt returner from Birmingham. Everyone knew him on campus as Hatch. Though most football players were destined to be Ques, his dad was an Alpha. Hatch was very disciplined, soft spoken, and had perfect manners. Rarely did student-athletes have time to establish worthy relationships with non athletes, so we appreciated Hatch's effort to break the mold.

After a couple of weeks of step practice, learning the Greek alphabet, and affording Kim and a few of her sorors ample laughs, we had a "come out" show in the Branscomb circle. "Come out," or probate shows, were always a sure way to draw a crowd, so most of Black Vandy showed up. Especially certain to attend were Greeks, present to assess potential aspirants. Apparently, joining an auxiliary group at an HBCU was taboo and the surest way to eliminate yourself from contention in a real fraternity or sorority. Black schools saw auxiliary group members as thirsty wannabes. These concerns weren't as big of a deal at Vandy, where Black Greek membership was so limited that being overly selective meant jeopardizing the viability of a chapter. Lots of people graduated from auxiliary groups to legitimate organizations at Vanderbilt. Still, the real Greeks liked to tease. And for good reason. The AKAs "skee-wee'd" and MIAKAs "wee-skee'd." They wore pink and green, while we wore black and green. Their hand signal was a solitary extended pinky, while our signal looked like the gun you'd make playing cops and robbers as a Kindergartner. In hindsight, being an auxiliary member was laughable. But tell that to a first semester freshman frothing at the idea of going Greek...

  I loved my social life at Vandy. I partied with the coolest people on and off campus. Taaka vodka remained stocked in my room. White Boy Rick, a red-headed, goateed stoner happily shared weed, Adderall, and ecstasy with me. I only tried Adderall after procrastinating on a computer engineering project with an impending deadline. Rick was my partner and we'd stayed up all night talking shit and burning CDs from pirated Napster tracks. No matter how many times I attempted to remind Rick of the next morning's deadline, he nonchalantly brushed off my insistence. "Trust me Meek. We'll just take these Addies and pull an all nighter." Reluctantly, I agreed. The next thing I knew we were creating a Flash website from scratch. This was back when Flash was cutting edge technology. Miraculously, we got an A on the project, it was actually pretty dope. *Maybe pills weren't so bad after all.* That incident motivated me to do my due diligence on ecstasy, the wonder drug even Bone Thugs was bragging about. If I was ever going to experiment with drugs, I figured college was the perfect time. Ecstasy seemed to be relatively safe as long as I stayed hydrated. So I got a couple of blue dolphins from Rick and popped the first one in the solitude of my room. I wanted to be sure MDMA didn't turn me into a bumbling idiot before I tried it socially. For forty-five minutes I contemplated kicking Rick's ass for giving me a placebo. Right at the moment I stood up to go confront him, I noticed the lights from my boombox seemed to follow my eyes. *Whoa.* Then I noticed the beats on Busta Rhymes' *Anarchy* sounded waaaayyy better than they ever had before. I started dancing in place, uncontrollably, with rhythm! The next trial was at a party the following weekend. I was a dancing machine. Ecstasy was dope. I just hated the lockjaw I suffered for several days afterward. *That can't be a good sign.* I was content with having the courage to explore, but knew popping Ecstasy wouldn't be a regular thing. Besides, I was haunted by my family history and wary of becoming addicted to anything.

Becoming a lazy drug addict and flunking out of college, after working so hard to make it there, wasn't an option. While I partied fairly hard, I was still conscious of trying to keep a respectable GPA. Unfortunately, I had no idea all of my classes were designed to weed out most engineering students. Chemistry and calculus were by no means foreign to me by the time I got to Vanderbilt. However, the introductory courses seemed to move at a breakneck pace. Even worse, virtually all of my professors were foreigners with extremely difficult accents. Seeking extra help from them once I started to struggle was fruitless. To complicate matters further, I rarely had the money to purchase all of my textbooks upfront. My friends from poorer families received full rides, while my friends from wealthier upbringings could afford to buy their books before classes began. I, on the other hand, fell into the income bracket that missed qualifying for an all expense paid college experience. Student loan money would first get credited towards my tuition and then any remaining funds would be disbursed as a check. Each semester I would purchase the books I could afford and then wait anxiously for my student loan reimbursement check to purchase the rest. Typically, half the semester would have gone by before I had the money to get all of my books. Finding cheap used books was easy, however it seemed publishers dropped updated editions like clockwork just to keep money flowing in. Syllabi always called for the latest textbook edition. Using last year's version of a textbook frequently led to frustration and confusion with page numbers. Regularly, I found myself behind in my studies. Instead of swallowing my pride and asking my classmates to share their books, I figured I would just work twice as hard at the tail end of the semester to catch up. That never seemed to go according to plan, I was always behind.

Words cannot express my disappointment in not being eligible to pledge Alpha Phi Alpha with Sebastine my second semester. Finishing first semester with a grade point average of 2.3, I failed to meet the minimum entry requirement of a 2.5. Though I would ultimately go to summer school (for the first time in my life) to retake a couple of courses and push my GPA past the threshold, I was deeply embarrassed. I looked to God for answers. Perhaps I was being punished for being too much of a party pursuing, foul mouthed, fornicating sinner, I considered. Unlike Watertown, there was no shortage of Black churches and Bible thumpers in Nashville. Tennessee was the buckle of the Bible Belt, with Nashville being the de facto capital of God's Country. There were churches on every corner, I had never seen so many. Virtually every Southern student I knew went to church on Sunday, even the ones I partied with on Saturday nights.

My MIAKA brother Jarrod never missed a service. I began riding with him to Born Again church on Trinity Lane in North Nashville. Born Again was exceedingly different from all the churches I had been to previously. Often hungover, I'd cram into Jarrod's little, white, bubble tint, clunker to make the journey. We were usually late and had to resort to creating a parking space in the dirt at the back of the parking lot. No matter how tired I was, entering the sanctuary instantly made me perk up. Walking in the door, my eardrums were delighted by the sound of a real Gospel choir, a deep contrast to the small assemblage of off key old ladies strewn together at Co-op City Baptist Church. Professional musicians conjured up the Holy Spirit with intense drumming, feverish keyboard tapping, sensational saxophoning, thumping bass, and effervescent guitar riffs. It sounded like the Gospel music Mshangwe listened to at Taft. I never considered choirs really performed like that in actual churches. In fact, the music and singing sounded even better live than it did on CD. Coincidentally, the greatest selling Gospel artist of alltime, CeCe Winans, was a congregant and sometimes led worship and praise. People would run up and down the aisles, lose their bearings, shuffle their feet uncontrollably, and sometimes pass out when the Born Again Church Choir whipped them into a frenzy. Twin Pastors Horace and Harold Hockett would spontaneously catch the Holy Ghost, speak in tongues, Crip walk, and push the whole congregation to let loose. Though the Spirit never inspired me to spazz, I thoroughly enjoyed the spectacle, while clapping and singing along to the lyrics projected on the sanctuary's large screens. Grandpa Alric and his Jehovah's Witness wife, Lucy, used to warn me about the crazed "holie rollies" who acted a fool in church. Well, I finally came face to face with them at Born Again… and they weren't so bad. In fact, they inspired me to be a man of God like no other church had. For the first time I felt an unexplainable connectedness, love, relief, and uplift. I also felt guilt for not being a better Christian. Shame caused tears to well up during the choir's gospel ballads. I'd feel my heart pound and a frog develop in my throat as the pastor's sermons convicted me of immorality and unworthiness. I knew I needed to change, *but at what cost?*

As soon as I got back to campus I would feel conflicted. Sinning in peace after experiencing Born Again's service was difficult. I came to college to wild out, not become a church boy. Giving my life to God meant giving up sex, drinking, partying, Hip Hop, and the friends with whom I enjoyed all of those things. I couldn't understand how my peers experienced these same types of church services then resumed their normal lives within minutes of leaving the parking lot. It's never been easy for me to believe in anything halfheartedly, when I commit to something it's full steam ahead. So I sought more knowledge in Christ to see if life would become more obvious. Afforded an elective course, I chose Religious Studies to get an academic interpretation of God's Word. I also started attending Reggie Madison's campus Bible Study.

Reggie was a Vanderbilt senior and a member at Born Again. His testimony was that he was off the chain his first two years in undergrad, a womanizer, and proponent of debauchery. Halfway through, Reggie found Christ and did an abrupt 180. He felt I had the same potential. As a matter of fact, God *told* Reggie that I was *specifically* the person to whom he should pass his baton. Therefore, Reggie selected me to be his understudy. As I grew stronger in my understanding of The Word, I felt the weight of "The World" being lifted from my shoulders. The sky seemed bluer, the birds chirped louder, and I felt like I was walking on a bed of clouds.

One of the Alphas, B. Taylor, was close to Reggie and also poured into me. He introduced me to Christian Hip Hop and even brought me to a "club" in Smyrna to watch live performances. Cross

Movement was dope and sounded more like the conscious rap groups I loved, than the overly preachy groups I expected. GRITS were from Nashville and had a fresh, original sound too. Swapping my explicit content for this new vibe didn't appear to be as painful as I perceived.

With Hip Hop out the way my only remaining vice was sex. I knew it would be my biggest struggle. Banging beautiful brown skinned beauties was at the top of my priority list for college. But now I felt guilty about my uncontrollable lust. Going cold turkey seemed extreme, so I figured I would just back away from the buns slowly by being less aggressive in my pursuit.

By chance, I came across Erin Boyd, a short, reclusive, bookworm from Atlanta, on the way to the bookstore. For the life of me I couldn't figure out how we'd never crossed paths as raisins in the Vanderbilt bowl of sugar. Once she mentioned that she lived on the Peabody side of campus, a twenty minute walk one only made when absolutely necessary, things became clearer. Not only did Erin live on Peabody, but she was also a transfer student from Florida State. *People transfer to other colleges mid school year?* Luckily, Erin's distance from main campus, coupled with her mid year enrollment, insulated her from the contempt many chicks held as a result of my *Collard Greens & Cornbread* appearances. Still, Erin didn't take me seriously out the gate. I was a year younger and anything I said, no matter how sincere, she took as game. She wasn't caught up in partying, fashion, or climbing any social ladder. Her main priority was finishing her pre-med track at Vandy and going on to become a neurosurgeon. Though I was going through my Christian walk, the thrill of the chase excited me. Initially, the only way I could get close to Erin was to study with her. We studied in the student center basement. We studied at the library. We studied in the Branscomb lobby. Eventually I wore her down with my charm enough to study in her room. Even then, Erin kept me at arm's length. I grew to trust her with my deepest secrets. She was less forthcoming and mysterious, but she cautiously gave me access to her heart. Before I knew it we had fallen in love. No matter how far I delved into Christianity I felt confident Erin would be understanding and supportive - even if it meant denying the pleasures of the flesh... down the line.

As I continued to seek answers from the Lord through classes, prayer, church, and Bible Study, I remember being inspired to write an essay titled, "Jesus - He's Us," while doing laundry in Vandy Barnard one Saturday morning. Clarion happened to catch me in the act and shook his head as if I had really gone off the deep end when he figured out what I was doing. It didn't take long for word to get back to the rest of the friends I had suddenly started neglecting. Running into Kim at a Black Cultural Center event, I was finally forced to confront the inevitable.

"Meek talk to me. What's going on with you?" Kim queried.

"Nothing. I'm just trying to figure some things out so I'm chilling."

Concerned, Kim continued, "You know I love you no matter what. Just make sure you're doing what's good for *you*... not people who are telling you what's good for you."

Manipulation and coercion I had never factored into the motives of my Christian mentors. Suddenly I questioned my naiveté.

Shortly after, I struck a nerve with my buddy Brookes. Being half Asian he had been exposed to his late grandmother's Buddhism. He challenged me on whether or not she, "the most loving, sweetest woman," he ever knew was going to Hell. Instead of providing a personal opinion I shared with him Born Again's church doctrine:

"The one who physically dies in his sins without accepting Christ is hopelessly and eternally lost, doomed to the lake of fire and therefore, has no further opportunity of hearing the Gospel or repenting. The lake of fire is literal. The terms 'eternal' and 'everlasting' used in describing the duration of the punishment of the damned in the lake of fire, carry the same thought and meaning of endless existence as used in denoting the duration of joy and ecstasy of saints in the presence of God. (Heb. 9:27; Rev. 19:20)."

So yes, technically Brookes' sweet grandmother was destined for Hell. Brookes blew a gasket. With tears in his eyes and anger in his voice he shouted, "You cannot tell me my grandmother was sent to Hell for not believing in Jesus! She was the most kind, giving person to everyone she ever met. You're insane if you believe that!" I agreed the church doctrine was exceptionally harsh. There was no way to reconcile these extreme Christian beliefs with what I felt in my heart couldn't possibly be true.

I sought answers from my mentors on how to justify conclusions like these moving forward. Like multilevel marketing mavens they had answers for *everything*.

"Before you die everyone has the option to accept Christ or not," Reggie would explain.

"But what about people in rural China or India who never get exposed to the Bible?" I asked.

"The Bible says no matter what, even those people will be given the choice."

Then they'd direct me to scriptures that backed up their statements in coded language. Most times this would dispel my skepticism. In the cases where Reggie or B. Taylor didn't have the answers, they would reach out to more knowledgeable Christians and get back to me. When I wasn't satisfied with those responses, I was pointed to Proverbs 3:5 "Trust in the Lord with all thine heart; and lean not unto thine own understanding." Suspending critical analysis seemed to be an essential component of faith. Wrestling with this technique began to wear on me mentally, spiritually, and emotionally.

On one hand, I wanted the comfort of knowing I was fulfilling God's purpose by being obedient to the Lord. On the other hand, I was reluctant to sacrifice my friends, objective mindset, and carnal desires because I got spooked into doing so.

Either Reggie sensed my hesitation to fully abandon "The World," or I was so proficient at living a double life that he decided to officially anoint me the heir to his Bible Study group. Unassumingly, I accepted an invite to his off campus apartment for what I believed to be post church lunch. Had I known Reggie had plans to formally pass his torch, I may have found an excuse to run from the situation. In an intimate ceremony after eating, he asked me to kneel before a Bible which lay on the floor next to a gold crucifix. Reggie closed the blinds and lit some candles and incense. *Oh shit, what have I gotten myself into?* Reggie began pouring out, "God has revealed to me that you are the one. He gave me a vision where I could see right through your chest into your heart. It was glowing brightly. Demetrius you are special and I am excited to have you continue the Lord's work on campus in my absence." Then he dipped his fingers into a vat of warm "anointment oil" and made a cross on my forehead. He asked me to close my eyes while he prayed over me. "Lord I know that you will use Demetrius to fulfill your purpose as he submits in obedience to your word…" Afterwards, Reggie hugged me with tears in his eyes. I knew I was in too deep.

But I kept going to church while sinning out of sight. I felt myself turning into one of the fake Christians I despised; the do as I say, not as I do breed of impostors. Authenticity greatly concerned me - I'm not a fake person, being myself has always been my schtick. I grappled with being a highly visible hypocrite, one foot in the church, and one foot in "The World." I wasn't ready to give up my life for a system I had not been completely sold on, a system that created lingering doubts and paradoxes. Whichever path I chose to walk, I felt I'd be letting the people I cared about down. I either had to be Meek or Meek Tha Freak. The two could not coexist.

During my time of internal strife, I stayed in touch with my good friend Lauren from middle school. Lauren did a better job of checking on me than I did her, a fact that haunts me until this day. She ended up enrolling at Pomona College in California since the West Coast perfectly complimented her carefree spirit. While I juggled my social and academic life, she always found time to call me. She even sent brownies and hand drawn artwork. Shortly before beginning classes at Pomona she was diagnosed with a rare form of cancer and forced to withdraw for chemotherapy. The diagnosis didn't seem to dampen her spirit though, it was just something she had to get through - she was tough, no biggie. When Lauren called to tell me she had beaten cancer into remission and was poised to head back to school, I breathed a sigh of relief. I knew she was a soldier, *of course she'd beat cancer.* Afterwards, she'd sell me on how dope it would be to visit Italy. Cruising the Mediterranean coastline occupied her mind. I guess the uncertainty that cancer brought inspired Lauren to want to see more of the world. And for good reason.

Not long after heading out to California the cancer returned. This time it was more aggressive. Still, I had no doubt Lauren would be able to defeat it again, she was the most optimistic person I knew. We didn't bother to dwell on the diagnosis because it was pretty much a given she'd pull through. I couldn't wait to get back to The Bronx so we could catch up face to face and shed our worries about cancer and religious judgment. But when I got home for the summer I immediately began a paid internship with ABC Sports Television. I got the gig by qualifying for a highly competitive placement in The Emma Bowen Foundation. As a result, I scheduled, cancelled, and rescheduled hang out sessions for two weeks. A Friday afternoon was finally carved in stone for Lauren and I to hangout at her place.

Sounding a bit weak, but still excited, she confirmed on the phone the night prior. The following day as I clocked out of work, I called to give her the heads up I was on my way.

To my surprise, her father answered the phone, a first, and said, "Hi Demetrius, I'm sorry but Lauren passed this morning."

Initially, the words did not register. "But I'm on my way to hangout," I insisted.

"Yes, she told me you were supposed to stop by. Unfortunately she couldn't hold on so she could say goodbye to you."

What? I just spoke to her.

"I'm sorry Mr. Martinez, I didn't realize Lauren was that sick," I mustered.

"She stopped chemo a long time ago. She couldn't take it anymore. She was ready for whatever happened next," he revealed.

I was devastated.

At Lauren's "homegoing" service, I spoke about the first time she warmed my heart with her smile in the back of Ms. Biallo's class. I joked about her insistence on paying her way on our first date. I disclosed how she was sending *me* brownies after rounds of chemo. As I spoke and peopled smiled at the fond memories, internally I questioned why God would take such a beautiful creature away so soon. How could I continue to believe in the crazy church stuff I was bombarded with in Nashville? Quickly, I had an answer… from none other than Lauren herself! Mrs. Martinez read a letter Lauren had written when she realized the inevitable was near. In it, Lauren asked us not to question God's will, as she did not. Lauren expressed excitement to see what the Creator had in store for the next chapter. The letter was absolutely beautiful, profound, and inspiring. *If Lauren could have faith in God, so should I!* Later, I went home to reflect on a drawing Lauren had sketched and mailed with a batch of brownies a few months prior. It was an abstract depiction of a feminine spirit dancing among the stars, set against the dark backdrop of the universe. I finally understood what it meant: our bodies may perish, but our spirits live on forever. I kept this in mind after Lauren's family spread her ashes along Italy's Mediterranean coast.

    I returned to Vanderbilt ready to teach Bible Study. Lesson plans should have been prepared over the summer, but I was content with winging it. All I had to do was open the Bible and let the Holy Spirit reveal new scriptural insights. That was my approach. "Men's Christian Bible Study - Wednesday 8PM" read the arial font signs I placed around campus. A handful of people showed up: Jarrod, Sebastine, a couple of freshmen, and Greg Hersey, the onsite facilitator of Campus Crusade for Christ. Greg quickly realized I was ill prepared to teach anything beyond surface level fundamentals. But he patiently encouraged me to keep going, imparting wisdom when my interpretations were off the mark. Soon, Greg became my new mentor. He was less fanatical and preachy than Reggie, something I liked. Imagining Greg angry was impossible. We shared a mutual appreciation for The Simpsons and cutting edge gadgets. The connection felt natural and I felt less pressure to be somebody I was unsure I could be under Greg's watch. Previously, I felt inept for not speaking in tongues or spazzing out from catching the Holy Ghost. Greg was a loyal Christian without all the theatrics. He brought me into his fold, bonding me with other students, men and women, under his tutelage. We studied and prayed together and even went on out of state retreats.

    For Greg and the gang I would have done just about anything… anything except decline to pledge Alpha Phi Alpha. As rumors swirled on campus the Alphas would follow Sebastine and Rashaka's Spring line with a Fall 2001 line, my Christian crew, knowing my intentions, lobbied for me to abstain from pledging. Despite a few of the girls being Greek and Reggie's close Alpha friend, B. Taylor, still present on campus, I was heavily pressured to resist the temptation to join the frat. They felt I was too weak in my faith to come out on the other side unjaded. As an Alpha, I would undoubtedly subject myself to parties, groupies, liquor, and general frat boy debauchery. Before I got "saved" that was my whole M.O. Knowing I would have to sacrifice those things as a real Christian, I figured I would still be able to do step shows, community service, and increase my political profile, while occasionally having an excuse to at least work the door at parties.

Resentment towards my super Christian friends kicked in swiftly. *Why won't they trust me to make my own decisions? I can control myself. I'm a grown ass man!* To justify heading down the trail I sought to blaze since high school, I grew increasingly weary of the Campus Crusade crew's judgment. My eyes opened and my critical thinking stopped taking a backseat to Proverbs 3:5. No longer could I suspend reality to accept the frenzied foot shuffling, Holy Ghost convulsions, and schizophrenic tongue contortions at Born Again. Weariness precipitated my backsliding into "The World." Reasoning with myself, I felt there had to be a healthy balance between faith and practicality. There had to be a way to reconcile being an Alpha and a Christian. After all, DMX was a devout Christian for crying out loud. No one could stop me from believing in God while living out my dreams and desires. I resolved to have my cake and eat it too.

Continuing a personal, less public relationship with Christianity was my solution. Though I made sure to pray before bed, I stopped breaking my neck to witness the often outrageous displays of divine inspiration commonplace at Born Again. I ceded the weekly Bible Study I inherited from Reggie to Greg. Had it not been for the fact that most people assumed I would be tied up pledging, the abrupt change may have heightened suspicions.

Under the guise of Alpha intake, I was free to redefine personal priorities. Disclaimer: Alpha Phi Alpha and all Black Greek Letter Organizations outlawed hazing in 1990. Wooden paddles, swung with the force of steroid era bats at the rear ends of nut clutching aspirants, were no longer to be used. Psychological manipulation, verbal abuse, bullying, and torture became illegal. Aspirants were instructed to report if they were ever lined up in height order and asked to lock arms in dimly lit garages. In addition, aspirants were not to be forced to smack their own foreheads thunderously for "smile wipes," nor ordered to recite tens of pages of Alpha history verbatim while balancing on one leg like a "Thinking Man," nor pressured to fetch the most inconvenient item, from the most inconvenient location, at the most inconvenient time, without money or transportation. Surely, juggling that type of stress, on top of maintaining good grades had to be a challenge of epic proportions. Had I been forced to endure *that* process I'm sure it would have tested my human limits. The primitive tribalism that emerges from the trials and tribulations of brothers in despair forges titanium bonds. So I've *heard.* A lengthy rite of passage style process, passed on to successive generations of men decade by decade, couldn't have crafted brotherhood more natural than that which resulted from post-hazing's two weekend cluster, conducted by the national governing body of A Phi A...

After nine weeks of going off the grid (for "probate show preparation") with my line brother, my ace, Angelo Christopher Lee, I emerged with an invincible spirit. Big Brother Iceberg Slim was born. No challenge was too great for me to tackle. Not only had I successfully crossed the burning sands of Alpha Phi Alpha, I had done so while rebounding from my struggles in biomedical engineering, busting a 3.4 semester GPA in my new major, economics. Lacking a passion for economics, I only made the decision to switch because it was obvious my brain was not hard-wired for the discipline and mundane grunt work engineering required. I knew nothing about economics, except that it sounded like I'd make money without having to face the frustrations of chemistry, physics, and calculus. If I wasn't going to be an engineer, doctor, or scientist, certainly I'd be respected as a businessman. Being a businessman sounded dignified, even if the term was so vague it lacked true definition. Enjoying newfound Alphahood was more of an immediate priority than figuring out a career though. I was convinced all I needed to do was graduate and life would work itself out.

Suite life with my boy Brookes and new associate, Nick Scott, was all about chillin'. Once we figured out financial aid qualified us for food stamps, it was on and poppin'. A utility closet was converted into a boom-boom room, where Brookes served Harris Teeter steaks and Nick rolled Memphis dank, while we drank Skol under a blacklight with our guests. Devin The Dude and 8Ball & MJG were often the soundtrack. Fortunately, my Alpha commitments forced me to venture out from the under the kush clouds. Brookes, a brilliant guy with a near flawless SAT score, struggled to make it to class. Nick, after finding himself on academic probation with Brookes, vowed to wait until after class to spark up. Unfortunately self control took a backseat to collegiate freedom and they were sent home to find motivation to continue at Vanderbilt. The old "look to your left, look to your right… one of you won't make it to graduation" adage seemingly proved true.

Chanting, "We party hard, we stay up late, but most of all we GRADUATE!" at parties with the bruhs reinforced the will to survive Vanderbilt's academic pressure cooker. *Survive* is all I was trying to do. I lost my inner desire to compete as hard as I could academically. Despite econ being a smidgen easier to grasp than engineering, my books being late still posed a serious challenge. Even worse, the econ professors were arrogant pricks who bragged about how many students lacked the mettle to persevere in their major. The White Greeks who relentlessly partied on Frat Row always seemed to do well on the exams though. Rumor had it they stored archives of old tests from which to study... old tests that varied little, if any, from current tests. Without friends on the inside, confirming the hearsay was impossible. Racist incidents on Frat Row drove me away from bonding with the Vandy's dominant demographic. Standing in line indefinitely, while droves of White students freely streamed in and out of parties, created resentment. My gold Vanderbilt photo ID didn't seem to grant me the same privilege as the non-melanated folks. In fact, they were never even asked to show their IDs for entrance to parties. On the few occasions I successfully parlayed entry to DKE (pronounced Deek), I could feel the crowded dancefloor disappear around me as if I was contagious. DKE was full of wiggers who blasted rap and threw costume themed Thug Life parties. Yet, only Black people who other Black people dismissed as oreos, were welcomed to party there. I guess I shouldn't have been so naïve to expect a school with a dorm named Confederate Memorial Hall not to play host to a contingent of bigots.

Shockingly, the administration awarded us a house on Frat Row my junior year. Since the local chapter of Kappa Alpha Order was suspended, supposedly for paying homeless men to beat each other to a pulp in their basement, the property was vacant. Occupying a frat house was a college dream come true. Wild parties and 24/7 debauchery were sure to abound. Sharing the place with the boneheaded Ques and sometimes weird Sigmas couldn't even stifle the excitement of acquiring a real frat house. Regardless of the university's designation, the NPHC (National Pan-Hellenic Council) House would undoubtedly become the Alpha Mansion.

Ironically, since its inception in 1865 Kappa Alpha Order was notorious for being racist. According to fraternal lore, "the founders listed Robert E. Lee's chivalry and gentlemanly conduct as an inspiration. At the 1923 Convention, Lee was designated as the 'Spiritual Founder' of the Order by John Temple Graves."[4] Yes, *that* Robert E. Lee, Commander of the Confederate Army during the Civil War.

Before J. Edgar Hoover undermined Alphaman, Dr. Martin Luther King Jr., and sabotaged the Black Panther Party through COINTELPRO, he pledged Kappa Alpha. Not surprisingly, Kappa Alpha didn't roll out the red carpet to welcome us, four Alphas, a Que, and a Sigma, to their home. The new arrangement wasn't in place for more than a few weeks before the tension led to a physical confrontation on the frat house steps. Alarmed by incessant banging on the glass front doors, I rushed to see who was causing the commotion. Immediately I noticed a tall, brown haired, young, Southern aristocrat insisting on entry to the building. Confused and perturbed, I cracked the door and asked, "Is there something I can help you with?" The dude aggressively pushed through the door and barged into the house. "Yo you can't just come up in here like that, what's your problem?" I shouted, hoping to alert Sebastine, Bichar, and Robert for backup.

"You're in my house… I can come whenever I damn well please," the White boy fumed.

Concluding he was obviously a disgruntled Kappa Alpha member, I advised "It's time for you to go bro," and gestured towards the doors he'd just barreled through. When he refused to move, I began pushing him backwards. Recalling my two semesters of Varsity wrestling, I backed him onto the porch. In my peripheral, I could see a couple more of his frat brothers approaching the scene.

---

[4] A Convivium Toast to Robert E. Lee

On cue, Sebastine and Bichar showed up to help repel the first asshole, then neutralize the threat from the other guys. Black versus White, we tussled on the lawn before spilling out onto 24th Avenue. Realizing they'd met their match, the KA members retreated, shouting profanities as they backpedaled.

A few nights later we were awoken by the sound of glass shattering in the basement. Atop the debris lay a brick. Running outside to ID the culprit, I noticed the trunk of my teal '93 Nissan Altima, a car I worked all summer to purchase, keyed. In large letters it read "KA," in smaller letters "therine." Though I was known for messing around with crazy chicks who fit the profile of car keying, window smashing loonies, no KAtherine's came to mind. Kappa Alpha retaliation was the only thing that made sense.

Shortly thereafter we became very close with Mona and Kristen, Vanderbilt's young, new, Greek Life administrators. Mona, a thick, tell-it-like-it-is Sista, and Kristen, a bubbly, energetic blonde, genuinely had our best interests in mind. They arranged a meeting between the NPHC (the governing body of Black Greek Letter Organizations, or BGLOs) and the White Greek organizations. I served as the NPHC's Vice President, a leadership position that sounded good for future resumes, but really wasn't all that rewarding. Typically, NPHC meetings were just two hour gripe fests, where BGLOs complained about being slighted by each other. However, this particular meeting forged a truce between us and KA, who couldn't afford to get into anymore hot water.

I hoped the meeting would finally inspire unity between all Greeks on campus, but afterwards we were still treated like invading Blacks, the tip of the reverse gentrification iceberg. Despite Frat Row's traditional rowdiness, our neighbors frequently called VUPD to complain about noise and unwelcome outsiders. Instead of addressing concerns with us directly, they complained to the administration about parking and had our guests towed.

Truth be told, we did draw a sizeable crowd, excited to party at Nashville's only Black undergraduate fraternity house. When I say "we" I'm referring to the good brothers of Alpha Phi Alpha, Kappa Theta Chapter. The Ques and Sigmas weren't as social and had no members able to draw students from around the city to party with them on campus. On the other hand, Bichar and I, (and to a lesser extent Sebastine), could be found in the TSU Student Center or on the yard at Fisk throughout the week. We were there so often I still run into people who swear we graduated from their Nashville HBCU. Having a frat house gave us an excuse to pass out flyers to every fine melanated college girl in Nashville. In no time, Bichar and I became the most recognized faces in central Tennessee.

Growing up in South Florida, the club promotion capital of the world, Bichar had a knack for guerilla marketing. We'd run a few thousand paper fliers at Kinkos then slide them under every door, in every dorm, at every school within driving distance. Venturing as far as MTSU in Murfreesboro, we would even place them under the windshield wipers of every car in the campus parking lots.

Our first promotions efficacy test came when Vanderbilt hosted Juvenile for a fall 2002 concert. *Unofficially* we threw "400 Degreez: The 'Official' Juvenile Concert Afterparty at the Vanderbilt Alpha Mansion." Six hundred people showed up to our two hundred capacity frat house. The party was so packed no one seemed to care that Juvenile never showed up. VUPD was so overwhelmed by the traffic we brought to campus that Metro Police arrived to assist… with a helicopter. *Success!!!* That night we became unsuspecting party legends who would rule Nashville's Black nightlife in unprecedented fashion.

With fame came groupies. Few female undergraduates could resist the golden proposition: "Why don't you come over to The Mansion?" Combined with the added effects of colossal twenty inch rims and the thundering bass exuding from Bichar's tinted, champagne colored Maxima, we batted close to a thousand upon pulling up to TSU and Fisk. On "Nasty Boy" Biggie bragged his Mercedes could fit "four in the back, two if you're fat"... well, we'd fit four in the back plus two on their laps. Many times we'd return to campus with enough women to share with the Ques and Sigmas. Our Kappa friends were on call for special emergencies (they declined to live in the frat house for reasons unbeknownst). There was never a dull moment. Instances where there were no female visitors are difficult to recall.

Miraculously, I maintained my relationship with Erin. She studied diligently in her room and was comfortably asleep when most of the frat house shenanigans went down. Since most of the Mansion visitors were imported from off campus, it was fairly easy to keep a lid on rumors. Not to say Erin didn't suspect anything when I claimed to be making Kinkos runs at 2, 3, or 4 am, but I generally steered clear of drama. Outside of a couple close calls, where good guy Sebastine saved me from total destruction, I was able to entertain the ladies, while keeping my main at bay. I loved Erin and felt guilty for being dishonest and disloyal. I knew I wasn't shit. But if I didn't get it out my system, I feared the inevitable resentment certain to come down the line. *When else would I have the opportunity to wild out like this?*

Newfound popularity made our chapter the target of ire and resentment from Tennessee State's Bloody Beta Omicron chapter of Alpha Phi Alpha. Being the coolest dudes at the largest HBCU in the state conferred a sense of pride and arrogance in TSU's Alphas. They felt Nashville was their city and even other Alphas should bow to their throne. While we certainly respected B.O's reign, we never got the memo that one Alpha chapter was superior to others. We figured if our Kappa Theta chapter of Alpha Phi Alpha shined, it was a positive reflection on all Alpha chapters. The hate was unexpected. A sibling rivalry developed. Kappa Theta would catch wind of B.O's passive aggressive efforts to sabotage our events and status through word of mouth. Mansion groupies were unsuspecting informants, relaying the salty pillow talk of our TSU brethren. Oftentimes we shrugged off the jealousy, making sure to be cognizant of B.O's intentions, while continuing to push Nashville's nightlife to unprecedented levels.

Unfortunately, fights were inevitable. There was unavoidable tension between our chapters. A phone argument between Bichar and an ex girlfriend, who dated a TSU Alpha, culminated in an off campus showdown between me, Sebastine, Bichar, our Kappa friend Gib, and twenty Beta Omicron bruhs. I was never more surprised than when I opened the door and a hallway full of angry Alphas pushed past me. The whole building shook as we rumbled for what seemed like thirty minutes. Despite the overwhelming odds, we escaped the scrap virtually unscathed. Spitting in the face of intimidation, we showed up in the TSU Student Center to pass out party flyers the very next day, to B.O's chagrin.

The hatchet was ultimately buried over brunch in Rand. After airing our grievances, it struck me that attending a prestigious PWI caused my brothers at TSU to view my chapter as nerdy elitists looking to exploit their market. Essentially we were considered less Black and incapable of fully grasping "real" Black interests. Though we were allied with the "cool kids" via fraternal bond, we were never supposed to usurp their authority. As outsiders, we were hated for being culture vultures. Of course, my chapter felt this thinking was absurd and divisionary, yet it resonated as a symptom of the greater Civil War being waged between Black folk and uppity Black folk. I wondered if the Jewels, who founded A Phi A at lily white Cornell, encountered similar resistance from Beta Chapter bruhs at Howard.

To test whether I was actually clueless about the "real" Black college experience, I took advantage of a poorly publicized exchange program between Vandy and Fisk. For a semester, I would earn six credit hours taking my English electives at Fisk. I loved Fisk. It was smaller than TSU and fostered more of a family type atmosphere. Had Taft been a predominantly Black boarding school it probably would have felt a lot like Fisk... In spirit at least. Fisk was way more cash strapped and the campus infrastructure reflected a lack of investment in modern upgrades. Still, Fisk appeared to be the site of momentous occasions in American history. Many of those occasions were commandeered by prominent alumni like Nikki Giovanni, John Hope Franklin, Ida B. Wells, and Alphaman, W.E.B DuBois.

Vandy's Kappa Theta and Fisk's Alpha Xi Chapter have always been tight historically. Alpha Xi embraced us as equals, frequently joining us in step shows, travel, and all aspects of brotherhood. Amongst Southern Black elites, the Fisk brand carries pride, power, and prestige; traits Alpha Xi personified through academic excellence, military precision, and unexplained magic. Though Alphas proclaimed to be "cold and cocky," Alpha Xi was confident, yet humble. Through osmosis, I hoped taking my two little old English classes on their yard would allow me to absorb some of their swag.

Of course six hours at Fisk wasn't enough to give me the full HBCU experience. Taft taught me that the *real* bonding occurred outside the classroom. But I did feel more comfortable participating in classroom discussions and conversing with the professors. Unfortunately, I assumed A Different World's Hillman was merely TV fantasy when declining to apply to Fisk in favor of Vandy. I likely cheated myself out of the opportunity to live in an all-Black community focused solely on enlightenment. I resented myself for not carefully considering the alternative.

For letting myself and the Black community down, I resolved to more consciously commit to Black empowerment. Ironically, it was a White girl, Sam, in my film class who convinced me to use Vanderbilt's resources for social justice. Randomly, I ended up in her group, along with another blond, Jessica, who suffered from a severe case of ADD. Tasked with filming and editing a one hour project, I struggled to figure out what type of production would best cater to our collective strengths and interests. For the comfort of my White female counterparts, I suggested doing a documentary on the Nashville music scene; that way, I could venture off and explore my love of Hip Hop while they studied the presumably White music they loved.

Fortunately, Sam had a better idea. Her and Jess, sophomores my senior year, were supposed to begin at Vandy with five-star football recruit Marcus Dixon. Before Marcus could suit up as a Commodore, his scholarship was rescinded following rape allegations in his hometown of Rome, Georgia. Vanderbilt dropped their offer to Marcus before he was given an opportunity to prove his innocence. Honestly, I hadn't followed the case much, as most of the drama unfolded two summers prior while I was interning for ABC Sports in New York. In the midst of traveling on the PGA Tour, and being repeatedly mistaken for Tiger Woods by White folks who swore they couldn't tell the difference, I remained oblivious to the injustice done to Dixon. After the parents of Marcus' Caucasian cut buddy, Kristie Brown, discovered their daughter had relations with the superstar athlete, he was falsely accused of taking her virginity by force. It didn't take long for the judge and jury to realize consensual sex had occurred. Marcus was acquitted of rape, battery, assault, and false imprisonment. However, since Marcus was seventeen and Kristie was fifteen, a minor, at the time of the alleged incidents, Marcus was nonetheless convicted of statutory rape and aggravated child molestation. Dixon received a mandatory minimum sentence of ten years under Georgia law. The ruling sent ripples of outrage throughout the Black South, catching the attention of the NAACP and Oprah Winfrey. Sam suggested we turn our attention there. *Did I really let a White girl beat me to exposing racial injustice?*

We set out to produce a documentary we hoped would explain why Marcus Dixon sat in a prison cell instead of our classrooms. As rookie investigative journalists we felt it was imperative to know why Vanderbilt rescinded Marcus' athletic scholarship before he was even convicted of a crime. We were surprised by how easy it was to schedule a meeting with Vanderbilt's head football coach, Bobby Johnson. Not believing it possible, I waited for Jess to fail after she picked up the phone and suggested, "We should just call him." Johnson's administrative assistant, a middle-aged White woman, was delighted to hear Jess say we wanted to interview the coach for our film project. She never even asked what information we hoped to attain, she just put us on his calendar. I doubted the conversation would have been as frictionless if *I* would have called. White allies can open doors simply through the common comfort of word pronunciation and inflection - *noted*!

Coach Johnson beamed with pride that three film students were interested in interviewing him for a documentary. Everyone else who interviewed the coach skewered him over Vanderbilt's abysmal SEC record. As we entered his office, two bubbly White girls and an unassuming, babyfaced Black guy, the typically stern Johnson smiled as if he were about to bite into dessert. We buttered him up with flattery about the interesting sports memorabilia and pictures adorning his workspace. He was happy to give us the backstory behind most items in his collection. After ten minutes or so, Coach

Johnson was eager to get the meeting knocked out so he could go back to football business.

"So how can I help you kids with this documentary?" he inquired.

Projecting it would be a highly sensitive discussion, I looked at Sam and nodded to encourage her to take lead.

"Weeellll... since you asked... we had a few questions about Marcus Dixon. Do you remember him?" Sam pried.

Coach Johnson's pale face immediately turned hot pink, "Yes of course. Where are you going with this?"

I chimed in with, "Do you know why Marcus' scholarship offer was rescinded before he was tried in court?"

Johnson grew panicked, he stood up from the leather chair behind his desk and asked us to turn our camera off.

"Look, I don't know what you kids are trying to pull but this is not what I had in mind. I'll have to politely ask you to leave," he fumed.

Exiting swiftly, we composed ourselves outside the building. A new excitement came over us - we were on to something!

With the Vanderbilt administration holding to a code of silence, we knew we had to be creative in securing footage and uncovering the truth. Nashville was obviously a dead end. I wanted to visit Marcus in prison to hear his thoughts directly but learned recording devices of any kind were banned. Poking around on LexisNexis, we found the home address and telephone number of Marcus' parents. They agreed to let us visit and interview them at their home in Rome, Georgia, a town notorious for its ties to the Ku Klux Klan. I considered the danger in me, a Black man, driving through Tennessee into Georgia with Sam and Jess. Running into the wrong cop or racist civilian could result in me becoming Marcus' cellmate, or even worse, deceased. Curiosity bested fear however. We piled into Sam's Civic without even booking a hotel. The plan was to get some footage with Marcus' family and then turn right around for the three hour drive back to campus.

The old adage "when in Rome, do as the Romans," took on new meaning. The highlight of a Georgia Roman's day was shopping at Piggly Wiggly. Instead of a skyline, Rome's most notable landmark was a set of three huge crosses strewn atop an unremarkable hill. I imagined these were the type of crosses the Klan burned on people's lawns when they committed terror. In fact, I speculated the Klan took pride in the intimidating crosses being Rome's most noteworthy feature. I struggled to understand why anyone bothered to live in this backwards ass town. Nonetheless, we had work to do.

Pulling into the driveway of Marcus's shotgun house, we were greeted by a burly White man. "Hi, I'm Marcus' dad Ken. I'm so glad you made it!" *Interesting.* Ken escorted us inside to meet his wife Peri, who was also White. *Whoa!* Ken explained he was Marcus' basketball coach during his middle school years. Marcus' biological mother struggled with drug addiction all her life, while his father rejected him as a mistake he wanted nothing to do with. As a result, Marcus was raised by his grandparents until he was twelve. It was then that Ken and Peri, responsible for getting Marcus to and from school for practice, adopted him. Briefly, I considered they saw Marcus as a meal ticket out of Rome, only adopting him because of his athletic prowess. As they divulged key details of his upbringing and the unconditional love they shared, I realized their intentions were genuine. They disclosed Marcus was a great kid and an obvious target of the town's racism. Like most teens, they admitted Marcus made juvenile mistakes:

"He mooned somebody trying to be funny. They suspended him for ten days. Then a girl said he got a little touchy feely after track practice once. Typical high school stuff ya' know?"

I believed them. They explained that Marcus knew his accuser Kristie from class. When her father, a known racist, found out they had sex, he flipped his lid. Fearing her father, Kristie claimed she was an unwilling participant when she was found having sex with Marcus in a school trailer. Based on what Ken and Peri disclosed, Marcus' arrest was unjustified. Everything they told us made us want to fight even harder to get Marcus exonerated.

After filming for five hours and eating several pizzas, Ken received a phone call from the NAACP. They wanted to know his availability for a rally they planned to hold on the steps of the Atlanta state capitol building in the coming days. Ken and Peri had missed so much time from work fighting for Marcus' freedom they were unsure if they could attend. "But I have three Vanderbilt students here that you should have at that rally," Ken professed. The NAACP was so thrilled to have us come speak at the rally they made accommodations for us to sleep at the home of the chapter president. We called Vandy to let our professors know we'd be missing a few days of classes. Most of them understood. Suddenly our day trip turned into an impromptu, indefinite journey.

Upon arrival in Atlanta we were greeted at the NAACP office downtown. Armed only with our camera and spirit, we blended in with the staff working feverishly to get out the word about the impending rally. Solidarity and hospitality were the themes of the day. After sunset we followed the president to his spacious two-story, four-bedroom home to figure out what we planned to say at the rally. Jess admitted she was terrified of public speaking, so Sam and I composed a joint statement. We knew we'd be flanked by the likes of the media, protesters, and counter protesters of Marcus. It was important not to say anything stupid. And it was a good thing we prepared, as we were asked to follow remarks by Atlanta Mayor Shirley Franklin, legendary Civil Rights hero Dr. Joseph Lowery, Ken and Peri Jones (who dropped everything to attend), and other prominent figures who demanded the Georgia Supreme Court overturn their ruling. When me and Sam's moment in the spotlight arrived, we used it to describe the disappointment we felt in Marcus not walking amongst us on campus. We kept it short and direct. The crowd cheered loudly at the conclusion of our brief remarks. "God bless you kids," some old lady yelled as we made our way down from the podium.

Returning to Vanderbilt with over ten hours of footage to edit, we felt we were doing something with the potential to alter the course of history. We spent days editing, debating, and brainstorming on how to showcase each scene. Jess frustrated me to no end with her constant loss of focus and random suggestions for edits. As someone who already despises working in groups, I blew up about how much she was slowing down our progress. She cried. Sam was disappointed it got to that point, but she was just as frustrated with Jess, so she understood. At the end of the day, the production earned us an A and props from the general student body. To the contrary, Vanderbilt administration remained silent, attempting not to create a stir amongst those who may not have previously questioned the school's rescinding of Marcus' scholarship. Marcus sat in prison for fifteen months before Georgia succumbed to mounting pressure and overturned his Aggravated Child Molestation charge. Upon release, he declined to consider Vanderbilt and elected instead to go to Hampton, an HBCU.

My involvement with the Marcus Dixon case occurred during my final semester at Vandy. It made a lasting impact on my desire to see social justice for Black people in America. I just had no idea how I could become more involved in the struggle as a Black man with no financial resources. I was broke throughout college and determined to sever my reliance on the Wendy's dollar menu afterwards. With pockets like rabbit ears, grad school didn't appeal to me at all. I wanted to start making money as soon as possible.

After enjoying four years of mild winters and Southern comforts, going back to New York didn't appeal to me whatsoever. I resolved to remain in the South. As classes drew to a close, I noticed how recruiters seeking corporate diversity primarily canvassed the campuses of Fisk and TSU. Companies didn't visit Vandy specifically to find top non-White talent. As well, there were no campus advisors with a particular interest in making sure every Black student graduated with a decent job offer. I was left to fend for myself in the wilderness. Closing out my bachelor's degree short of a 3.0, getting recruiters to acknowledge my existence was impossible. I was invisible. Settling for corporate leftovers was the only option. Northwestern Mutual offered me a job selling life insurance to seniors. I didn't see how my baby face would be useful in that space. Being confined to an office all day was also unattractive. I turned down that offer, reluctantly signing with Dell to sell computers for its Small & Medium Business Division. Though I would be stuck indoors, at least I'd be pushing something cool: technology. Working for a Fortune 500 company like Dell sounded amazing to my parents, Nana, Grandma Gloria, Grandpa Alric, and Uncle Greg, who all made the trip to Nashville to witness me, a family anomaly, walk across the stage. In fact, working for Dell seemed like a big deal to anyone outside of Nashville. Natives knew the deal though. Dell, with its high turnover and low base salary, was beneath the expectations of a Vandy graduate. I took no pride in revealing to classmates I would be employed there. Between war protesters interrupting Condoleeza Rice, and Chancellor Gee quoting motivational Seussisms from Oh, the Places You'll Go, I feared for my future. I thought life would become clear once I finished college, yet here I was in a fog of uncertainty.

Frat Brothers
(Left to Right: Renauld Clarke, Robert Boxie, Dr. Cornel West, Me, Sebastine Ujereh Jr.)

(Me and Bichar Myrtil)

CHAPTER SEVEN

THE PLANTATION

You can work to the bone but don't put all yo eggs in one basket
We don't never get a piece of the pie
Work 50 years, retire then die
Stay po', rich folks is the criminal
But you don't wanna hear me tho' so
Thank God it's Friday, ain't it what we live fo'?
Nigga gotta get up out the plantation
Same job that my pop had before me
I'mma pass it down to my seed fucked up situation
             -dead prez "W-4"

    The forty day lapse between graduation and receiving my first paycheck was a fight for survival. After using my graduation gifts to pay my first and last month's rent at a roach shack next to TSU, I was flat broke. A hundred and sixty-eight thousand miles of back and forth between New York and Nashville, impromptu college road trips, and the daily wear and tear of plowing through potholes between Vandy and campuses all over the city, finally wore on my '93 Altima. Every time I cranked the engine there was a fifty percent chance of my rusted hooptie starting. Mojo, the mischievous black mutt I found running down West End Avenue junior year, protested eating Ramen noodles by running away at any available opportunity. The three-hundred dollars I wasted on Mojo's obedience school remains one of life's worst investments. His rebellious personality and ungratefulness pissed me off even more while I scraped to survive.

Credit card offers flooded my mailbox, as if Visa and Mastercard smelled blood from outer space. With my new PYT, Lynnette, still in undergrad at TSU, I felt asking her for financial support was unreasonable and unmanly. Besides, I've always despised asking people for help, even in times of dire need. So I finally succumbed to Capital One to float me until my first Dell direct deposit.

Lynnette was a gorgeous, modelesque, red-bone with a sole left cheek dimple from Dayton, Ohio. Though I *knew* it was impractical to expect a long term relationship with someone who still had three years of undergrad remaining, I was smitten by her airiness, long legs, and commitment to fun. Before graduation, leaving Erin, a responsible, ambitious, determined, future pediatrician for Lynnette, a young minded, fashion obsessed, TSU freshman, was difficult. But Lynnette's looks complimented my ego and challenged me to hold her attention, considering she had an endless supply of Negroes trying to holler. Unlike Erin, who was unpretentious and comfortable being a homebody, Lynnette demanded the finer things in life - things that typically came with a cost. While I got through most of undergrad without having to spend a dime on dates, I knew it would be impossible to keep Lynnette satisfied without taking her out to the movies, P.F. Chang's, and the like. I quickly swiped my way into a couple grand of credit card debt courtesy of my new relationship and lack of income.

By the time I got to Dell I was starving for cash. Training couldn't go by quick enough, I was ready to hit the floor and earn commission. Even living in the hood, a base salary of twenty-eight grand wouldn't be enough to sustain my cost of living. Training dragged on and on for what seemed like forever. It was easy to recognize who would excel at the job - the people like me foaming at the mouth to hit the phones. Ali, a twenty something Persian, tired of hustling used cars for his dad, seemed especially determined. "It's all about volume… take more calls, close more sales," he explained in his subtle Middle Eastern accent. Simple enough. I believed wholeheartedly in my sweet talking skills. People would buy something from me no matter their background, race, class, or gender. Thus, Ali and I, anxious to build our fortunes, begged our instructors to hit the queue early. We grew increasingly frustrated by their refusal to let us flourish.

Since my training class started a week after the rigid pay cycle began, it took three weeks to receive my first paycheck. Desperate for the dinero, I checked my mailbox before and after lunch. When the check finally arrived, at four o'clock in the afternoon, I viciously ripped off the perforated edges. To my horror, six-hundred dollars was garnished by the state for a long forgotten traffic violation. The ticket in question was only two-hundred dollars, but the court costs, interest, and collection fees caused the penalty to balloon. The State of Tennessee didn't leave me with enough money for rent, groceries, or my credit card bill. I was completely distraught.

Luckily my frat brother, Alton, a TSU bruh who also landed at Dell, looked out for me. Any resentment I felt from prior skirmishes with Beta Omicron evaporated. Alton was a great guy who truly adhered to the tenets of manly deeds, scholarship, and love for all mankind. He loaned me the cash I needed to make it to my next paycheck, refusing to take no for an answer. A few days later, when my car died in front of the building's main entrance, Alton towed me with his tiny Toyota Tercel. I was forever grateful. I repaid Alton with unconditional friendship. Seeking to absorb his strengths, I studied his obsessive compulsive neatness and efficiency. His apartment was immaculate and carefully organized. Alton's ability to navigate a computer or anything related to technology was unprecedented. He seemed to live above the fray of conventional human expectation.

Thus, I was shocked to learn Alton had spent time behind bars. He was the epitome of "has his shit together," *how could this be?* Well, a few years prior, Alton also lacked the funds to pay off outstanding traffic tickets. With no wages to garnish, he was locked up for a month to repay his "debt to society." Finding out Alton, a great guy, was a casualty of America's idiotic incarceration craze made me furious. To avoid becoming a victim of circumstance, out hustling the justice system was imperative.

Once I finally hit the sales floor I got my hustle on. Observing Alton made me lightning fast on the computer. I employed Ali's strategy of taking as many calls as humanly possible during my shift. Out the gate, members of my training class started dropping like flies. Shaken by unruly customers, a grueling Monday through Friday work schedule featuring a mandatory bi-monthly Saturday shift, and the complexities associated with understanding computers well enough to sell them, people disappeared daily. Some quit, but most were asked to pack up their desks and walked out mid shift. Often, I would sit down at my desk, glance to my left or right and notice a barren desk where a co-worker sat moments ago. Colleagues who weren't recent college graduates came through Spherion, an extremely cutthroat temp to hire agency. Anytime we saw the tall, White, Spherion overseer roaming the floor, we knew somebody was getting canned. On the other hand, Dell direct hires typically vanished without warning. All employees walked on eggshells in fear of getting the unexpected boot.

Vandy privilege and work ethic made me assume I was insulated from impetuous termination. Dell gloated about the Vanderbilt graduates it employed. From the beginning to the end of my shift I took call after call. I did everything I was instructed to do in training as precisely as possible.

Everything was all good until my manager, a young blonde, two years removed from taking calls on the queue herself, approached me at the end of my shift one evening.

With a concerned look in her eyes she offered, "You want to stick around here longer, don't you Demetrius?"

Confused, I responded, "Yes of course I do. Did I do something wrong?"

"No, you're doing exactly what we asked you to do, but nothing more."

Still unsure what she was implying I asked, "Is there something else I should be doing?"

She put her arm on my shoulder and said, "your shift starts at 11 but the bell starts ringing at 6am. I can't tell you to work more hours, but if you plan to remain employed I suggest you figure it out."

Whoa.

By suggesting overtime in coded language, my manager hinted Dell expected me to give my blood, sweat, and tears to the corporation. Working until 8pm during the week and waking up early to work Saturday mornings was already taxing. I barely got to see Lynnette or do anything I liked to do. I considered her words, then the fact that finding another job in George Bush's economy was nearly impossible. Besides, I needed a new car and Lynnette liked eating at J. Alexander's. I could use the extra commission. I resolved to work bell to bell, fourteen hours a day, six days a week.

Work began to consume my every thought. Even when I slept, I dreamt about work. Panicked that I lost a sale I would wake up hyperventilating, only to realize I needed to hit the shower and beat the traffic rush to the office. In the shower, I would talk to myself and have mock conversations with clients. The same thing was happening to Ali. We'd joke about it… after the bell closed for the day. In any event, we were crushing it. Our work efforts consistently beat out rising quotas. For the first time, I finally had enough money to pay all my bills on time. I could finally take Lynnette on dates without having to worry about eating Ramen noodles for the rest of the week. Furthermore, I was able to get rid of my hooptie and buy a Lexus from Ali's dad. It wasn't a new Lexus, but it was the same GS 300 Jay-Z drove in his Dead Presidents video; an upgrade signifying my entrance to Big Williedom. Oh, and it had twenty inch rims, the classy type. Gainfully employed, I finally felt like a successful Black man.

Now that I had a little money, I was finally able to travel. I joined the fellas in Cancun for Memorial Day Weekend. Rushing to work when I returned, I hydroplaned at the 440 to I-24 interchange, totalling the Lexus. Its bald, low-profile tires demanded attention weeks prior. In trying to beat everyone to work, I never found time to dedicate to non-revenue generating tasks. Every minute not spent at work was a minute wasted not making money.

Lucky to escape serious injury or death, I went to Carmax the next day with a busted chin and broken hand. I would have gone back to Ali's dad, but this time I could afford a warranty and something with lower mileage. Lynnette tagged along and helped direct my attention to the luxury vehicles. Prior to walking on the lot, I'd set a budget of ten grand for my next whip, so a new luxury car wasn't on my radar. But after running the numbers, accounting for my income and credit, I qualified for a loan up to 40K. To my dismay, the salesman disclosed this within earshot of Lynnette. She had her eye on a green BMW with tan leather interior.

"Don't you like this? It's only twenty-five thousand!"

Suddenly, I could hear Cadillac Don and J-Money singing "inside peanut butter, outside jelly." Against my better judgement, I agreed to test drive the Beemer.

The ride was silky smooth and I found myself asking the salesman, "How much would my payments be on this?"

He tapped his calculator a few times then showed me the screen.

"$500 a month?! Nah, I'll look at something else."

He smirked then said, "It's your call. Based on your income you should be able to easily afford it. I get paid the same commission no matter what, so it doesn't matter to me."

Lynnette stared at me intently, communicating how bad she wanted me to buy the car.

"What the hell... I'll take it."

Getting screwed on my interest rate mattered little. To pay for my newly acquired toy I knew I just had to hustle more at work. Right on time, I received a promotion to Dell's mid-market business division. After two years of talking to rude, computer illiterate, small business owners, I was relieved. The promotion meant interacting with IT managers and Chief Technology Officers at companies with two to five-hundred employees. I no longer had to explain the difference between a hard drive and RAM. These clients were more knowledgeable and typically purchased higher end equipment, like servers and storage devices. Dell assigned an account set of thirty companies, tasking me with a monthly million dollar hardware, software, and peripheral quota. Despite having to sell this massive amount of equipment, I had faith in my work ethic to get it done.

Unfortunately, in the short two years I had been employed with Dell, the company went from being the world's leading computer manufacturer to ceding market share back to HP. Dell had overly ambitious expectations, an aggressive growth curve our trainers bragged was unprecedented, yet boldly attainable. To cut costs and promote expansion, Dell outsourced most customer service and technical support operations to India and Central America. Loyal customers frustrated with talking to "Mike" in Mumbai left by the boatloads. Business suffered immediately. Quotas increased, while clients fled for the hills. Dell executives panicked and pressured sales managers to stave off the mass client exodus. In turn, salesmen like myself took the heat becoming micromanaged and scrutinized even further. Dell became Hell.

In the ensuing panic, managers and teammates shuffled around to different teams. Somehow I ended up with Stacy, a forty-something blond few people seemed to like, as my manager. Wine, I assumed, was her only friend. The left wall of my cubicle was transparent and doubled as the right wall of Stacy's cubicle. Nerve wracking, annoying, and juvenile is how I would describe sharing a glass wall with my boss. I imagine zoo animals, perpetually locked in their clear cells, feel the same contempt for their observers. In any event, Stacy established her ground rules upfront. Basically, no fun was to be had between the hours of 8am and 5pm. The only chit chatting on the row was on the phone with clients, lunch breaks could not go a single minute beyond the allotted hour, and a daily summary of our client interactions had to be submitted before heading home. *Happy, happy, joy, joy.*

Less than two months into Stacy's dictatorship I sought escape. A client convinced me to create a LinkedIn profile, after raving about how the new social media site brought career opportunities her way. Unfortunately, it didn't bring me the instant success she promised, so I hit the job boards, Monster and Careerbuilder, trying to be as discreet as possible to avoid detection by Dell recruiters.

Though Nashville was emerging from the shadows of obscurity to become a major city, it was difficult to find any employers that piqued my interest. Working in a call center made me nauseous every morning. I knew I needed an outlet for my creative thought. After hitting a dead end in my attempt to get back into TV with cable's Country Music Television, I finally made some headway at Tennessee's best public relations firm, McNeely, Pigott, & Fox, reaching a third round interview. A few months prior, I gave myself a crash course in writing press releases for a fledgling t-shirt company my frat brother, Tre, asked for my partnership in. My press releases were good enough to garner attention from newspapers and radio stations far beyond Nashville. Thus, the opportunity at MP&F seemed promising. Andrew Maraniss, an executive at the firm, took a great interest in me. He was in the early stages of writing *Strong Inside*, a biography on Perry Wallace, the Black Vanderbilt basketball legend who integrated the SEC. With no Black men on staff, I fashioned I might be MP&F's Perry Wallace. However, the economy dictated otherwise. Despite Andrew pushing MP&F's partners to bring on another associate, he was rebuffed due to the economic slowdown the country continued to battle under the Bush Administration.

Trapped and frustrated at Dell, resentment towards Corporate America pushed my attention to Tre's t-shirt company. Inspired by a Black Masculinity class at Vandy, where Tre learned about A. Philip Randolph, Dr. King, and other notable Black leaders, Tre saw an opportunity to tie together his passion for fashion design with Black Empowerment. Randolph founded radical monthly magazine The Messenger in 1917, a publication described by the United States Department of Justice as "the most able and the most dangerous of all the Negro publications." He would then go on to threaten America's bigotry under FDR's Administration by developing the March on Washington Movement in 1941. Roosevelt absconded from the threat by issuing Executive Order 8802, which banned discrimination in the defense industries during World War II. Nevertheless, Randolph was determined to gain full equality for our people. Unsatisfied with the sluggish progress being made, the time for Randolph's March on Washington would eventually arrive on August 28, 1963. There, Martin Luther King Jr. delivered his famous "I Have a Dream" speech, which drew a report from J. Edgar Hoover's FBI Domestic Intelligence head, William C. Sullivan. Sullivan, at Hoover's urging, distributed a memo stating:

> "Personally, I believe in the light of King's powerful demagogic speech yesterday he stands head and shoulders over all other Negro leaders put together when it comes to influencing great masses of Negroes. We must mark him now, if we have not done so before, as the most dangerous Negro of the future in this nation from the standpoint of communism, the Negro, and national security."

A. Philip Randolph and Dr. Martin Luther King Jr., two advocates for civil disobedience, equality, and uplift, were guilty of none other than being dangerous Negroes. They wanted to destroy White Supremacy and encourage Black Empowerment. So did Tre. So did I. So did Sebastine, Frank, Gary, and Gib. It was Tre's idea that spreading the dangerous Negro spirit through t-shirts would wake up the masses. Despite my subconscious desire to see Black people on equal footing, I was probably the first person fully awoken by the concept. I figured somewhere down the line, after I'd made enough money to live comfortably, perhaps I'd run for office and be able to create change for my people. Yet here I was with an opportunity to promote change immediately in a cool way. No matter how radical it sounded, I was indeed a dangerous Negro... in my mind at least. Why not push theory into practice? On this premise, dangerousNEGRO Black Empowerment Apparel (dN|Be or dN for short) was born with the aim to raise social consciousness through graphic t-shirt messaging.

While my entrepreneurial fire raged with dangerousNEGRO, my frustration continued to mount at work. The final straw came one stormy day after a contentious email from Stacy. Keep in mind we literally shared a cubicle wall. Despite our uncomfortable proximity, she decided to chastise me electronically for being four minutes late to work. The very same morning, Nashville experienced a typical, severe, spring thunderstorm. My puppies, Dominoe and Paris, terrified of the weather, refused go for their morning walk, disrupting my morning routine and making me tardy. Their mom, Cheecago, had birthed them unexpectedly before going missing during a thunderstorm at Lynnette's grandmother's house in Dayton, Ohio. Cheecago was found dead a few miles away the next morning from a lethal chest wound. They *hate* thunderstorms. In any event, after they finally did their business, I rushed down Murfreesboro Pike to get to work as soon as possible. The day started out like any normal day. I checked my voicemail then email, followed up on leads, prospected for new business, contacted clients, yada, yada. Then I went to lunch. I lived close enough to the office to go home for lunch and make it back comfortably within an hour. Upon return, I was greeted by an email from Stacy so long it took more than a few seconds to scroll to the bottom. All day she had sat next to me divided by a thin sheet of glass and said nothing. Her email indicated she wanted to create a record of my reprimand. I was all too familiar with the signals that precipitated an employee being abruptly escorted from the building, while holding a small cardboard box overflowing with photos of their pets and significant others. As I read the email it was clear this was Stacy's intent. She started with:

> "Demetrius, you were late to work this morning. We are down for the quarter and I like to know that my agents are committed to giving their full effort. Walking into work at

8:04 tells me you are not giving this job your full commitment."

By this point I was seething. Blood pressure going through the roof, I continued to read all the way down to the bottom, where it was highlighted that my next tardiness could result in anything up to, and including, termination. Hastily, I pushed away from my desk and stormed to HR to complain about how unreasonable it was for Stacy to send her email. They pretended to care. I pretended to believe they might have sympathy.

During my tenure, I worked hundreds of hours of overtime, running myself crazy behind unreasonable clients and expectations from the company. Revenue upwards of twenty-million dollars could be attributed directly to my effort in that timespan. Never did I receive an email thanking me for working like a slave, bell to bell. I accepted the fact I was merely a minion, an underling trapped by financial dependence. Sure, I could have left one day without knowing how I would sustain a living, eat, or survive - the same dilemma faced by my Virginia ancestors daily. But jumping ship required a masterful plan. Grateful for never having to endure iron chains, whips, physical abuse, and torture, it was difficult for me to deny the parallels between America's foundational slave plantations, and the corporate plantation I could not escape at Dell. For a minimum of eight hours a day I toiled in a cubicle, careful not to invoke the wrong tone with authority, or draw unnecessary attention to myself. I kept conversation light and impersonal, code switching to indicate my Blackness did not pose a threat. Boarding school and college prepared me well for this.

But I was too smart to remain a wage slave. Frederick Douglass proved slaves possessed the intellectual capacity to function at a high level, independent of America's prescribed limitations for a

Black man. Like Douglass, I was highly skilled at speaking and writing, and knew they held the keys to my liberation. After one of my dangerousNEGRO press releases landed a prominent feature in the Indianapolis Recorder, my partners and I were contacted by a Black charter school to speak to their students about our company. Thrilled people saw the meaning in our name and appreciated our efforts, I prepared a short speech, took a day off, and made the four hour trip up 65 North. Sebastine happened to be in grad school at nearby Purdue, while Gary, the African childhood friend he recommended join our team, conveniently resided in Indianapolis. Gary, a street networking genius, arranged our first photoshoot with then obscure urban photographer Mike Boyce, to coincide with the school visit.

From the time we stepped foot in the building, the energy at the charter school was electric. Kids in burgundy polos and khaki trousers raced down the halls to greet us. Black kids. I found my purpose. Over the loudspeaker the principal announced a schoolwide assembly. The halls were soon flooded with even more Black kids. They piled into the gymnasium where their teachers used rehearsed attention gaining techniques. The school's principal and founder, a fine, educated, chocolate Sista, took the floor and introduced us like rockstars. A handful of kids snickered when they first heard the words "dangerous Negro," a reaction I anticipated would be even more prominent amongst the immature middle schoolers. However, it was clear a majority of the school's teachers had educated them on our monicker beforehand.

Naturally Sebastine, voted dN's president due to our confidence in his moderation, was first passed the mic to give a brief overview of our company. The audience responded with enthusiastic applause after Sebastine's intro. Nervous and self conscience of his Zimbabwean accent, Gary followed with the details of how he became apart of dN, and as a master networker, what his role was to the team. Excitement grew in me as the kids clapped for Gary, indicating I was up next.

I wasn't nervous at all. I felt comfortable... at peace. Like a tree drawing on sunlight for expansion, I absorbed the kids' energy and fired it back like a hadoken. Scanning the rafters, I made purposeful eye contact with as many as I could. As if I had found the key to triumph in life, I preached an equation of ambition plus determination equals success. I never fully wrote out my speech, opting instead to reference bullet points I scribbled on index cards. Improvisation had always been one of my strengths, organization a weakness. Excelling at sales bolstered my ability to read an audience and feed off the randomization of any series of responses. Directing those responses towards laughter, intrigue, and motivation were my goals. I wanted the kids to know I understood them, their challenges, and their upbringings. I was just like them - a little goofy, a little nerdy, with street smarts, and a desire to rise above my family's misfortunes. And they could be just like me - an entrepreneur who swore off all haters and defeated the system. This was rewarding. This made a difference. This is what I wanted to sell. *Screw computers.*

It was just a matter of hatching my escape plan from Dell, a difficult task considering Nashville's limited career opportunities. I knew I needed to be in a larger city. A city with more jobs, cooler stuff to do, more diversity, and more people. Better weather than Nashville would be a bonus. Despite being firmly implanted in the South, Nashville had annual snow and ice storms that paralyzed the city with the slightest precipitation. If I were to move, I was determined never to see snow again. I always felt snow conflicted with my African genotype. Freezing is my least favorite feeling. So I considered moving to the West Coast. I didn't consider Florida because there were too many New Yorkers there. Other New Yorkers annoyed me. They were always in a rush to go nowhere, cutthroat, rude, loud, obnoxious, volatile, and cold-hearted. San Diego sounded like a place I could avoid all that.

One of my teammates, Patrick, a White dude the same age as me, suggested I look him up in Houston, while being escorted from the building by security holding a cardboard box of his belongings. Two minutes prior, he had arisen from his chair and shouted, "I can't take this shit anymore!" I nodded, then shook my head and smiled in disbelief at Patrick for finally snapping. I was jealous knowing I could never get away with quitting in similar fashion. A Black man can't just blow his top and flip off his oppressive employer. The risk of being blackballed for the rest of our corporate career is way too high. Furthermore, we're rarely in the position to fall back on cash reserves or family members until we find alternate employment. I certainly wasn't. I would have to have more tact.

Though Sebastine moved there to work for Schlumberger after earning his Master's in Engineering, I never seriously considered Houston as an option, before Patrick planted the seed. Texas sounded more politically backwards and country than Nashville. After watching Tennessee Senate candidate, Harold Ford, get railroaded by dirty attack ads stoking White fear of a Black man getting cozy with White women at the Playboy mansion, I was sick of dealing with honky tonk racists. Sebastine loved Houston however. He advised me to come see how progressive H-Town was before writing off his newfound home. Afterall, it was the fourth largest city in America, and while inebriated in undergrad, I loved listening to DJ Screw tapes. *I wonder if all the girls look like Beyonce?* A visit couldn't hurt.

With New Year's approaching, I was determined not to extend my Nashville residency beyond 2006. I attacked the twelve hour drive to Houston with the vigor of Harriet Tubman on the underground railroad. I'll never forget watching the enormous downtown skyline pop out of the shadows, as my Garmin GPS, a Christmas gift from my mom, guided me down 59. The sprawling metropolis exceeded my expectations. Houston's skyscrapers dwarfed Nashville's. Certainly there had to be countless job opportunities sprinkled throughout the impressive, modern, glass and steel structures. *Interesting.* I imagined myself perched in an office on a high floor overlooking the city. That would sure as hell beat the boring, single-story, industrial complex of Hell Dell. Houston was an upgrade off the strength of the skyline alone.

Even after spending a significant amount of time promoting and attending parties in undergrad, the wondrous bass, wobbling backsides, and wild unpredictability of nightlife still kept my attention. Houston's club scene severely outpaced Nashville's. There were clubs and stripclubs scattered throughout the city. Before Bichar had the courage to drop out of med school at Meharry to open up Atlantis, his own nightclub, Nashville had one, maybe two, consistent options for clubbing. Houston had too many to count.

For New Year's there were an infinite number of options for parties. Sebastine recommended we check out Fox Sports Grill inside the Galleria. "Really? A sports bar? Inside the mall man?" I quipped. Sebastine pulled up the flyer for the event on Indmix, a Houston website solely designed to let people know what was poppin' in the city. Biz Markie would be deejaying at the Fox Sports Grill for New Year's. *Biz Markie?! In Houston?* I thought back to my first album purchase, his *Goin' Off* album. Biz Markie was a legend. Surely he could be spinning in New York, Miami, or Vegas, but of all places, Houston won out. Houston was an official city.

Still, I was curious to see what the people were like. All I could think about was UGK repping Texas with their "country fried rap tunes." *Could these people even appreciate the greatness of a Biz Markie?* The opening DJ kept the crowd engaged with Fat Pat, Lil O, and other local artists to whom I was ignorant. The sound was different, but it was actually dope. I came to realize the artists who had just begun to emerge on the national scene - Slim Thug, Paul Wall, and Mike Jones, were just the tip of the iceberg for Houston's own brand of Hip Hop. The Houston interpretation was majorly slept on. But did Houston *really* understand Hip Hop?

Once Biz finally hit the wheels to usher in 2007, I was surprised to see the crowd furiously gyrate to every East Coast jam he played. Voluptuous Sistas, with cornbread fed booties, sang each song verbatim. Tall, well dressed Brothas rocked side to side, spilling Hennessy on their wing tipped Stacy Adams. It was like partying in New York with better looking people. Houston understood Hip Hop. Houston loved Hip Hop. Hip Hop lived in Houston.

***

Seeing all I needed to determine Houston was a logical destination for relocation, I went back to Nashville to break the news to Lynnette. She would have to complete her final semester at Tennessee State alone, while I blazed a new trail for us a thousand miles away. Save for an ugly interruption caused by a confessed sin with her high yellow, Iota, ex-High School sweetheart, we had been living together for the greater part of two years by this point. She never found out about my cheating, so it was difficult not to take her back on account of her honesty. I loved her. I also secretly struggled with whether she was the right woman for me. Though we could mutually appreciate superhero flicks, she liked cheesy horror movies and I liked documentaries. She wasn't fond of my pets either. But she was bad, a bombshell. And we both preferred flat wings, sometimes frustrating when drums were in the mix, but nonetheless a telltale sign of our compatibility. Despite her bad spending habits, attention seeking, and flirtatious nature, her guilty conscience usually steered her towards confessing her indiscretions. I could live with that.

Besides, I loved her family. Even her bullish mom Theresa, who repeatedly encouraged Lynnette to heed the advice of God Himself, who spoke to her in her Trotwood, Ohio dreams: "Demetrius ain't the one for your daughter." Her father Bryan and I were practically inseparable. He loved Hip Hop as deeply as I did. After welcoming Lynnette at fifteen, Bryan tirelessly worked two to three jobs at a time, but never lost his passion for the music. In 1993, his Dayton area rap group, WESTSIDE, put out a self titled album. The lead single "And That's All She Wrote," created a buzz locally. Obviously I found that to be dope, though I never heard the record. Bryan and I were only ten years apart, so Bryan was like the missing generational link between my Dad and myself. He understood and respected the old school, while being a diehard fan of more modern acts like The Lox, and later, Slaughterhouse. An East Coast purist in Ohio's midwest, Bryan and I only diverged on our views of Southern rap. Though we both loved Jeezy's raspy voice, sly charm, hardcore lyrics, and co-sign from Jigga, Bryan was disappointed by Southern rap's hostile takeover of Hip Hop. I certainly agreed the music on the radio was wack and there were indeed a preponderance of "garbage ass rappers" being bred, but I could also move beyond my initial reluctance to embrace the wit of a post-Hot Boy Lil' Wayne.

Wayne was the favorite rapper of Red, Lynnette's red hued little brother on her mom's side. Having lived away from New York for close to a decade, my relationship with my half sibling, Dontae, was virtually nonexistent. Red was the little brother I always imagined I'd have. He was handsome, athletic, and fascinated with everything I did. He called me all the time, communicating with me more often than he would Lynnette. I gave him advice on girls, as well as his first fake ID, which was really the New York State driver's license I fished out the rubbish bin when I was finally forced to get a Tennessee license. Whenever he came to Nashville I'd let him borrow my clothes, which usually fit him better anyway, and sneak him into the club. After he finally graduated from high school, family tradition dictated he would only get help paying for his first semester of college. From there he would be on his own, expected to somehow scrape together a method to fund the rest of his studies. Having watched Lynnette struggle with school as she juggled working long hours at Dillard's, Bank of America, and Red Lobster, I absolutely despised the policy. When Red couldn't afford to continue his studies at Sinclair Community College, he faced family pressure to join the military, as his mom and other relatives had. I discouraged him from fighting for a country that didn't fight for him. He listened. We were tighter than real brothers.

  Red would usually stay with Lynnette's Uncle Mike and Aunt Charlotte off Haywood Lane when he came to town. Uncle Mike was the brother of Lynnette's mom Theresa, sharing the same thick, distinctly Black nose they inherited from their father. Being the only blood relative Lynnette had in town, Uncle Mike served as her surrogate male protector. He treated me like Will Smith's Mike Lowery in Bad Boys the first time Lynnette brought me over for Sunday dinner. Though he had to pretend to be unruly, I knew Uncle Mike liked me. He was too joyful of a Christian to mask his smile and exuberance for an extended period. Naturally nurturing and warm, his wife, Aunt Charlotte, treated me like family from the get-go. Also a New York transplant, our common backgrounds automatically conferred mutual respect and prompted nostalgic discussions. I felt comforted by the remnants of her accent and looked forward to her East Coast home cooking. Aunt Charlotte and Uncle Mike felt like my real life family. Their adorable toddler, Alexia, was my niece.

Christian and Vic, Lynnette's younger sisters on her Mom's side, and Brenee, her younger sister on her Dad's side, were my younger sisters too. Whenever I visited Ohio, I was happy when they tagged along to Rooster's for wings. None of the interaction was forced. We genuinely enjoyed each other's company. At Theresa's house, we'd play Uno or Phase 10, then watch movies until the wee hours of the morning. At Bryan's house, Brenee would hoop with me in the driveway. When Bryan's protective mom, Grandma Linda, was not butting heads with his Jehovah's Witness wife Donyale, she would also come by to hangout. That was rare though. We'd usually drive a few blocks through the neighborhood to spend separate quality time at Grandma Linda's. She usually watched the dogs and kept a bed ready for me. Grandma Linda adored me almost as much as her beloved son Bryan. Because Bryan and I had such similar personalities, Linda and I had a natural grandmother-grandson bond. She said I reminded her of a younger Bryan. While Bryan was at work, and Lynnette caught up with friends and family, I'd take Grandma Linda to run errands. Sometimes we'd stop by the public school from which she retired after years of being an underappreciated lunch lady. When I was back in Nashville I would call to check on her, often to see if she'd caught the day's LeBron highlights.

I wasn't as close with Lynnette's maternal grandparents as I was to Grandma Linda, but I still admired them. Her grandfather, a reserved, handsome, brown-skinned man, known for his signature wide brimmed fedoras, beamed when he recounted Dayton's heyday at the height of GM's car manufacturing dominance. By the time I visited the city, all that remained were relics of glory days past. The gorgeous, two-story, Tudor home he shared with his wife was one of them. She was pleasant, graceful, and easy to mistake for Phylicia Rashad. From her, Lynnette inherited her left cheek dimple and sweet nature. Lynnette confided in her when Theresa was trippin', being judgemental, and overprotective.

During Lynnette's annual family reunion, which alternated between Dayton and Toledo, I never felt out of place. Her cousins, aunts, and uncles all greeted me as one of the family. We even went to church together. Everyone knows a family that prays together stays together. I was more attached to Lynnette's family than to Lynnette many times. Leaving her in Nashville to forge a path in Houston was a necessary maneuver to determine how connected we were as individuals. I needed to know if our relationship was simply one of convenience and comfort. Were we holding each other back from growing? Was Lynnette capable of being completely independent? I wanted to explore my independence as well, albeit in a long distance relationship sustained purely by night and weekend minutes. If we could survive that, we could survive anything.

CHAPTER EIGHT

dangerousNEGRO

I wonder if the spirits of Bob Marley and Haile Selassie
Watch me as the cops be tryna pop and lock me
They cocky, plus they mentality is Nazi
The way they treat Blacks I wanna snap like paparazzi
We're the children of a better God searchin' for better jobs
-Common "Real People"

    Without a clear plan I resigned from my job. I didn't have an opportunity lined up in Houston. All that mattered was getting off the Dell plantation, even if it temporarily required ending up at another plantation, a necessary evil considering dangerousNEGRO was not generating the kind of profit necessary to provide a dividend. With my boy Lawrence Watkins' Great Black Speakers Bureau flourishing, paid speaking engagements fell my way though. I just needed to bide my time at a day job until my speaking career became my primary source of income.

    Perhaps I might even like another day job and coordinate a way to have dual incomes. Certainly everyone didn't work at a plantation like Dell. Some people seemed to love their jobs, or at least didn't find them unbearable. For almost as long as I'd been alive my dad worked at the VA Hospital. My mom worked as an administrative assistant at William Mercer in Midtown until her promotion to compensation analyst, a decades long journey which found her juggling school, her career, and parenting while obtaining her Bachelor's degree, the prerequisite for escaping menial labor.

People just don't subject themselves to seven years of night classes if they don't believe there's a place for them in Corporate America.

Maybe there was a place for me too. Working in a skyscraper on a high floor like my mom sounded appealing. I'd sit in an office downtown gazing at pedestrian ants below. Houston had dozens of tall buildings.... Buildings full of jobs! After a week long visit, I secured three H-Town job offers. *Wow, I was wanted.*

I wouldn't be fooled into joining another plantation this time around though. Enterprise begged me to sign on as a "Management Trainee," but their long hours and job description raised my antennas. Washing cars and running around to accommodate impatient clients on Saturday mornings sounded too plantation esque. Enterprise talked a good game but the job was too easy to decline.

Looking elsewhere, Chase extended me an offer as a personal banker, after I passed their math exam and interview. Ironically, I interned with Chase's Global Asset Management division in the Fox News building across the street from my mom one high school summer. The following summer I spent in their Financial District building off Wall Street, performing dull tasks I can't even remember. Here I was with an economics degree, from Vanderbilt, considering a personal banker position that only paid twenty-eight grand a year. Of course there was room for growth, as the soror who fast tracked me through the interview process, Wynter Patterson, became a regional manager in less than five years. But I couldn't get past the fact I would be bored to death helping people fix overdrafts and sign up for online banking, while giving up my Saturday mornings. Plus I knew working for Chase would require my full dedication if I hoped to attain any level of clout within the organization. Elevating dangerousNEGRO and my public speaking career were higher priorities, priorities which would take a backseat to something I wasn't passionate about if I chose Chase.

That left Transperfect Translations as the remaining option. Headquartered in Manhattan on Park Avenue, enthusiastic Millennials filled the company's roster. Transperfect's office in Houston sat on the forty-second floor of the white Continental Airlines building downtown. The building next door, taken over by Chevron when Enron collapsed, looked like something out of The Jetsons, with its modern design and reflective teal glass. Featuring a circular bridge suspended above Smith Street, it connected employees to another building and a parking garage across the street. I imagined how dope it would be to walk under it everyday on my lunch break. The Continental Airlines building, though awkwardly shaped, was no slouch either. Its high speed elevators made me feel like a superhero, launching me over four hundred feet in seconds.

When I entered Transperfect's door a gorgeous, blonde haired, blue eyed woman greeted me. I recognized her voice as Dana Sanders, the enthusiastic regional sales manager who phoned after my Careerbuilder submission. Previous exposure to the finest of fine White girls at Taft and Vanderbilt, hadn't prepared me for a White woman this fine. Ever since Meredith played me in high school, I was long past my attraction to most White women, but Dana was the most stunning I had ever seen. She had fuller lips than most and dimples in both cheeks. Petite, with just enough meat to make Brothas turn their heads, Dana was a stone cold fox, a very professional fox who could easily pass for a Stepford Wife had she not worn pantsuits. Her movements were brisk, motivated by ambition and espresso. She smiled to expose her perfect teeth, while she stared me in the eyes, listening intently to my previous sales experience. Considering the contempt I held for Stacy, my previous White female manager at Dell, I imagined I would run away from any opportunity to be managed by a White woman again. However, Dana was different. She was forward and assertive, not passive aggressive like Stacy. In further contrast, Dana was upbeat and bubbly, while Stacy was drab and depressing. I felt wrong to have assumed all White female managers were the same.

Furthermore, Transperfect was not the same as Dell. Transperfect flew employees to sales trainings in New York and corporate galas in San Francisco. Traveling made me excited. Even better, day to day tasks wouldn't confine me to the office all day. The job required cold calling businesses, attending networking events, visiting prospective clients, and delivering convincing presentations; all tasks that would help hone my public speaking skills. Most of all, the product, translation services, could be sold with integrity. There would be no need to stretch the truth or sell clients materials they didn't need. Either they had important documents requiring a competent human to translate into another language, or they didn't.

Still weary, I was determined not to let Corporate America pimp me this go 'round. When Dana offered me the account executive position at 35K plus commission, I told her I'd have to entertain other options. Afterall, not only was Enterprise offering the same deal, but my base salary at Dell climbed to 40K by the end of my tenure. Surely a salesman of my calibre deserved at least the same base salary I earned at my last gig. Dana told me *all* account executives started at 35K. Reminiscing on how silly I felt upon discovering several of my White co-workers negotiated higher entry level pay at Dell, I refused to be that naive again. I was relieved when my ballsy resistance led Transperfect to meet me halfway with a base salary of 38K. Not a total victory, but nonetheless a small triumph. With commission, I was sure I could clear at least fifty grand annually. Not bad for a first year sales rep with no established pipeline in a new city. I took the job.

In order to break my lease at swanky Nashboro Village, (a "master planned community" on a golf course), afford the move, and have funds to sign a new lease in Houston, I liquidated my 401K. Eating the exorbitant tax penalty on the withdrawal felt like rape, but I saw no other options. Leaving Nashville with the payday loans I became accustomed to juggling would surely haunt me. Thus, I paid off the loan on Murfreesboro Pike, then the one on Bell Road, and vowed never to get sucked in by predatory lenders again. With the money I had leftover, I couldn't just leave Lynnette hanging, so I paid the deposit for the new apartment she would need in my absence. She made me feel guilty about abandoning her and the young couple to whom we had grown attached, Shawn and Malarie. Our weekly game nights would cease to exist. Of course I would miss those things, but I reminded Lynnette we knew we couldn't live in Nashville forever. It was time to spread my wings and fly, for the both of us. So I packed my little green Beemer to the ceiling, carving out just enough space for Dominoe and Paris to stick their noses out the window, and made the twelve hour descent to H-Town.

Upon arrival, me and the dogs went into city shock, as cars on Richmond Avenue whizzed past us at fifty miles per hour during our first walk. Recounting my visits back to New York during my high school and college years, I knew it would take a few weeks for my pulse to adjust to the faster paced lifestyle. People were less patient and more aggressive in bigger cities. Experience told me I would reacquire those traits in due time.

My new apartment complex was more crowded and less attractive than the last two I lived in back in Tennessee. There was hardly any grass for the dogs to poop, the outside of the units were painted puke yellow, and some terraces leaned in directions that suggested shoddy construction. Jokingly, I referred to the complex as Turtle Pointe Projects when the topic of my dwelling came up around Sebastine, and his future wife Kiran's, educated friends. The whole room would burst into laughter because everyone knew how sketchy the apartments on the corner of Richmond and Dunvale looked. Most of them lived in nicer complexes just blocks away, in the Galleria area extending from I-610 westward to Gessner. But the rent for my seven-hundred square foot, two-level loft, with a bedroom overlooking the living room was only $525. I couldn't believe how inexpensive it was to live in Houston's most bustling area. Surviving New York's ghettos gave me the confidence to live just about anywhere. Anybody in Momma's projects would have traded places with me in a heartbeat.

Ten miles were all that separated my Galleria area apartment from Transperfect's downtown office. Little did I know it would take more than ninety minutes to travel those ten miles during Houston's hellacious rush hour. I had to leave home no later than seven o'clock to make sure I got a parking spot in a crumbling, condemned, parking garage four Texas sized blocks away from my job. For only $5 I could park there all day. Occasionally, I would arrive to see the city had padlocked the entrance due to the exposed steel protruding from the potholes and decaying concrete inside. Somehow the janky, Middle Eastern owner would have it back open by the next morning.

Unfortunately, parking in the garage attached to our building was not an option. Dana said the company was not willing to foot the bill. However, as soon as Dana was beyond earshot, Blaire, also an account executive, and the only other employee in the office, revealed Dana's parking claim was bogus. A year older at twenty-six, bleached blond and very Caucasian, Blaire kept it real with me, while maintaining her alternate corporate persona. Dana never questioned her loyalty. She deserved an Academy Award for pretending to enjoy Dana's presence. Blaire's parking in the building garage was paid for and she felt my slighting unfair. "You shouldn't have to sweat your ass off for four blocks after you park," she fumed. Suggesting I pressure Dana to get funds from corporate to cover parking, I thanked Blaire for looking out for me, but I knew better than to rock the boat in a sales job as a Black man. Sure, I successfully negotiated a higher starting salary, but that was prior to my employment, back when I had the upperhand. Salespeople, especially Black ones, had high turnover rates and Transperfect was no exception. According to Blaire, the previous account exec that sat in my seat lasted less than two months. Certainly, I planned to outlast him. So I remained mum about the parking disparity. I also kept quiet about not being granted the vacant office between Dana and Blaire's, which had an impressive floor to ceiling view of Southwest Houston. Awkwardly, I sat at a desk in the reception area, surrounded by copy paper and facing a bare wall. No matter, I was just there for the paycheck. I figured I would earn my way into the vacant office sooner or later. Corporate hazing was to be expected. I entered the job with great intentions to redefine my future and prove Dell's horribleness a fluke.

Dana stuck to a strict daily regimen. First thing in the morning, she clicked on mail merge > ctrl-P to print letters and address labels from the cold call lists she constructed the evening prior. She loaded a thick stack of paper into the letter folder and waited for every sheet to be creased perfectly into thirds. From there she stuffed each envelope by hand, licked the back, and loaded stacks into the Pitney-Bowes postage machine. The whole process took about an hour for robotic Dana who could do the routine in her sleep. For non-black belt letter stuffers, who had to contend with the folding machine screwing up creases and the postage machine getting jammed, the undertaking was a two hour ordeal.

"Blaire, we have to do this everyday?"

"Does the sun always rise in the East D?"

Shit.

I hated tedious, monotonous tasks. During the final summer of my ABC Sports internship I nearly lost my mind applying stickers to marketing materials and auditing expense reports. The repetitiveness drove me insane. In order to endure the mind numbingness of the letter stuffing burden, I threw in my earbuds and nodded my head to dead prez' "W-4", while continually reminding myself this was just my job; dangerousNEGRO and public speaking made up my real career.

Not only was grunt work in the office frustrating, but maintaining my relationship with Lynnette was becoming cumbersome. I could sense her resentment in our phone calls. Considering the trove of trust issues stemming from previous deceit, I became highly convinced she would step out on me again. Everyday she seemed more distant. The inquiries stemming from my insecurities certainly did nothing to make her miss me. Clearly this was the case when I drove twelve hours to surprise Lynnette on her birthday. Instead of being excited to see me, she seemed especially perturbed. I knew something had changed. Still, I visited when time permitted.

During one of my back and forths between Nashville and Houston, I got pulled over on Highway 59 in East Texas. From half a mile away, I could make out the alternating red and blue lights of a police car emanating from darkness at the bottom of the hill I descended. An obvious speed trap, I eased off the gas and checked my speedometer to make sure I wouldn't be the next sucker collared at the hill's basin. No sooner than I passed the highway patrolman, who had a Mercedes detained, another cop approached me from the rear. *Got to be kidding me!* I was confident I hadn't exceeded the speed limit... well at least not by enough to warrant being pulled over.

Getting stopped in rural East Texas at three in the morning was definitely not on my bucket list. I imagined it would have to be much worse than the routine, unwarranted traffic stops I faced at the hands of the NYPD anytime I returned to New York. The worst of those incidents found me, Eddie, Louie, and Darryl lying face down in the snowy street while "New York's finest" unjustly searched my mom's Bonneville for money, drugs, and guns. That particular stop was prompted by the new shearling coat I copped on Delancey Street for fifty-percent off the day after Christmas. The first question the White officer asked upon approaching my window, weapon drawn, was "Where'd you get that flashy coat?" His follow up: "How about you guys step out so we can search your car?" His Latino sidekick searched our pockets, while trying to convince us he was doing us a favor - not trying to hurt us or get us in trouble. When we were finally free to go I demanded the White cop's name and badge number. He laughed and told me to go fuck myself. New York's Pricks and Dicks were beyond reproach under Giuliani's two terms of terror.

Based on the state's reputation for executing Robin Harris' "Gotta Go - Gotta Go" death penalty philosophy, I knew East Texas cops had to be exponentially more racist and dangerous than the NYPD. Even worse, I actually *had* a gun in the car this time. The first gun I held was at my boy Louie's crib in Co-op City. His dad kept a deer hunting arsenal. Based on the gun clapping narratives of M.O.P, Mobb Deep, Black Moon, and a great majority of my favorite Hip Hop artists, Black masculinity required me to be prepared for the instance I might have to cap somebody; even if guns terrified me deep down inside. After Tank taught me to shoot in high school, my fear turned into machismo.

The South's lax restrictions and pro gun culture inspired me to purchase a 40 calibre pistol from a Confederate flag clad gunshop on the outskirts of Nashville after undergrad.

"Trust me, you don't want a 9 millimeter... you might as well get something that's gonna take somebody out if you need to use it," I remember the snaggletoothed, Redneck salesman advising.

Having to kill somebody frightened me, but I followed his logic.

"How am I supposed to transport this in my car without a concealed handgun license?" I asked.

"All you gots to do is make sure the bullets and the gun are in two separates parts of the car. If you keep the gun in the glove compartment, then keep the clips and ammo in the trunk, you got it?"

I nodded.

Fast forward a few years to my three am traffic stop near Nacogdoches, Texas. The gun was in the glove compartment, the clip in the trunk, as I was taught. Texas had lenient gun laws according to everything I heard, but in this instance I questioned the validity of my sources. Fear that *these* cops might conspire to arrest me regardless of my compliance with the law elevated my heart rate. New York cops lied and planted evidence all the time, there was no telling how much more devilish Texas cops had to be. Despite taking the circumstances into consideration, I admitted I was carrying a firearm when the officer asked.

"Where'd you get this car?" he probed.

"I bought it from Carmax."

"What are you doing in Texas with these Tennessee tags?"

"I recently moved to start a sales job in Houston," I responded.

By this point Dominoe and Paris barked furiously in the backseat, as the pale officer aimed his flashlight in our eyes, while probing for signs of impropriety.

"Do you consent to us searching your vehicle?"

Politely I informed him, "I would prefer that you not, because it's late and I have to be at work in Houston first thing in the morning."

"We can do this the easy way or the hard way. If you decline the search I'll just have your vehicle impounded until we can get a search warrant. You'll miss work tomorrow for sure. So I'm gonna ask you again, do you consent to us searching your vehicle?"

Shaking my head in frustration I said, "Go ahead. But you'll be wasting your time because there's nothing illegal in my car."

With his gun drawn he yelled at me to exit slowly, with my arms raised. He then turned his attention to Dominoe and Paris, "I'm telling you now I will shoot those goddamn dogs if they make a move towards me when you take them out." Rightfully, they wanted to rip the cop's head off due to his aggressive posturing. I was nervous they would lunge towards him despite my urgings to remain calm and stop barking. I cracked the backseat door to grab their leashes, wrapping them around my arm several times to limit their ability to approach the scared officer. There wasn't enough rope to get within a foot of the cop. Of course, they still tried. "Take them up in the grass on that hill or I promise I will shoot them dead," he assured. We sat on the hill for two hours while the asshole cop, and the two additional patrolmen he radioed for backup, ransacked my car searching for something they could use to take me to jail. Another cop arrived to test my forty cal for fingerprints. A few months prior, Bichar fumed he had been the victim of a cop planting weed in his car after he broke down on Interstate 40 and summoned the same officer for help. I was all but certain my fate would be the same, or worse, based on the officers' dogged determination to find an excuse to take me to jail. Wondering what would happen to Dominoe and Paris while I was in lock up consumed my mind. Finally, the asshole cop gestured for me to come down the hill to get back into my trashed car. Offering no apologies, he handed me a ticket for doing 55 in a 50.

I got back to Houston with just enough time to put the dogs in my apartment and head straight to work. Barely keeping my eyes open as traffic crawled down 59, I made it to work about ten minutes late. Dana allowed me to turn on my computer and check my voicemail before summoning me to her office. She asked about my weekend with Lynnette in Nashville, pretending to show genuine interest, before promptly transitioning into an interrogation of why I was late to work.

"The traffic today was the worst I've ever seen," I mentioned.

"But I got here early somehow didn't I? I want you to figure out a way you can get here earlier ok?"

I gritted my teeth, nodded my head, and exited her office. Blaire, who surprised me with her unexpected resignation a few weeks prior, obviously made the right decision to leave.

With Blaire gone, Dana could devote her full attention to driving me crazy with her micromanagement. It mattered not that I successfully cold called and arranged product demonstrations with new businesses, or that I closed deals with previously elusive companies, I could feel Dana's breath on the back of my neck at least fifty hours a week. Flashbacks of Stacy at Dell brought back anxiety. Micromanagement and I simply did not jive. The uncertainty of when dangerousNEGRO and/or my speaking career would spring me from corporate America made Dana's suffocation even more frightening.

***

The only thing keeping me sane was the confidence I had in my entrepreneurial endeavors. I had reason to be optimistic. dangerousNEGRO was taking off in Houston. Sebastine and I secured consignment deals with urban boutiques End Zone and KS Fashions in the Third Ward, as well as, 467 Street in the upscale Galleria.

Then, after a concert at Warehouse Live, a chance encounter with Jay Ellis, Bun B's Rap-A-Lot affiliated booking manager, opened the door to me being featured in Mike Jones' "Turning Heads" video. You can see me hanging out the passenger side of a slab rocking a dN *Definition* tee for about 1.5 seconds in the final production. Two weeks later Jay Ellis called me to share the news he successfully placed a *Smart Is The New Gangsta* tee in Bun B's "That's Gangsta" video. (Justin Giboney, my business partner in Atlanta, conceived *Smart Is The New Gangsta* while performing legal services as an attorney. It quickly became our most popular design). "That's Gangsta" featured Sean Kingston and led as the single to Bun's II Trill LP. If you pull it up on YouTube you'll see a husky, dark-skinned dude rocking the black and white colorway at twenty-four seconds in. Following the video's release, dangerousNEGRO had Houston on lock. More and more frequently I'd run into random strangers wearing our shirts. People were thrilled to find out I was one of the minds behind the company when I approached them, though I got a better rush out of simply complimenting their dope shirt selection and asking where they made their purchase.

While studying for his PhD. in chemistry at Stanford, Tracy was doing the same in the Bay Area. In between experiments, he somehow found time to identify a local, Black screen printer, which would take our production process to the next level. Oakland's Big Printing was able to produce tees with our own tags in them! It sounds like nothing now, but back then, having our own tags sewn into the shirt collar was groundbreaking. Custom tags made us a legitimate streetwear line. The embarrassment of trying to get store owners to carry our shirts with Hanes, Anvil, or American Apparel tags was over. No longer would I have to beg a dry cleaner or seamstress to wrestle with cutting generic tags and sewing dN tags in their place. dangerousNEGRO was real. Stores in The Bay respected our legitimacy when Tracy approached them for rack placement. Accounts were opened on the West Coast.

Similarly, Gary was doing his thing in the Midwest. He kept up the momentum after we flooded the Indianapolis Black Expo with t-shirts the two previous summers. A social butterfly, Gary, AKA G-Money, was a staple of the Indianapolis club scene. All the promoters knew Gary, as did most of the women and hood figures in Nap. He was an influencer. Gary made every Black person in Indianapolis want a dangerousNEGRO tee. When celebrities came to the club, he always made sure to have a shirt on hand to slide them on their way out. Gary was fearless in that regard, unintimidated by the prospect of rejection or embarrassment. A natural salesman like me, he could finesse his way into or out of improbable scenarios better than anyone I've ever met. I've never paid to get in an event with Gary; his gift of gab has always opened unseen opportunities or created a necessary diversion from which we could benefit. Somehow a few guys too cheap to pay club admission would end up in VIP rubbing shoulders with our favorite entertainers.

When I heard Common and Ludacris would be headlining my alma mater's homecoming concert, I knew I had to be like Gary; those guys were getting shirts by any means necessary. Though I had graduated, I was still cool with Mona Hicks from the Greek Life office. She got promoted and had more juice by the time the concert came around. One of her new responsibilities was to make sure celebrities, particularly the Black ones, received the university's utmost hospitality. I followed her like a shadow the day of the concert. As I calculated, I found myself backstage face to face with Ludacris for a photo op. Though I was a little nervous and didn't want to come across as a male groupie, I took the sight of Luda's blinged out Africa pendant as an affirmation. Surely, he'd be receptive to wearing dangerousNEGRO Black Empowerment Apparel. Except he wasn't. When I asked if he could take a picture holding up the shirt I brought for him, I was surprised by how nonchalantly he refused with a straight "nah." *Well, alright.* Obviously Luda had no idea I made most of the women in my class permanently look at me sideways for regurgitating his most memorable bars from "Ho" on VUTV my freshman year. In the pic we ended up taking, Luda stared blankly into the camera, while I beamed with pride for managing to document a brief encounter with one of my favorite rappers, in my own dN tee. Maybe he had a rough day. Maybe he had a contract with another t-shirt company. Maybe he was sick of people making requests to exploit his celebrity. I'm not sure, but my mission was accomplished, albeit partially. Demetrius Walker and dangerousNEGRO could be mentioned in the same sentence with a superstar.

    The encounter with Ludacris further motivated me to find Common backstage. I never forgot how down to Earth he was when Mr. Hall and I had lunch with him in New Haven seven years prior. Maybe he'd even remember plucking lentils from his plate with injera if I reminded him. Once Mona headed to her seat to watch Luda perform, I opted to stay behind to make sure I would cross paths with Mr. Com Sense. Off to the left of the stage, in the tunnel leading back to Memorial Gym's locker rooms, I watched Ludacris rip the stage from less than twenty feet away. I might as well have been invisible as his entourage, including his Baby's Mother and young daughter, barged past me while exiting the stage. Something told me I would see him again under different circumstances in the future. No matter, I turned my attention to finding Common. Patiently, I sat in a chair by the door everyone had to walk through before climbing four steps up to the stage. With a tan *Definition* tee strewn over my right shoulder, I tried my best to appear inconspicuous. When a Caucasian

State Trooper entered the hallway to make sure it was clear, I looked at him, waived, then quickly made eye contact with the floor, as if I was an overworked student upset I wasn't in the crowd. He fell for it. I knew I was home free when his olive green, Dudley Do Right hat turned its attention to the opposite end of the hall. For what seemed like an eternity, but was probably just a few minutes, I waited for Lonnie Rashid Lynn, Jr. to rear his head. Suddenly I looked up and there he was. Solo. He looked contemplative like he was trying to remember some new lyrics. I figured it was a bad time to break his concentration, so I simply stood with my hand on the door knob to assure him I was only there to assist in his stage entrance. The crowd erupted in a frenzy when the DJ dropped the "Go" instrumental. Showtime. Doing my best Geoffrey from the Fresh Prince impression, I swung the door open and invited Common to step through. Before he burst onto the stage, he made sure to acknowledge me with a sincere, smiling "Thank you." I watched his whole set through the door's window, surprised he was able to be so energetic while performing "conscious" music. After forty-five minutes of performing his classics, he exited the stage exhausted, dripping in sweat. "You still here?" he asked jokingly, surprised I was still waiting at the door. At least a few hundred times I had rehearsed what I'd say before giving him the shirt. I was supposed to remind him about the Hip Hop summit at Yale and lunch with Mr. Hall, but in the heat of the moment a fearful inner voice assured me he wouldn't remember.

Just give him the shirt and keep it brief. Okay, I got this.

"You inspired me and my friends to make this. We're big fans of your music."

He threw the shirt over his shoulder but didn't say anything. I figured he might use it as a sweat rag. Before I could say anything further, his publicist, a thirty-something White lady, appeared to drag him off to a radio interview with 101.1's Dolewhite & Scooby. At 6'3, I doubted he would even wear the shirt, considering it was a medium (the last *Definition* tee I had in stock). Regardless, knowing Common knew about dangerousNEGRO excited me. Maybe he'd tell other important people about it. Maybe he'd mention us in public, or even better, give us a shout out in his next album's liner notes.

Nothing could prepare me for the moment I turned on MTV's Total Request Live with Carson Daly and noticed Common rocking the *Definition* tee under his black, nylon Gap jacket. He had just signed an endorsement deal with The Gap, yet there he was showing support for us, the little guys. I did a double take before frantically dialing the fellas to tell them to turn the channel. Whoa, this was huge! A few hours later MTV uploaded the video on its website, along with a green room headshot of Common in the shirt. The words of the *Definition* could be made out clearly. I emailed the clip and headshot over to Angel at ConcreteLoop, an exploding Black celebrity gossip blog. The site drew hundreds of thousands of unique visits a day. Angel found Common wearing dangerousNEGRO newsworthy. This was it - dN|Be was about to take off!

Common rocking dN considerably elevated our profile. Somebody at BET took notice and sent an email to our info account asking if we would be interested in shooting a segment for their series, "The 5ive," hosted by Alesha Renee. *Of course!* The choice was obvious to me, though Justin and Chairman Tre cautioned we risked alienating our core fanbase, who took issue with the coonery pervasive on Black Entertainment Television. In 2007, BET was known for selling its soul to the White opportunists at Viacom. A host of corny, unflattering Black reality shows modeled after MTV's predominantly White shows swept the network. Baby Boy, with f-bombs dubbed over and replaced by "fool," and n-words awkwardly replaced with "brotha," aired with commercial breaks most evenings. Despite the potential consequences, we all agreed the exposure received via BET outweighed upsetting our supporters who despised the network. Afterall, it would have been hypocritical to criticize BET for not showing more positive programming, then decline to allow our fledgling Black empowerment clothing line to reach the masses.

In return for more rack space, Sebastine and I agreed to film most of our segment at End Zone Fashions. Former NFL player Bobby Taylor owned the store, which offered University of Houston students a convenient urban wear outlet. Two blocks away on Scott Street, KS Fashions, directly across from Wheeler Baptist Church, also agreed to the same deal. KS, named after its street legend owner Kerry Stubblefield, was actually closer to U of H, but significantly more hood and less inviting. But they were gracious enough to carry our line, so we repaid our debt of gratitude by including them in our BET spotlight, although briefly. Ninety-nine percent of the clip was filmed at End Zone.

Sebastine was extremely nervous about being broadcast nationwide. Four shots of Crown weren't enough to calm his nerves or stem the sweat dripping from his forehead. On the other hand, I was ready for my moment in the spotlight. *It was about damn time!* The cameras were there to spring me from the plantation.

Overly excited, I stumbled over my words more than a few times. Sebastine's bad nerves also created reasons to retake a few scenes. Luckily the film crew, the same guys who filmed the Mike Jones "Turnin Headz" video a few months prior, liked me. Pure happenstance, I had no idea BET hired them before we showed up. Reuniting with the same professionals responsible for keeping a platinum selling artist relevant felt like the universe aligning to propel us towards success. They assured me they would edit the footage to make us look dignified.

Nervous about looking corny or suspect on television, my worst nightmare was Black people questioning my sincerity. Anticipation of the final edit wore on my nerves. Unfortunately, it took weeks for the footage to be edited. At least that's what I was told every time I requested an update. With each passing day I grew more and more skeptical BET would air anything featuring the title "dangerousNEGRO." Would the higher ups at Viacom be daring enough to absorb potential backlash from people misunderstanding our name? Probably not.

We were well aware of how controversial the term dangerousNEGRO was, specifically for older folks who could remember "Negro" losing its footing to "Black," and consequently "African American." For them, it represented taking a step backwards. During my first radio interview, an angry, Black, middle-aged, male caller said we were "inflaming White people's worst fears and reinforcing negative stereotypes." From that moment forward the only times we ever seemed to get this feedback was from pre-Generation X Black folks. It was a delicate issue for anybody who lived through the era of being referred to as a Negro. The BET clip had to convert the naysayers.

After five weeks of holding our breath, our segment finally aired on The 5ive. Alesha Renee made sure to smile when she announced:

> "What's up everybody and welcome to The 5ive. I'm your host Alesha Renee. Today we're bringing you up on brand new websites, web clips, artists, gadgets, fashion, and so much more that you need to be up on right now. Rolling into our number five spot is a new line that we came across that stands out - dangerousNEGRO."

She made sure to fully enunciate and pause briefly between the two words "dangerous" and "Negro" before proceeding with:

"Whereas most lines only make a fashion statement, dangerousNEGRO makes a political statement as well. dangerousNEGRO.com is the home of empowerment apparel. It's not just a place to shop, but it's also a spot for news and info and so much more about what's going on in the community. It's socially conscious style, with strong messages on t-shirts, bracelets, and so much more, and it's our first pick of the day. Knowledge is power, so you guys act like you know about The 5ive's dangerousNEGRO.com."

Wow! We were totally blown away by Alesha's thorough introduction. Off the bat, it was evident the producers of the show wanted dangerousNEGRO to be portrayed in a positive light. Already in the crosshairs of the conscious Black community, it's safe to say they needed us to look good as much, if not more, than we did. And the segment truly delivered.

It starts out with me and Sebastine introducing ourselves outside of End Zone Fashions. I invite the television audience to join us inside to find out what dangerousNEGRO is all about. Sebastine gives a brief summary of our basic premise, before I go into the significance of our name. We introduce a few of our most popular shirts, *Smart Is The New Gangsta* and *Young. Gifted. Black*. During the clip, the producers weave in a bunch of historic visuals for reference. Unexpected special effects add further flair to our talking points. The 5ive did dangerousNEGRO justice.

***

The details of The 5ive segment were relayed to me over the phone by Tracy, as I didn't get to watch it when it originally aired. My life had completely changed in the five weeks it took for the clip to debut on BET. Dana finally drove me over the edge at Transperfect, so once again, I found myself leaving another company without a definitive source of income. Basic cable had to go. I was never much of a TV watcher once I entered adulthood anyway. Sitting in front of the idiot box made me feel guilty about being unproductive. Besides, the internet was more exciting and worthy of my attention; it curved to my interests at any given moment. Thus, I didn't actually watch the clip until a week later, when I received a copy in the mail - from my father. Out of all people who caught the broadcast, my father was the only one who randomly had a DVD recorder to accompany his TiVo. I used the disc to upload our television debut to YouTube, my favorite emerging web medium. Surely it'd go viral, I figured.

If only there was a way to upload the video to Facebook so the rest of my friends and family could spread the word. That feature wouldn't emerge until a few years later. Though I initially resisted the urge to join Facebook, due in part to getting catfished on its predecessors College Club and Black Planet, I succumbed to peer pressure and joined the social network. Being in a long distance relationship, Facebook provided a convenient way to keep up with Lynnette. Our daily phone call often felt like a chore, with details missed, omitted, and forgotten. On the contrary, I could login to Facebook and see what was happening on Lynnette's wall in real time. Most of all, I could see my attractive, potential wife's pictures, constant reminders of the life awaiting. There was no firewall blocking Facebook's transmission at work, so I would often check in on the latest developments during my lunch break.

Soon I discovered Dana considered me to be on the clock as long as I was sitting at my desk. A non-paid, one hour, daily lunch break apparently only counted when I vacated the office. To Dana, butt in seat meant slave on duty. One day as I slurped gumbo at my desk, I noticed Dana creep behind me to pick up a ream of copy paper. Since I had thirty minutes left on my break and I didn't feel I was doing anything inappropriate by scanning Facebook, I thought little of it. A few moments later she asked if I had my mail merge ready to print solicitation letters.

But I'm on my break?!

"Yes Dana, I'll get the merge ready as soon as my break is over."

Five minutes later I heard her walk out of her office to fetch a stapler from a cabinet near my desk. Considering Dana always had at least two staplers on her desk, she was obviously spying. Nevertheless, I was determined to use the full sixty minute period allotted for my mental respite. No sooner than she returned to her desk did she request:

"Demetrius could you come to my office please?"

Despite still having ten minutes left on my break I obliged. When I walked in, Dana's face was red. She looked like her head might explode, as she reached into the pit of her belly trying to find the most politically correct words to express her anger.

"Let's get one thing clear Demetrius. When you are in this office I own you, do you understand?"

Shocked, it was impossible for me to hide how stunned I was to hear Dana voice this out loud. My eyebrows instinctively rose as high as my hairline, the white of my eyes completely exposed. I always assumed she internalized those thoughts and ran them through an HR filter before verbalizing them, but to actually hear a White woman tell me she owned me, with a straight face, was the most surprising moment of my life.

Before I could offer a response, Dana continued, "How do you think this situation is working out?"

Looking Dana in her blue eyes I voiced "It's not."

I considered walking out and slamming the door, never to be seen again, but the more rational side of me won out.

"Consider this my two week notice. I'm sure you'll need some time to find a replacement..."

I lasted three more days before I found it unfathomable to return to my desk after lunch. I called HR in New York to apologize for not being able to finish out the terms of my resignation. They understood. Dana had a reputation of running salesmen off...

The dangerousNEGRO Team
(Left to Right Top: Justin Giboney, Tre Baker, Gary Mavindidze, Me. Bottom: Sebastine Ujereh Jr, Frank Robinson. Missing in Action: Tracy Holmes)

CHAPTER NINE

ROCK BOTTOM

My life is full of empty promises
And broken dreams
I'm hoping things will look up
But there ain't no job openings
I feel discouraged hungry and malnourished
Living in this house with no furnace, unfurnished
And I'm sick of working dead end jobs with lame pay
And I'm tired of being hired and fired the same day
-Eminem "Rock Bottom"

Stomach rumbling, I stumbled to the empty refrigerator. Knowing the only items inside were a box of baking soda, a pitcher of tap water, and a month old onion, I still hoped for a miracle. Maybe Jesus would have mercy on me and turn my pitcher of water into wine, so I could at least drink away my hunger. *Nope... no miracle today.* I slammed the fridge closed. There I stood in my barren kitchen, temple against the cold, white wall. Frustration, fear, exhaustion, and disappointment slammed into my conscience like a doomed meteor reaching its inevitable fate. A fallen star I was indeed. *How did I allow myself to get to this point?* I was a posh prep school alum, a Vanderbilt graduate, an "exceptionally gifted" individual. Yet at 25 years old I hadn't figured out a way to prevent myself from starving to death.

Suddenly, I felt something I had only felt twice before. Circa 1988, the first time occurred as I watched Littlefoot lose his mother to a ruthless Tyrannosaurus Rex in The Land Before Time. Years later, Lauren's premature death conferred the same absolute sadness. With my head against the wall, I felt warm tears roll down my cheeks onto the wooden floor. Jigga ran through my mind: "This can't be life / This can't be love / This can't be right / There's gotta be more / This can't be us." *It couldn't be me... right?*

Before I could assess the magnitude of that question, Dominoe and Paris knocked over their empty bowls in protest of their master's unwillingness to feed them. As Telemundo, (one of the four channels I could get with decent reception) blared, I sunk into an even deeper depression. I had less than no money, my bank account reflecting red, negative digits. I already owed Sebastine six-hundred dollars, and every family member I could think of was asking *me* for cash. So I pulled a page out of Beanie Sigel's rhyme book, ascended the staircase to my bedroom, and "ate sleep for dinner."

At 7 A.M. my cell phone sprang me from sleep as scheduled. Not that I really needed it, my circadian rhythm was so tuned to the corporate ritual I typically awoke right before the annoying chirp sounded. Still hungry, I reluctantly limped towards my tiny second floor bathroom. En route, I looked at my emaciated body in the mirror. Having a metabolism as high as mine, missing a few meals amounted to a rapid reduction in weight loss. I hopped in the shower using my razor thin slice of Irish Spring as my facial cleanser, shampoo, conditioner, and body wash. Afterwards I brushed my teeth, grimacing in pain as the bristles ran across my rear molars in need of urgent care. No benefits meant anbesol was my dentist. I didn't have enough money for my bottled half ounce dentist though. I reached into my closet to grab a pair of slacks and a collared shirt. One of my socks had a hole in its heel. Only I would know.

Per daily protocol, I rushed to walk the dogs, then left them in the apartment to watch Telemundo and bark at unsuspecting passers by. It was now time to sit in rush hour traffic on the way to the 100% commission sales job I found out of desperation on Craigslist. Yes, I was that desperate, and Pop Labs, a search engine optimization and marketing firm on Houston's west side, posted an extremely convincing ad.

    Clicking on my seatbelt, I backed my green 3-series out of my customary parking spot. A yellow dot illuminated next to the E on my gas gage. As the gate rolled open to release me to Richmond Avenue's morning drudge, I turned on the radio. Too many commercials. Reaching under the seat, I found The Blueprint and skipped to track six. "I'll sell ice in the winter time / Fire in hell / I am a hustler baby / I'll sell water to a well." Motivation was what I needed and this was it. *Something was getting sold to someone today by any means necessary.*

    On the way to the office I picked up Kevin. I was in bad shape, but he was even worse off. His '96 Buick LeSabre had a cracked head gasket and was on its deathbed waiting for the plug to be pulled. No sense in making him find some quarters to take the bus since I had to pass his general direction on the way to the plantation. As I approached the corner of Harwin and Bonhomme, I spotted Kevin's thin, dark-skinned frame in the distance. A fitted White Sox cap adorned his scalp to hide his desperate need for a haircut. His goatee had grown out of control and was in urgent need of a shave. Lucky me, I could never grow facial hair - one less expense I had to worry about. He opened the passenger side door and cheerfully greeted me with the same words from the day before, "I really appreciate this ride man. My car should be running next week."

    We were both Hip Hop heads so we could appreciate each other's musical insight on the way to work. Kevin was also a college graduate, and Greek, having pledged Sigma at Texas Southern. There he studied radio, television, and film production.

Though we shared common interests, Kevin's life was more complicated. Kevin had a two-year-old daughter that stayed with his baby's mother out in Katy. He was under constant pressure to provide as a father. Despite Kevin's circumstances, he was somehow more optimistic than I was about working on the corporate plantation for no pay.

Walking into the glum lobby of the black, trapezoidal building overlooking the corner of Beltway 8 and Westheimer, Kevin boasted about how confident he was he'd close a deal by week's end. "I got a couple people ready to pull the trigger... just gotta push them over the edge," he mentioned. Riding up the cramped elevator, I couldn't help but notice the look on everyone's face. Eyes remained glued to the digital display as the numbers illuminated each floor in ascending order. Zombies, mindless zombies addicted to Starbucks. Only Kevin and I remained on the ascent to the 25th and final floor. He told me everyone saw how hard I was working and found my persistence impressive. "You just had some bad luck with your deals closing. I bet like five in a row will close soon. Just watch D, it's gonna happen."

We walked out the elevator and through the large glass doors. Kevin stopped to flirt with Bianca, the thick-bottomed, redbone receptionist. She was definitely fine, and her New York accent reminded me of home. But I knew better than to try my luck. First, she distributed every paycheck in the office - mines were non existent. Second, Bianca lived with her boyfriend in upscale Jersey Village, I couldn't compete with that. And last, I learned from the disaster of dating an older co-worker when I was nineteen, that mixing business with pleasure was a mistake. So I made a B line for the tea in the break room hoping to satisfy my persistent hunger. At the minimum, I figured a sugary cup of tea would keep my stomach from eating itself for a few more hours. I ended up in line behind Ronnie, a husky, part-time barber and aspiring musician, who sat next to me on the sales floor. To no avail, Ronnie checked all the cabinets for bags of tea. Coffee, which I despised, was the only remaining item of sustenance. *Coffee or death?* Coffee it was. As I contemplated how to proceed with making my first cup of java, Silver, one of the veteran closers entered the break room. He looked just like Ryu from Street Fighter II. "You don't know how to make coffee? You gotta be kidding me. Get out the way."

For five minutes I listened to Silver hype his coffee making expertise. Once the batch was ready, he poured it into my tiny styrofoam cup, added five packets of Sweet'n Low, mixed it in with a skinny red straw, and encouraged me to drink. Within seconds of my first sip, I found myself gazing into the bottom of an industrial sized garbage can. The excessive Sweet'n Low shocked my taste buds, making me regurgitate the remaining contents of my puny stomach. I was surprised there was even anything left in the tank to puke out. Hearing the laughter of my co-workers, I lifted my head out the garbage can and tapped the water cooler for a small cup of water. The last morsel of nutrition I owned was at the bottom of a Hefty bag.

From 8 to 8:30 every morning, Gene, the company's president, gathered up the sales team like a caffeine-crazed border collie, herding us in the training room. Plantation days always commenced this way. Paying an uncanny resemblance to Bud Bundy, Gene masterfully channeled Vince Lombardi. Never have I met another person who could consistently motivate a workforce to give their blood, sweat, and tears for peanuts.

"Demetrius, as a level one rep, what is expected from you on a daily basis?" Gene asked sarcastically.

"Two-hundred and fifty phone calls, four hours of talk time, and at least three T.Os" I rattled off.

"Holy shit!" Gene exclaimed, "someone in this room has a brain. That's surprising because I looked at the call stats and the turnover sheets from yesterday and not one of you dimwits was able to do it. All I ask you to do is dial at least two-hundred and fifty phone numbers from the leads I give you. Everyday. The leads are good… I paid a lot of fucking money for them so I know they're good. I guarantee there are at least three good leads to turnover every day. I'm not even asking you to think, I gave you a script to follow for Christ's sake. Just qualify the leads and turn them over to the closers. That's it. How fucking hard is that? Don't I treat you to free beer every Friday? Is this how you pricks repay me? I could hire some goddamn chimps to do a better job."

Chuckles erupted from the closers at the back of the room, while Gene continued his rant. He pointed to Anna, the newlywed, pint-sized blonde we all suspected he was banging and said:

"Everyone look at her. She started out just like you. By doing what I told her, she became a closer in record time. As a matter of fact, I just made her your sales manager because she listens, unlike you turds. Anna, do you have any comments for these schmucks?"

I watched everyone collectively roll their eyes as Anna parted her lips to speak:

"You guys are making too many excuses. Just stick to the script and make sure you're getting here on time for work. Stop coming back from lunch at 1:05. Be in your chair with your headset on at 1. This isn't a game. Anybody in this room could be in the same position I'm in. There's a lot of money to be made here. My last commission check was twelve grand. All of you are capable of doing this, just follow the script."

Gene interrupted to add, "This is the real world, do you think we're being too hard on you? Let me show you how you I should really treat you."

Gene flipped the light off, then cued the projector hanging from the ceiling. I glanced at the West Houston skyline right before Anna dropped the blinds to kill the beaming sunlight. Pressing play on the conference room computer, Gene smiled devilishly. Squinting my eyes I could see 2 nubs emerge from the corners of his receding hairline. Instantly, we all recognized the scene on the screen. Blake, played by Alec Baldwin, was about to go in on a bunch of whiny sales reps in Glengarry Glen Ross. "Only one thing counts in this world… Get them to sign on the line which is dotted!" Baldwin exclaims during his verbal shellacking. We'd seen the clip dozens of times. It never got old, we loved it each time. And when we weren't watching Alec Baldwin yell "ABC: Always Be Closing," we were watching Ben Affleck grill new stock brokers during orientation in Boiler Room. Strangely, these scenes always convinced us our circumstances weren't that bad, and the verbal abuse we received at Pop Labs was necessary for motivation. Like battered women, we would have felt like Gene didn't care about us without the foul language and degradation. Meeting Gene's expectations were more important than making money.

Marching to my seat on the sales floor, I'd recall Gene's rags to riches testimony about how he went from selling shoes just a few blocks away, to starting his first multimillion-dollar web company. He had no formal college education. At eighteen he got his wife pregnant, beginning his career as a teenage parent. Yet I was twenty-five, childless, and had a Vanderbilt diploma on my living room wall. Gene constantly admitted he wasn't as smart as me and confessed his irrational decision making as a young adult. Something finally clicked in young Gene though. Being broke angered him enough to work his way up to a seven-figure bank account balance... with help of course. White men always had access to help. Finding someone to invest at least a few thousand dollars into an idea was easy. As a Black man, I found myself with no one to call for assistance in escaping the plantation. I was on my own.

Upset with myself and my circumstances, I vowed to hustle my way to the top. Instead of settling for two-hundred-fifty, I burned through three-hundred phone calls sniffing for potential deals. Gene's deceptive telemarketing script read:

"Hi John, I'm calling about your Google account."

Baffled, the lead would usually respond: "my Google account?"

"Yes, your Google account. You are the business owner right?

[If not, try to get past the gatekeeper. Do not give her any information. If unsuccessful in getting to a decision maker hang up without leaving a voice message. Once the decision maker is on the line proceed.]

"Great. We're noticing that your company is not showing up on any of the search engines under the organic or paid listings. Are you doing any advertising? Well, you're not getting any exposure online and your competitors are stealing all of your business. How much are you spending?"

The goal for me as a level one rep was to qualify two things – 1) Was I speaking with the business owner? 2) Have they been spending at least five-hundred dollars a month on advertising? If the answer to both of these questions was yes, I was required to transfer the lead to one of the "closers," a senior rep with God level persuasion skills. Gene recruited most of his closers from a prison mentoring program. Anthony, a forty-five-year-old dead ringer for Fleece Johnson, had a serious drug problem. He would close deals then disappear for days on drug binges. Gene could never fire him because he was a magician on the phone. Scotty, an athletic, soft spoken WASP, served time for fraud. On the phone, the word "no" didn't exist to him. I once heard Scotty close a lady who spent the first twenty minutes of their conversation cursing him out for making her unproductive. Closers were professional conmen with a skillset perfect for the job; they ingeniously kept people on the phone for hours. The most reluctant clients would become putty in their hands. Fear, uncertainty, and doubt were the three emotions Gene encouraged closers to pounce on. I was intrigued by their ability to swindle small business owners into four, sometimes five-figure SEO and SEM contracts.

New reps, fresh off the street, would fumble through lousy leads, barely qualify them, then turn them over to the closers, who would somehow convert lemons into lemonade. During my stint at Pop Labs I sent the closers tons of qualified leads. For some reason or another, they were never slick enough to close my deals. This left me frustrated, broke, and literally starving. So I decided to take matters into my own hands one day. On call two-hundred-seventy-six, I expertly skirted past an unsuspecting gatekeeper with the perfect combination of flattery and flirtation. She passed me on to her business' owner, a middle-aged air conditioning guru in Dallas. Impressed by my infiltration of his cold call defense, he asked:

"This is Bob, what can I do for you?"

"Hi Bob, I'm calling about your Google account. You are the business owner right? Great. We're noticing that your business is not showing up on any of the search engines under the organic or paid listings. Are you doing any advertising?" I asked unconsciously.

"Yeah, I'm all over TV here in Dallas. Why what's the problem?" Bob asked.

"Well, you're not getting any exposure online and your competitors are stealing all of your business," I explained without any knowledge of who his competitors were or where they were coming up on the search listings. Sales reps on my level didn't even have computers, so it was impossible for us to perform a Google search to check whether our assumption was correct. At this point we were required to send the qualified lead over to a closer, rendering a computer irrelevant anyway. Regardless, after Bob declined to hang up in my ear, I pushed on.

"This is very serious Bob. You're missing tons of prospective clients for your AC company. If you're not on the front page of a Google search your business is virtually invisible. I'm gonna get you on there."

Bob seemed to be amused, "And how do you plan to do that Mr. Walker?"

Got em'!

We continued talking for forty-five minutes, while the closers motioned and begged me to turn the lead over. There was blood in the water. Ignoring them and trusting my empty, rumbling stomach to guide me to success, I closed Bob on a $1500 per month contract. Before the call ended, I respectfully declined his offer to sell air conditioning units for his company in Dallas.

Once Bob faxed back a signed copy of the contract, I strutted into Gene's oversized corner office. He could have very well been a vampire, as he always kept the blinds closed blocking all daylight from the spacious, triangle-shaped office. Mirror tint lined Gene's windows facing the sales floor, so no one could ever tell if he was really in there. Knowing he could see us, but we couldn't see him, we always worked as if he was present. At this point, I cared not if I was walking in on a business meeting or an inappropriate groove session with Anna, I was there to get a check cut immediately. Though I closed my deal mid pay cycle, waiting another week for commission was not an option.

"Gene, I just closed a deal by myself, I need you to cut me a check today."

He smiled like a proud father on graduation day and said:

"Demetrius you're different than most Black guys I know. I'm not trying to be racist, but the truth is I'm used to them coming in here and asking me for handouts, favors, and gifts they haven't earned. Ya' know, Kevin comes in here and gives me his fucking pitiful sob story every week and begs me for lunch money. But you don't. You only become more aggressive and hungry to succeed as the weeks go by. Because of that, I'm going to go ahead and cut a check for you."

In a commission only sales job the motto is "you eat what you kill." I took the check and walked out the building partially offended by Gene's broad generalization of Black men, but mostly proud I had stalked and killed my first prey. To me, the check was like a masters degree in sales from the School of Hard Knocks. I would have framed it had it not been for my need to cash it, pay bills, and buy food... posthaste.

The following Monday I went back to see whether I could catch another great white... with a toy fishing rod. Halfway through the day, I became sick at the idea of fishing through another ten-thousand leads just to find another deal. Nauseous and mentally exhausted, I walked over to Anna's desk and simply told her "I quit."

Anna genuinely felt bad when she hugged me and responded "I understand. I'll let Gene know when he gets back."

I tried to wait for Gene to come in, but there was no telling whether he'd show up or enjoy the day playing golf somewhere. Though I valued the aggressive sales tactics I acquired, I knew my brilliance was worth more than the mental and physical strain I suffered on Gene's plantation. Once again, I was leaving a job with no definitive plan for generating income. But since I was at rock bottom, I knew things couldn't get any worse if I left. With my newly acquired sales skills, I was determined to climb out the deep hole I was in, inch by inch.

CHAPTER TEN

THE LIGHT

Make a business for yourself, boy, set some goals
Make a fat diamond out of dusty coals
-Big Boi (Outkast) "Bombs Over Baghdad"

After I left Pop Labs I made finding a decent, full-time job, my full-time job. I refused to settle for anything without benefits and a base salary. Long, painstaking hours applying to openings on LinkedIn left little time to focus on dangerousNEGRO and my speaking career. Every business demanded an individual cover letter to accompany my resume. All this, after already requiring a candidate to type every detail about previous employment on an insanely long job application. I hated the entire process. I felt like I was selling my soul at a slave auction to another plantation; only this time I had to tap dance to snag a massa who'd pay for my dental visits.

Nobody cared that I went to one of the country's most elite boarding schools or a top twenty university. Leaving three companies in the span of a year made me toxic waste to most employers. Good opportunities failed to fall in my lap. Head hunters never called me for the cushy consulting gigs my friends bragged about. Sketchy sales jobs I was trying to avoid were the norm instead. There was an offer to sell "miracle" headlight defogger to people at gas stations, and an offer to sell "insurance products" with Primerica. Finding a job I could be proud to discuss in public seemed impossible.

Finally, I got a call from Idera, a software company housed out of a plantation style mansion in Montrose. The irony of interviewing for a position in a building dressed as a relic of the Confederacy, was striking. Corporate bondage would literally make me a House Negro this time around, I deduced. But judging a book by its cover is seldom a good idea. Once I entered the building for my interview, I realized most of the staff was progressive.

Damon Tompkins, a bespectacled, rugged, yet refined, MMA hobbyist, was extremely welcoming as he stared me in the eyes from behind his Christian Dior frames. He had wealthy, enlightened, White guy swag. Damon, a Philly transplant, detected the subtle remnants of my East Coast accent and we instantly clicked. The night before, I stayed up studying Idera's website to prepare for any curveballs Damon might throw my way. Fortunately, Damon's ADD kicked in so intensely that my cursory knowledge of how Idera's software eliminated SQL Server headaches for Database Administrators was never exposed. Instead we talked about art and politics. Impressed with my wisdom of his two favorite topics, Damon called in Idera VP, Jim Legg, to engage in the conversation. Legg was more of the country club aristocrat I came to know well from Taft and Vanderbilt. "Wow, you really *are* as smart as Damon said you were. You ready to work?" I was more than ready. It was time to get back on my feet.

When Jim left the room, Damon told me HR would prepare a formal offer, based on my previous experience. I froze when he asked what my salary expectations were, figuring it to be a trick question. Aim too high and risk being priced out of contention, or low ball and shoot myself in the foot? I decided to play it safe and say I expected to make about 40K in base salary, with the majority of my income being made in commission. Damon said I was right on target with my estimate.

Two days later the offer letter came in the mail. I was a little surprised to see an official offer of 30K for my base salary. Since my first year out of undergrad I hadn't had a base salary that low. I weighed whether I should counter. *Shit, I'll take anything right now, I'm starving.* So I left it alone and accepted the position. I met Damon once again to submit my paperwork and he seemed pained.

"What did they offer you in base salary?" he queried.

"30K," I revealed.

"You've got to be fucking kidding me. They only did that because you're... You know what, nevermind. I'll take care of this for you."

Damon barged out the meeting room to confront Jim Legg in the hallway. Listening intently, I could hear Legg say "well he was gonna take it Damon. It couldn't have been *too* low." Realizing I was probably within earshot of their conversation, Damon pushed the door shut so they could finish. A few minutes later, Damon returned to reveal my base pay had been increased to 40K. He apologized profusely for "the assholes in upper management" trying to take advantage of me. I was blown away. Maybe I was wrong about corporate America. Maybe there were people who actually cared there. Damon earned my unconditional loyalty that day.

Idera's office environment was pretty chill. There wasn't a strict dress code or people breathing down my back all day. My whole team, including Damon, my sales manager, sat in a dimly lit corner of the office cracking jokes all day. On our lunch breaks, we'd alternate between playing outdoor basketball at Spotts Park or lifting weights at 24 Hour Fitness. No one stressed about being back at our desks within an hour. Every Friday we were even allowed to bring our pets to the office. (I declined because my half breed pits, Dominoe and Paris, don't play well with others. Nevertheless, a pretty cool perk). There were frequent holiday celebrations with beer, crawfish, and attractions. And they were fun, unlike the compulsory "celebrations" I experienced previously.

Outside the office, I even enjoyed being the only Black guy at Happy Hour in Midtown. Between shots of Fireball, the fellas and I took turns flirting with Samantha, the fine, bubbly, Asian office manager. Bob Riley, my lanky, 6'4 teammate (in the office and on the court), cherished these opportunities to talk politics. Bob, a lifelong Republican, enjoyed debating with me because I was the only person comfortable enough to vocalize my differing opinions in a nonthreatening manner. Everyday we learned something from one another. Bob would turn me on to the fringe politics of Ron Paul, while I would make the case for an unlikely Obama presidency. We butted heads on the rights of all citizens to have access to quality education and healthcare, things Bob felt were reserved for people who "earned" them. Though he disagreed that the life, liberty, and pursuit of happiness mentioned in the Bill of Rights equated to free doctors visits and quality public schooling for all, I illuminated Bob's White Privilege in ways he had never considered. His genuine interest in hearing about The Bronx, boarding school, and being a Black man allowed me to open up. When he attempted to cite MLK, as most Republicans do, to explain his disagreement with affirmative action and why people should only be judged by the content of their character, I told him about King being called "the most dangerous Negro in America." And then I told him about dangerousNEGRO and my experiences running the company with my friends.

Throughout my years in corporate America, I kept dN a secret from my White coworkers because I feared they wouldn't understand it. I didn't want to be labeled the angry Black man who only tolerated White people in small doses for a paycheck. Most of all, I never wanted the White guys in upper management to learn of my secret life as an entrepreneur and question my dedication to the job.

Negroes with plantation exit strategies were largely expendable. So I told Bob to keep dN a secret between us. That lasted maybe two weeks before Damon approached me with pointed questions about the eye of Ra on my polo shirt. Through ADD fueled rants on the row, Damon showed he was sympathetic to the plight of oppressed people on numerous occasions. Instinct informed me it would be safe to open up to Damon about dN as well. Of course I didn't dare tell him my vacation and sick days were used for speaking engagements around the world. I dismissed my trip to Africa as just a lucky opportunity to go on a safari in Tanzania, while stopping in Ethiopia and Kenya along the way. Truthfully, after speaking at the New York Institute of Technology I was asked by the Africa Travel Association to meet in Arusha with leaders of over thirty countries to discuss strategies for bolstering Black American tourism to the continent. Camera phone pics of rhinos, wildebeest, and lions were all my Idera officemates needed to see. Though I was open about being the cofounder of a Black empowerment t-shirt line, I avoided any indicators I was trying to dismantle White Supremacy.

The day finally came when I could hold back no longer. There was a spirited debate in the office about police brutality and unjustified homicides by police in Houston. Russell, a volunteer firefighter, and a few other guys in the office, felt police should receive the benefit of the doubt in most instances. "Bad things happen to bad guys." They left no room for the possibility Black people were overwhelmingly treated unfairly due to racist policies which valued Black lives less than those of others. Frustrated, I gave the full play by play of how I was assaulted by officers in Indiana the week prior. I omitted the details of me being there for a speaking engagement.

The evening before I was set to speak, Gary convinced me to join him for the opening of a friend's new club in downtown

Indianapolis. Considering the foot of snow on the ground and the subzero windchill, I was hesitant to partake. But it never takes much convincing to get me to a party, so I obliged. Upon arrival, we were greeted by a block long line of shivering patrons. Gary, notorious for never waiting in lines, motioned for me to follow him to the front of the venue.

"My boy is gonna come get us in."

As we approached the club entrance three Black police officers with bad attitudes stopped us. "Where the fuck yall think yall going? You better get to the back of that line," the tallest of the uniformed bullies shouted. He was about 5'8. Gary, cell phone to his right ear, extended his left arm to politely create space between himself and the irritable cop.

"I understand sir, but the owner is coming downstairs to let us in right now, I'm on the phone with him."

Taking offense to Gary's noncompliance, the officer grabbed Gary's extended arm and proceeded to place handcuffs on his wrist shouting, "This is our block and I told your stupid ass to get in line."

Stunned, I complained "whoa, whoa, whoa. Is all that necessary officer?"

Apparently my hand grazed the cop's chest as I pleaded with him to cease cuffing Gary. I felt a thud hit the back of my feathered Triple Fat Goose hood. *Did somebody hit me with a snowball?* Fist clenched, I turned around to realize I'd been punched in the back of the head by the shortest of the trio. "Really?" I stared down to ask him. Suddenly the third cop clocked me in my left ear from the periphery. Blood gushed from my torn earlobe, as the blow ripped out my cubic zirconia earring. I felt a barrage of body shots from both officers until I voluntarily submitted by stooping to my knees and locking my fingers behind my head. The circulation in my boney wrists was cut off by the unreasonable tightness of the steel shackles placed next. I was yanked from my snow covered knees to my feet and pinned against a police car. Through the window I could see Gary sitting in the backseat, hands behind his back. Furious, but conscious of my surroundings, I turned around to fume about how badly the officers overreacted. I looked them in their eyes and told them I was one of the good guys, I was only in town to motivate college students to strive for greatness.

"Shut the fuck up. That's what you get for putting your hands on a police officer. Keep talking and we'll take you to central booking."

Putting my hands on a police officer? At least fifty people on line in front of the club could vouch that any contact was inadvertent and caused by the "tall" officer's snap judgment. The cops made me stand with my back against the police car, threatening me with greater violence every few minutes if I so much as opened my mouth again. After two hours, they walked me down an alley at the rear of the club, where I was uncertain what they would do to inflict further damage. They unlocked the handcuffs on my wrists and told me to walk forward without turning around. "If we see you around here again it's a wrap for you." I found Gary waiting a block away, grateful we both escaped jail and serious bodily harm.

On the way back to Gary's place we recounted how crazy the whole ordeal was. There's no way two White guys would have been treated the same way by the officers. Gary, the consummate optimist, tried to find a silver lining, "at least the chicks saw us get handcuffed. They like bad guys. Our street cred is sky high now." I started to laugh but the pain of my torn earlobe thawing out in the car's heat stifled my snicker.

When we got home I was too distracted to go over my workshop notes. I kept replaying the incident over and over in my head, trying to figure out how the situation could have played out differently. The next thing I knew it was 6 am and time for me and Gary to drive to Terre Haute for a series of workshops and a grand finale lecture. Unprepared and exhausted, I counted on my improv skills to power me through the day. Indiana State brought me in for their Black History Month program, and as their keynote speaker I was slated to provide several hours of motivation to underclassmen through interactive seminars and a closing speech. The speech was the easy part. I had a forty-five minute canned presentation equipped with powerpoint slides, music, and video memorized. Through countless speeches at other schools, I knew how to work a crowd properly for maximum joke response and emotional impact. On the other hand, the workshop piece was new and it didn't take long for my lack of preparation to show through. Locked in a large classroom with approximately sixty students, I had no idea how to facilitate a discussion long enough to fill up the ninety minute blocks I was assigned. The index cards I failed to review the previous evening ended up containing nothing more than empty bullet points, ideas I failed to elaborate on enough. I burned through them in less than thirty minutes. When they proved ineffective at generating a sustained discussion, I resorted to awkward question and answer sessions - about anything in the universe. The disappointment on the Student Activity Coordinator's face was obvious. I was disappointed in myself too. Even the standing ovation and autograph requests I received later at my keynote's conclusion did nothing to temper the displeasure I felt in not delivering my best. Half of me wanted to reject payment for a lackluster performance. The other half knew I needed the money because the commission checks at Idera weren't bountiful. They'd given me the shittiest territory to scour for business - Nebraska, The Dakotas, Montana, Wyoming, and Idaho.

At least I gave them a new perspective on how race factors into police encounters. Besides me, few in the office ever had their cars searched, let alone a physical altercation with those assigned to protect and serve. "Fuck The Police" wasn't just a catchy song for people like me, it was a justified sentiment in many regards. Still, when I described how an HPD bullet narrowly missed my temple, as it errantly traveled through my back door and into my freezer, coworkers dismissed it as a fluke. "They were trying to shoot a dog and they missed. They couldn't tell you were Black from outside your house." Nevermind why police officers were flippantly firing rounds in my neighborhood (Alief, TX) in the first place, but I digress.

Idera was the best place I ever worked. I felt valued as a person. People were interested in my worldview there. They appreciated my presence in and out of the office. I looked forward to debating Bob and discussing art with Damon, who measured my scalp and sculpted a custom Batman mask for me out of clay. For the first time, my White coworkers were really my friends. So of course I was devastated when I received a call from Damon shortly after New Year's 2009 explaining I was being let go. George W. Bush had brought the economy to the brink of collapse, everyone was tightening their books, trimming fat, and laying off personnel. I knew the decision was purely business and not personal, so I had no hard feelings when I hung up Damon's call. I could tell he felt terrible about the whole thing. Honestly, I sensed something coming in the weeks prior as Damon inquired about my financial stability in private conversations. Shooting the breeze, Damon would disclose "everything's fucked up D. People are losing their homes. These jackasses are bailing out the banks. Is everything good with you? You got your bills in order?" I told him I was doing alright and even moving my mom down to Houston since her company laid her and thousands of other people off in New York. All the more reason I'm sure Damon felt awful when he had to break the news I'd be joining my mother on the unemployment line.

Looking on the brightside, I was finally free to invest all my energy into dangerousNEGRO and my speaking career. With all other partners sidetracked by Corporate America, dN sorely needed a full-time employee if we were ever going to take it to the next level. The time was now. Between my modest savings and unemployment checks, I was confident I could sustain a living, while cold calling stores to open dN accounts, and ringing schools to secure speaking engagements. If I applied the same effort I made at my former jobs to my own endeavors, success had to be in reach. I went right to work creating call lists from Google and LinkedIn. I hit the road and drove to Dallas with t-shirts, determined to be a successful outside salesman. Opening two accounts on the city's outskirts sent my confidence to the moon. Within weeks I was able to add accounts in Opelousas, Austin, and Beaumont. After e-stalking Barry Pener, the decision maker for Harold Pener's Man of Fashion urban wear chain, dN earned rack space in stores in Kansas City, Indianapolis, and Richmond, Virginia. Laughed out of stores in Nashville a couple years earlier, I even landed an account at the legendary Phatkaps. Though the accounts all placed small orders due to the down economy, I was on a roll. I could see the light.

With my newfound freedom I also had time to construct my first speaking website, DWalkerSpeaking.com. Besides serving as a digital business card to fortify my credibility with schools, it became an outlet for my personal takes on politics, entertainment, and pretty much any bottled up thoughts I was excited to spend a few hundred words sharing. I could voice my opinions on Spike Lee vs Tyler Perry, the reasons I opposed Blacks enlisting in the military, and my experiences volunteering with transracial adoptees in Colorado, without attributing the thoughts to the entire dangerousNEGRO team. We didn't subscribe to a monolithic way of thought. Several of my partners were more reserved, conservative, and concerned my differing viewpoints could have ramifications for their day jobs. On the other hand, even though Tre and I saw eye to eye on most things, he was more radical in many respects. Thus, DWalkerSpeaking.com liberated me from the opinions of all others.

Even with the new attention I got online, booking speaking engagements was still tough on my own. My old pal Lawrence Watkins was able to line up a few gigs for me through his more prominently established Great Black Speakers Bureau, but outside of Black History Month, my calendar remained relatively empty. I thought back to my days at Pop Labs when I burned through three hundred calls a day trying to find a single opportunity. Unfortunately schools were a tougher nut to crack. Most colleges and universities carouseled the same handful of popular Black speakers around the speaking circuit. And those same speakers were now signed on with Lawrence's company. Competing with the likes of Dr. Cornel West, Tavis Smiley, and Magic Johnson for keynotes was daunting. In order to stand out, I positioned myself as the low budget/great value option. A middle school in Depaul, Illinois brought me in to facilitate entrepreneurship workshops. The University of Northern Michigan flew me to the frozen upper peninsula, where only six students showed up, one of whom was the student activities coordinator who booked me.

Still, there were some inspiring highlights. Yale brought me in for a Master's Tea, an informal, town hall style lecture. Speakers are usually up and coming musicians, actors, activists, or innovators chosen directly by the students themselves. It was a great honor to be on the list of people like Hanson (the Mmmbop guys) and Hallie Haglund (a writer from the Daily Show). After speaking at Yale I seemed to get a few more unexpected requests. Out of the blue I heard from my high school mentor Mr. Hall, who invited me to keynote his Black male empowerment initiative in Iowa. Now a full fledged professor, I stayed in a spare bedroom at his home with his wife and two well-behaved children. It felt like a reunion with a proud uncle. The fact Mr. Hall, better yet Dr. Hall, would allow me to headline his event made me feel like I was on the right track career-wise.

Unfortunately, the Great Recession made every organization pinch its wallet. Skittish schools went into a panic and slashed budgets for most nonessential expenditures, i.e motivational speakers. Clothing retailers refused to place large orders because merchandise was slow to move. Young Jeezy's proclamation, "It's a recession, everybody broke" rang true. Nobody was caught dead making it rain anymore. The down Bush economy had everyone in a funk. Paltry unemployment checks, small speaking fees, and meager clothing commission made it impossible to pay bills and help support my transplant mom. The light started fading as I realized a return to the plantation was inevitable if we were going to survive.

CHAPTER ELEVEN

BREAKING INDUSTRY RULE #4080

> It's in our palms but we can't seize it
> Within our reach but we don't reach it
> Don't tell me that I can't be it
> I haven't won till it ain't even
> I ain't leaving till I ain't breathing
> No apologies, no tears
> No emotions, no fears
> Look at my face you can't even see the years
> But carved in the tree are the words "I was here"
> -Rhymefest "Familiar Faces"

If I was going to take another day job, I was desperate to find something I could take pride in, preferably something that impacted society in a positive way. Voila… LinkedIn came through in the clutch with a climate change speaker position. My friends in oil & gas considered me a tree hugger over my refusal to work for one of their companies. It was too much of a moral conflict of interest. Despite living in the nation's energy capital, I despised the obvious greed surrounding the whole industry. While everyone reeled from the Great Recession, the oil & gas giants saw record profits. It became clearer and clearer that 9/11 was just an excuse for an overseas resource heist. It angered me that the US government insulted the public's intelligence with their weapons of mass destruction hoax. Evil people, I refused to be a cog in their machine. So interviewing to be a climate change speaker opened the possibility I could personally begin cutting the tentacles of the United States' oil & gas leviathan. I made it through three rounds of the extremely competitive interview process. Everybody was desperate for a job so the competition was stiff. In the end, I flubbed a question about whether I wanted to have kids. Trying too hard to be funny, I laughed about not wanting the responsibility of raising a child anytime soon. Instantly I knew I'd just blown the opportunity. Pictures of the interviewer's kids came into focus on the shelf behind his desk. The whole premise of the job was to talk to kids all day. Elementary school kids, middle school kids, and high school kids. Ironically, I actually longed to be a Dad. *Damn.*

A few weeks later, Theresa Kialoa, a recruiter from the University of Phoenix, contacted me about a corporate liaison position. Already skeptical about for-profit institutions, I found their attraction to me, a career salesman, odd. But I needed a job, and there were worse things I could peddle than education. During my interviews, the University of Phoenix sold me on the value it provided to non traditional students, who either dropped out of school due to hardships, never thought they could get a degree, or needed the school's flexible schedule so they could continue to work full time. I drank the Kool-Aid. I couldn't wait to sell potential students on those ideas. When offered 40K plus quarterly performance based bonuses, I gladly accepted the position.

Government was my assigned vertical. Cheerfully, I called on city and county offices, convincing them to allow me five minutes to present the university's life changing offerings. I loved the job. The majority of the day I was out the office using my public speaking skills to be what I deemed an "education evangelist." Saving people from ignorance was my calling. Even the police, who I'd grown to despise through years of unfavorable encounters, could be converted. Some mornings I'd be up before the crack of dawn to catch an HPD roll call, where a staff sergeant would give me time after the days' pertinent announcements to advocate for continued education. Officers could apply their training hours to credit towards a degree, and those who did obtain degrees qualified for higher salaries with each level of attainment. It was an easy sell. I would tear off lead cards and pass them out to everybody in the room after each presentation. Miserable in their jobs and frustrated with their pay, the majority of the room would hastily fill out the lead cards. More than a few told me they were looking for ways to escape citation and arrest quotas. They were only cops because of limited employment opportunities. I promised an enrollment advisor would call them within forty eight hours to discuss majors, financial aid, and how to proceed with registration. The more registrations, or REGs (pronounced like edges with an r) a corporate education liaison like myself produced, the more we were compensated when bonuses rolled around. Since the government had made it illegal to earn commission on each REG, this was the loophole most for profit institutions exploited.

  Occasionally my evangelism was met with resistance, and even hostility. Several employers saw the University of Phoenix and its competitors as mere diploma mills. Former students complained their degrees were worthless, leaving them in debt without the coveted jobs they needed to repay their exorbitant loans. I dismissed them as sadly misinformed and victims of their own lack of ambition.

  To prove them wrong I even enrolled in the MBA program, taking classes a few floors up from my office in the evenings. I needed a new challenge anyway. I found the professors to be competent and the coursework to be relatively rigorous. Half the students were motivated, working professionals looking to advance in their careers. Over time, it became apparent the other half were lazy and unqualified to be in anybody's classroom. They showed up with no knowledge of the course material, expecting their fellow students and professors to pick up the slack for their lack of motivation. I despised these students; they were the knuckleheads who sullied the University of Phoenix' reputation. But the university was indifferent. It didn't matter who sat in a seat, a genius or an imbecile, as long as they qualified for federal financial aid. Suddenly my eyes were opened. University of Phoenix could care less if students were capable of keeping up with the curriculum. In fact, they didn't care if students graduated at all. Once the university received a student's grant or G.I. Bill money, it was a wrap. Account funded, on to the next sucker.

Needless to say my enthusiasm for the job eroded. The plantation tricked me into being a loyal servant once again. Poverty pimps preying on pupils for public funding, I would no longer be their mindless hireling. I did the minimum required to remain employed, while rededicating the majority of my energy to dangerousNEGRO.

The timing couldn't have been more perfect. Gary became buddy-buddy with Kanye West's collaborator and childhood friend, Rhymefest, after a chance encounter at Cloud 9 in Nap. Everyone knew Rhymefest shared a Grammy with Kanye for co-writing Jesus Walks, and their collaboration on Brand New even motivated me to cop Rhymefest's Blue Collar LP during my days at Dell. Rhymefest fell in love with our dangerousNEGRO tees, so we frequently supplied him with shirts to wear on tour and press runs.

Eventually Gary and Rhymefest built such a rapport that he became just 'Fest' and spilled his record label frustrations. J Records botched the release of Blue Collar, his debut. Creative differences while crafting a follow up project made the prospect of releasing another album with J Records unfathomable. The label and Rhymefest went their separate ways. The record industry was imploding on itself anyway. Napster and its next generation offspring,

Limewire, made it virtually impossible for rap artists to go gold or platinum like they had just a few years prior. Artists began leveraging the internet to release music independently, without the record industry's red tape and pressure to stick to a formula. Even better, instead of making pennies per album sold, artists could make a few dollars per unit moved independently.

    Fest was convinced he would thrive as an independent artist. He already had a Grammy under his belt, he was personally connected to several of the biggest names in Hip Hop, and his post-Blue Collar mixtape, Man In The Mirror, a Michael Jackson dedication album produced by Marc Ronson, was deemed a classic in many circles. All Fest needed was web savvy and someone to invest about fifty racks into the production, marketing, and promotion of his next project for it to be successful. He told Gary the success of dangerousNEGRO's independent clothing hustle was proof Black men could generate profits in the digital era with the right amount of drive and promotion. A conference call was arranged to explore the opportunity. Fest gave us his pitch, but honestly he had us at hello. Each dangerousNEGRO partner was a Hip Hop enthusiast in some regard. When we weren't clashing on the direction of dN, we were exchanging music, or engaged in lively debates about artists. After the call, our only question was how we would raise the 50K Fest needed to finish the album and get it to the masses. Come hell or high water the funds would be found, we wouldn't allow an opportunity to be Hip Hop legends float away.

    Despite working full time, I personally had no funds to contribute to the Rhymefest project. Being the brokest member of the crew was frustrating. I felt like I was always playing catch up on bills; bills that never stopped coming when I plantation hopped myself into unemployment during The Great Recession. Foolishly committing myself to luxury lemons, with their high car notes and maintenance, I never had spare change. Insurance, student loans, rent, utilities, cable, cell phone, and groceries ate the majority of my income. I had no choice but to be cheap. The only time I got new clothes was when my mom picked up garments a size too large from Banana Republic with her employee discount.

To the outside observer I was doing alright for myself. dangerousNEGRO was known on campuses nationwide. Sebastine and I had appeared on BET, we won MillerCoors' Urban Entrepreneur business plan competition, and had online features with Black Enterprise and AOL's Black Voices. dN had tens of thousands of Facebook fans and stores in major cities carried the line. I cut work to travel on the Extreme Entrepreneurship Tour, where using dN as an example, I pushed the merits of escaping the corporate plantation. In reality I was a hope dealer, no better than a dope dealer. I hadn't yet figured out how to sustain a living as a full time entrepreneur, yet I peddled that narrative with the optimism it would one day ring true. Family and friends hit me up for money, believing I obviously had my shit together. How sadly mistaken. Ensnared in debt, I was sick of being broke.

Finding a partner with whom to combine incomes and build wealth seemed like a solution to the only thing holding me back from real success. Dating and trying to impress women was unnecessarily expensive. Most of all, it was a distraction from building the empire I envisioned from childhood - the one that included the lamborghini hanging on my wall in Co-op City. If I was going to escape the rat race I needed a supportive mate to lighten the load and keep me motivated.

When it didn't work out between me and a fellow university employee, an AKA reading from Steve Harvey's "Think Like a Man" relationship manual, I kept the two Christmas kittens she rejected as symbols of my need to compromise. The perfect woman didn't exist.

Everyone had flaws and I needed to accept another's as much as I hoped a woman would accept mine. Most of my friends started to marry off and have children, surely they had a leg up on me in figuring out life. Feeling left behind motivated my pursuit of a life partner. The next good looking, honest woman, who liked pets was getting wifed.

At work I wasn't the only one who didn't have relationships figured out. Esmeralda, the petite, feisty, four-foot-eleven, Mexican chick on my team was blindsided by a divorce. We unexpectedly became good friends after sharing notes from church. Over lunch margaritas at Guadalajara, Esmeralda would find strength in Joel Osteen while I quoted Pastor J, the hood's favorite preacher. She became my work wife. When the emotional stress of her divorce was too much to bare, we'd take a walk so she could vent and cry. In return, Esmeralda counseled me on what type of woman she thought I should look for. One weekend we were both in such a funk we agreed to party our pain away. Riding shotgun in Esmeralda's SUV down Washington Avenue, I spotted an ATM from which to withdraw valet fees and potential cover charges. A frigid January night, I approached the ATM to find a shivering Beyoncé doppleganger dancing to keep warm in a shimmering mini dress.

She never saw me coming as she shouted to her waiting friend over her left shoulder, "Girl I hope nobody sees me out here dancing like this!"

Taking my cue, I smoothly countered, "Nobody but me."

Covering her mouth in disbelief, the sexy redbone shouted, "Oh my God! I'm so embarrassed!"

From there I assured her no judgment was cast, I was freezing too. "Maybe we can hang out some other time in warmer conditions," I offered. She took my phone and entered her details: Sabrina

Babineaux. Esmeralda said she was cute. "Yeah, she's bad," I confirmed.

Subsequent calls and texts proved Sabrina met the criteria of my wife checklist. Physically, she had the Texas beauty that attracted me to the state in the first place. Long legs, curves, clear skin, and a perfect smile, *what more could I ask for?* Secondly, she seemed trustworthy. I suspended my judgement on her having an uncomfortable amount of male friends. The old Meek would have classified a high male friend count as suspect. The new Meek was less judgmental. Finally, Sabrina owned a dog, a mean, beige chihuahua named King. I didn't care that King was a gift from a previous relationship, Black women who love dogs are rare. If I had a dollar for every girl who hid until my dogs were confined to another room, I would have had enough to invest in the Rhymefest project.

While Sabrina and I fast tracked our relationship, my partners and I raised the funds to get the Rhymefest album in motion. Our winnings from the MillerCoors Urban Entrepreneur business plan competition formed the core of our funding. Partners, friends, and family filled in the remainder. Money ready, we flew up to Soundscape Studios in Chicago to get Rhymefest's signature on the dotted line. I was so excited, I documented the whole trip on the handheld camcorder we used to film our step shows in undergrad. Descending the dark staircase from the building's lobby to the basement, I could sense I was entering another realm, maybe the fabled 36th Chamber. When the door opened at the bottom of the landing, I could hear a female vocalist *going in* on the Fast Life Yungstaz "Swag Surfin" instrumental. Entering the dimly lit foyer, I could see the attractive young singer through a large, glass window. *Now this is a real studio.* Michael Kolar, Soundscape's founder and chief engineer, gave us a quick tour revealing the history behind the building. Twista, R. Kelly, Crucial Conflict, and pretty much every notable artist in Chicago recorded at Soundscape at one point or another. A relic of the Prohibition Era, the basement had small hidden rooms behind one of the main rooms. Computers and audio hardware replaced the booze that sat there decades earlier.

    After our tour, we entered a small conference room where we sat around a roundtable waiting for Fest to finish taking a dump. About ten minutes went by before Fest burst into the room guessing, "You must be Meek. Yoooo I need that jacket homie!" referring to the olive green military garment emblazoned with dangerousNEGRO and a huge black fist on the back. I stood up to give him a pound, removed my arms from the sleeves, and handed it over to him. Fest loved the jacket so much it would become his wardrobe for the album's cover. Jacket secured, Fest went around the table matching faces with the names and voices he'd heard over the phone for the past few months. Eventually we got to the contract review stage. Our in house attorney, Justin, had drawn up a standard, boilerplate entertainment contract. Fest cringed and became visibly agitated. "This looks like the same shit J Records handed me. I'm disappointed." We weren't expecting that response. Our goal was to give Rhymefest full creative control of the project, while making it a fair deal for everyone involved. The last thing we wanted was for dN|Be Entertainment to be another oppressive, plantation-like record label.

    "There's certain language that has to be in there legally. We're not trying to trick you into anything," Justin explained.

    "Nah, I'm not signing this until we put it all in plain English," Fest pushed back.

    A red pen was passed for Fest to make line edits until he was content. Once adjusted, both sides initialed the changes and Rhymefest signed the revised document. We finally exhaled.

Rhymefest's second album, El Che, would be released on dN|Be Entertainment and distributed by EMI.

    Signing a Grammy Award winning artist like Rhymefest to a record deal was a dream come true. Somewhere in the back of my mind I always knew I was destined to be involved in the Hip Hop industry. From the time I peeled the plastic wrap off my first album, I analyzed the lyrics, persona, originality, and approach of emcees. Tucked away in my cerebral were thoughts on how artists could connect with the masses more effectively. dN|Be Entertainment coming to fruition confirmed the metaphysical Law of Attraction. The universe provided every resource necessary to launch the project. Justin drew up the contracts, Tre constructed the websites, and Gary, Sebastine, and I brainstormed daily with Fest over our strategic and tactical plans. Additionally, I handled press release writing, media interaction, and management of Fest's Facebook fan page. In turn, Rhymefest brought Konee Rok, his trusted video producer to the team, as well as Shadowkat Nightson, his audio advisor, and Donnie Boyd, his personal assistant and future wife. The team meshed seamlessly. Rhymefest was receptive to our ideas, like releasing the album on cassette for collectors and convicts alike. After I secured Saigon through Twitter DM for a verse on "Give It To Me," Fest loved our idea of hosting a contest to open up the third verse to a fan. Though Fest ended up selecting Adad, some random, mediocre kid he mentored, after our team spent countless hours reviewing the hot sixteens piled up in our inbox, it was still cool to bring innovation to the game.

    For a group of rookies, my partners and I held our own. Leading up to El Che's release, Sebastine served as our liaison to Rosehip Records, the shadowy label that served as our plug to EMI. For brokering the distribution deal, Rosehip received twenty percent of the album proceeds. Rosehip was frustrating to deal with because they slowed the stream of information between dN|Be and EMI. Getting a release date from EMI for the album was a nightmare due to lack of communication by Rosehip. Sebastine handled the stress well, diplomatically resolving issues.

    Luckily, I got to do more fun stuff like getting Fest booked at SXSW, a good look for underground artists, burgeoning newcomers, and music purists. My whole Houston crew made the two and a half hour drive to Austin to witness Fest perform on Sixth Street. Yelawolf, who would later sign to Shady Records, helmed by Eminem, Rhymefest's most well known battle victim, opened the show. From a second floor section, we watched Fest deliver a couple joints from Blue Collar before engaging in a freestyle. The small crowd hung on his every word. Afterwards, we went to some industry party at a mansion in the hills, where I embarrassed myself by introducing Brooklyn rapper, Curtains, to Fest as New Orleans rapper, Currensy. The faux pas made for a good laugh. Still, the hubris of graduating from fan to Hip Hop insider only fueled my ego. Rockstar lifestyle was within reach.

    While waiting for a release date from EMI, we put out two mixtapes, The Manual and Dangerous 5-18, the latter of which was supposed to inform fans of the date the album was dropping. Both mixtapes were warmly received online. To add to the excitement, Konee Rok crafted a visual treat with the first 3D animated Hip Hop music video for "Say Wassup," El Che's lead single featuring Phonte. Konee Rok followed up with "One Hand Push Up," a video that appeared to be shot in one take with Fest hilariously shaving, taking pictures, and receiving parking tickets with his left hand, while doing hundreds of push ups on his right. A visual for "Prosperity" came next featuring Fest being dragged through the TV screen by a televangelist (played by Fest). Videos for "Chicago," "Talk My Shit," and "City is Falling" also made it to YouTube. Our goal was to make a video for every song on the album, though it became impractical on our shoestring budget as time went on. The videos that made it online created a buzz in a Hip Hop market becoming more and more saturated by the day. The mixtape momentum, combined with six dope music videos, and generally positive reviews from reputable outlets like Spin, Billboard, and HipHopDX gave us reason to feel optimistic about El Che's release.

Unfortunately EMI threw a monkey wrench in things, confusing fans by pushing the album's release back to June 4, 2010 after we had already drilled May 18th into their minds. CD shipments were severely limited due to EMI's lack of confidence in El Che moving units. Still, with CDs quickly becoming relics of yesteryear, we thought digital sales would pick up the slack. Anticipation of Soundscan's first week totals gnawed at my soul following El Che's release. Having studied numbers for similar artists, I guessed the LP would move about 15,000 units. I'd never been more off target in my life. Only 2,200 fans picked up the project. Not even my Dad bought a copy.

Sure, there were glaring flaws with the album. Fest pressed for Little Brother assisted "How High" to be the second single. Though I wasn't impressed with the track, Fest envisioned it playing in coffee shops in Europe. It never gained traction, nor did Konee Rok bless it with a visual treatment. Furthermore, I begged Fest to drop "Agony" and "Last Night" in favor of hard hitting, unreleased cuts "Do It Again" and "Heard It From Me." Fest was unmoved. Sebastine and I labored over El Che's sequencing for days before submitting the tracklist we felt made the album flow seamlessly. Contractually having the last word on all creative input, Fest ignored our suggestions. Sebastine and I didn't hear the final product until we received copies in the mail right before the album dropped. In his attempt to formulate a theme and cohesiveness on El Che, there were random skits featuring Fest being stalked by federal agents that made no sense. On the album's cover, Fest clutches his head in contemplative thought as he gazes at Frederick Douglass' My Bondange and My Freedom, Ralph Ellison's Invisible Man, and an assault rifle covered by Fidel Castro's patrol cap. El Che's cover art symbolized liberation from a major record label, but the substance of the album did little to liberate minds, one of the core tenets of dangerousNEGRO. In our excitement to produce the project we neglected to encourage more revolutionary rhetoric that might have appealed to our established fanbase.

The marketing of El Che was botched as well. The little we had to spend on marketing primarily went to Facebook, which was just starting to leverage its advertising power. While pay-per-click ads worked for boosting fan page followers and spotlighting t-shirts, it didn't translate into album sales. I pushed for more banner ads on HipHopDX, SOHH, and AllHipHop.com, but with no financial skin in the game, I was rebuffed by my partners.

We needed a hail mary. Jimmy Kimmel promised Fest he could come back on his show anytime, so we crossed our fingers for the appearance to be the the gamechanger that ignited sales. Fest gave a memorable performance of "City Is Falling" with live band Zzaje before throwing on the dN jacket I gifted him and performing "Celebration," freestyling his last verse with Spinderella scratching live. Viewers responded swiftly, as sales surged for a week. In the end, it still wasn't enough to make us all rich and spring me from the plantation...

With Rhymefest, Movie Director Reggie Rock Bythewood, and Killer Mike

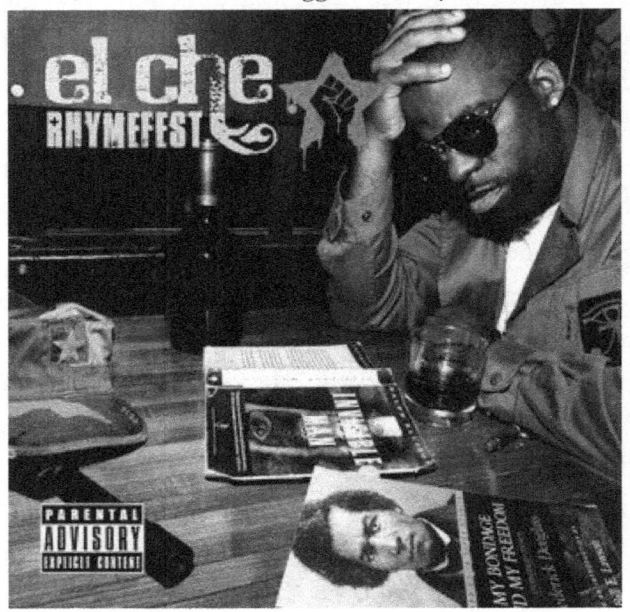

El Che Cover Art

CHAPTER TWELVE

ASHES

If there's anything I can say, to help you find your way
Touch your soul, make it whole, the same for you and I
There's not a minute that goes by that I don't believe
We could fly, but I can feel it in the wind
The beginning or the end
But people keep your head to the skyyyyy
-Cee Lo on Outkast's "Liberation"

Sabrina challenged me in ways that drove me crazy and made me question my flaws. Despite running a record label, while simultaneously taking care of my mom, working at University of Phoenix, finishing the MBA I committed to there, and completing a nine hour graduate certificate in Nonprofit Management at Texas A&M, she made me feel like I wasn't doing enough to keep her happy. Every time I went out of town for speaking engagements she turned into a huge brat, blowing up my phone, and accusing me of neglect. Never had I experienced such intense emotions from a partner. Sabrina wanted me all to herself, and as much as it annoyed me at times, I couldn't dispute that she loved me. I considered she was probably right, I was so driven I didn't give her the attention she deserved. When she finally stopped demanding my attention, choosing instead to hang out with a mysterious new group of friends, I was skeptical of her intentions, yet relieved I had breathing room.

The breathing room turned into open air, ultimately culminating in the dissipation of our eleven month whirlwind romance.

Liberated, I was free to redirect my attention to my career. The only problem was, I hated my job, and being an entrepreneur wasn't putting food on the table. Moral conflict made me check out mentally at University of Phoenix. As mounting federal restrictions strangled the for-profit behemoth, we were coached not to communicate with the media. Scandals stemming from investigative reports had the university on the hot seat. I had to buy time until I figured out my escape. Surely a better opportunity with more virtuous aims and a higher salary existed somewhere.

I turned to church for answers. Sebastine introduced me to Pastor J's Higher Dimension, tucked away in the hood of Southwest Houston, when I first moved to the city. It was a natural transition for Nashville transplants accustomed to hearing Mount Zion's Bishop Joseph Walker at one of the three locations he preached at on Sundays. Lynnette introduced me to Mount Zion before I relocated to Houston. We'd drive to the largest of Bishop Walker's churches, the seventeen-million dollar, five-thousand seat, monstrosity on Old Hickory Boulevard. I admired her commitment to tithing there. Bishop Walker often appealed to the congregation, of which a sizeable portion were broke Tennessee State, Fisk, and Vanderbilt undergraduates, for funds to buy a chopper. Instead of suffering through traffic between the three separate locations of his baptist church, Bishop Walker wanted to hop over it in his helicopter.

His mentee and fellow Que, Pastor J, hadn't reached that level yet. After completing his B.A. in Bible and Sociology at Nashville's American Baptist College, Pastor J only had *two* church locations. A block away from Higher Dimension's main location, the seven-hundred seater on Club Creek Drive, prostitutes slowly strolled down Bissonnett in broad daylight, wearing daisy dukes. Rundown apartment complexes, occupied by Blacks and Mexicans who hang dried their laundry on their balconies, surrounded the church. The neighborhood's decrepitude gave Pastor J street cred, along with his swagger, youthful appearance, and fluency in Ebonics. Pastor J liked to mix-match designer clothing and accessories. After service he could usually be found in the lobby shaking people's hands wearing Fendi shades and Gucci loafers. Afterwards he would whisk away in either his Escalade or Mercedes, flanked by a caravan of support staff, to the Katy campus, housed out of a middle school gymnasium. Gossipers revealed Pastor J lived in a lavish four or five bedroom house, nestled comfortably in the suburbs. "Of course he does. Why should nice cars and homes only be reserved for doctors, lawyers, and entertainers?" I'd explain to Sebastine, who began to struggle with his support of Higher D. Nonetheless, Pastor J's flashiness didn't interfere with the sense of calm I experienced upon entering the sanctuary. The weight of the world instantly disappeared from my shoulders. The choir, led by now popular and controversial chart topping music director James Fortune, made the hairs on my arm stand up. Sometimes I fought back tears, as their heavenly voices, crisp, cutting, and confident, could only be divinely inspired. For the first time in my church going life I actually began to sing along, with conviction. Emotions freshly tilled by praise and worship, Pastor J would then take the stage to spit hot fire. His sermons usually started off calm, the focus being on a simple concept or specific verse from the Bible. As Pastor J continued on, he would slowly deconstruct the short passage, providing alternate translations of words from Greek, Hebrew, and Aramaic, until scripture took on meaning no one previously realized, yet should have been so obvious all along. Pastor J would decode scripture and "make it plain" for the congregation. His words would pierce through my soul, convicting me of my sins, while giving me an option to pursue salvation. For this comfort I began to pay tithes, calling them my "peace bill." I'd proudly trot to the front of the church to drop ten percent of my income into the woven wicker baskets. I'd come back on Wednesday nights for Bible Study to sow further seeds in the collection plate. Seeing my devotion, I was approached to join the Singles Ministry. Maybe I'd find a virtuous woman there. After all, Proverbs 18:22 stated "Whoso findeth a wife findeth a good thing, and obtaineth favour of the LORD." I joined.

Church strengthened me when I was weak. Despite being bound to the plantation and failing at love, I was inspired to follow God's plan, a plan that inevitably included the extravagant excesses promised by the prosperity gospel. I only needed to be obedient, allow The Lord to forgive me, and in turn forgive others; even those I had given up on. Though I promised never to look back, I swallowed my pride and called Sabrina. During our breakup, not being able to crack the code on making her Biblically submissive ate at my brain. The challenge intensified my interest. Five years her senior, I concluded I should have given exception to her immaturity and focused more on her potential. I wasn't perfect and there was no reason I should have expected Sabrina to be either. I was willing to give it another shot if she was.

After two or three weeks of reconsideration, we rekindled our romance on Valentine's Day over dinner. We agreed to leave the past in the past, which was easier said than done. In the three months we were separated, Sabrina dated one of her "just a friend" new acquaintances, while I entertained a brief tryst with a University of Phoenix Enrollment Manager, a mature, hard working Nigerian-American woman from a good family. Communication with these people was ordered to cease and desist. Trust issues lingered in the background, as we attempted to forgive and forget, however. A March drive to Dallas for my old pals from Nashville, Shawn and

Malarie's wedding, was initially marred by incessant calls and texts to Sabrina's phone from a mysterious "just a friend" figure. She refused to answer. Catching myself being judgemental, I gave Sabrina the benefit of the doubt. I wanted us to enjoy the wedding without there being tension in the air when I introduced her to my friends. We watched the small ceremony intently, comparing notes on what we liked and didn't like throughout. The whole time, we imbibed on spirits at the open bar. Tipsy and in love, we were turned on by the security of having life figured out.

Four weeks later Sabrina's period was late. The thought of reaching the full manifestation of adulthood gave us optimistic energy. We were both excited when two blue lines appeared on the CVS pregnancy kit, confirming we would be parents and tied together forever. There was no reason to argue further, dwell on the past, or stress about the future because this was it, our life partnership was secured. The timing couldn't have been any better since I was days away from closing on the house I picked, with Sabrina's approval, in the suburbs of Katy. Having started the tedious home buying process eight months prior, finally assuming the title of homeowner was a declaration of manhood.

While I couldn't lay claim to accomplishing the American Dream, that rags to riches story which typically includes riding the wave of capitalism to greener pastures, realizing the African American Dream of getting out the hood was almost sufficient. The first night we spent in the two-story, tan brick house made me feel like I accomplished everything my ancestors wished I would. Laying in bed with my arm around Sabrina, my child in utero, I stared up at the twelve foot ceiling soaking in serenity. Twenty-eight-hundred square feet of space sheltered me, and my soon to be family, from the elements, threats against our bodies, and the world's wickedness.

I lived two houses down from the beginning of a cul-de-sac on a safe, quiet street in the suburbs, a dramatic upgrade from rapidly disintegrating Alief, Co-op City, and East New York. Paris and Dominoe finally had the backyard I promised they'd have for the past six years. Cuddles and Chill Will had a whole neighborhood of rabbits, birds, and other cats to chase. Next door to the left was a middle class Mexican family, to the right a hard working Filipino family. Across the street were The Reynolds, a White family with a small fishing boat parked in their driveway. At the end of the cul-de-sac was a Nigerian family, with two lanky teenage boys who shot hoops relentlessly in their driveway. Otter Trail Lane was the mythical melting pot of gold found at the foot of an elusive rainbow. What place more fitting to bring a child into the world?

Or so I thought. It wasn't until Sabrina and I moved in together that I realized my personal limits. Never had I recognized how much I valued personal space, autonomy, and silence. Perhaps it was apparent when I found boarding school to be an attractive option. Or maybe when I had no qualms about going to Vanderbilt, nine-hundred miles away from my family. In any event, the realization I perfectly enjoyed being a free thinking Black man, able to independently decide how to navigate life, and lay foundations for future seeds, conflicted with Sabrina's seeming need to possess the full majority of my attention.

My mom, in her final two semesters of nursing school, occupied one of the three bedrooms we had upstairs. Frustrated with not being able to secure a compensation analyst position in Houston, she decided to become recession proof, enrolling at Houston Community College before completing her BSN at University of Houston-Victoria. Sitcoms always seemed to exaggerate the tension existent between spouses and mother-in-laws. Mama Payne's not so passive aggressiveness towards Gina was simply fodder for laughs I thought. In real life, tension between your wife and mother is the best formula for stress. Though they would never openly address their beef, the discomfort was palpable. Sabrina would come home from her pharmacy tech job to find my mom watching cable on the plasma she'd brought from New York, her sole pre-Texas possession. Minimal words would exchange before Sabrina disappeared into our first floor master bedroom to watch television separately. When I finally got home I was attacked from both sides. "Can you at least try to have a cordial relationship with my mother? Once nursing school is done we'll have the whole house to ourselves," I'd plead to no end. Pregnant and wildly emotional, Sabrina would accuse me of putting my mother's needs above her own. "You're having my child, we're going to be together forever. A few months isn't going to hurt us in the grand scheme of things. Can you just be patient for me?" Her silence indicated she couldn't.

    I figured Sabrina would fall in line once I finally proposed. Neither she nor I wanted to bring a child into the world without being married first. Being unwed parents would have made it appear we didn't have life all the way figured out, like we were just shacking up - unacceptable. The stigma of being a baby daddy or baby mother just didn't jive with our upbringings. After formally asking Sabrina's father, Joe, for her hand, I went to Zales to finance a chunky, princess cut diamond ring. The proposal had been plotted several times from the moment I met her at that Wachovia ATM on Washington Avenue. I knew if Sabrina was indeed the one, it would only be fitting to ask her to marry me there, the same place our romance began. Finding an excuse to randomly end up at the same ATM was only a minor challenge. I told her to get dressed for a movie date off I-10. En route, I received a scripted call from my homeboy Reo, who had "just caught a flat." As we pulled up to the scene, Sabrina noted the coincidence of the location. "Yeah, that's funny right?" I asked matter of factly. Once I grabbed my crowbar from the trunk, I asked Sabrina to follow me and use her cell phone to light the area. As we walked past the front of the now Wells Fargo ATM, I stopped to tie my shoe. Oblivious, Sabrina started to continue to Reo's car before I called her back. By this point I had wiggled the ring box out of my pocket and opened it to display the rock.

Sabrina covered her mouth with a shaking hand, "Oh my God. Oh my God, is this really happening?" she asked rhetorically.

"This is where we met and this is where I'm hoping we'll start our new journey. Will you marry me?" I asked, as Reo secretly filmed the whole thing.

Still shaking in disbelief, Sabrina finally responded, "Yes, of course," before gaining her composure and adding, "It's about time. I was wondering what was taking you so long!"

Immediately the wedding had to be planned. The sooner the better. I didn't want Sabrina's stomach showing before we walked down the aisle. Our shotgun wedding needn't be remembered as a rushed affair covering for a great mistake. I wanted people to respect the fact me and Sabrina had it all figured out and we loved each other... before the kid forced us to become eternally tied. We chose fourth of July weekend because we knew everyone would be off work and have an extra day to fellowship with family. Promptly, I called the must knows: Grandpa Alric, Grandma Gloria, Nana, and my father. For such a major life event, a three month notice fell within the minimally acceptable indication range, I figured. Next, I contacted my best men, Sebastine and Bichar. They had both already married, and I had finally caught up to them in life goals.

Though we had little money, Sabrina and I were determined to have a memorable wedding. A free consultation with a professional wedding planner gave us the idea to consider non traditional locations. Once she mentioned The Heights Theater, a quick Google search proved it was not only unique, but inexpensive. Bonnie and Clyde were rumored to have hid there after robbing the former Heights State Bank. Sabrina was my Beyonce and Hov's " '03 Bonnie & Clyde" instantly sounded in my head. Hip Hop always pointed me in the right direction so the The Heights Theater was an obvious venue choice. The wedding planner fulfilled her utility and we set out to arrange things on our own. Sabrina's parents would pay for the alcohol and DJ, and I'd foot the bill for the rest.

Lacking confidence we could plan it all alone, Sabrina's Aunt Debbie voiced her concerns and stepped in to assume the role of wedding coordinator. As expenses increased, so did the tension between me and Sabrina. Like most women, she envisioned a fairytale wedding, where she wore the perfect dress and shoes, and every detail conformed with the precise magical vision she's had since childhood of wedding her hunky, athletic, soul mate. It was obvious I was not *that* guy, yet I was *the* guy she would be joined with, so fulfilling as much of the vision as possible was critical. On the other hand, my top priority was staying out the red. Decorations, flowers, plateware, and invitations were not important to me whatsoever. "Ten years from now nobody will remember that stuff," I pleaded to a sulking Sabrina. Pregnant and emotional, Sabrina responded with overwhelming rage. Arguments were no stranger to our relationship, considering the trust issues that remained a consistent theme. However, wedding planning, pregnancy, and living under one roof fueled emotions so intense I feared for the viability of our pending marriage. In fact, I slept very little leading up to the wedding, concerned it was a mistake. But it was too late. My family, friends, and I had already spent lots of money making arrangements to witness the nuptials. Frozen, at the seat of my bed with my head in my hands, I concluded I had to go through with it. I threw on the oversized white tuxedo I should have tried on days prior and headed to The Heights Theater. The show must go on.

I walked into the venue wearing aviator shades, the kind Jay-Z would wear, to hide my self doubt. Taft buddies Mshangwe, Venroy, and Mike were there to greet me with college buddies Sebastine and Bichar. Reo and Jonathan, my Houston confidants arrived a little later. As did Sabrina's older brother Taurus, a 6'2 truck driver, who we agreed would round out my roster of groomsmen to better represent the fusion of our families. In exchange, my sister Sabree joined Sabrina's bridal party. Her childhood friends, Othello and Anthony, upset they were not allowed to join the bridal party on Sabrina's side, settled for being ushers. Terry Mackey, my "sands" from Fisk's Alpha Chi chapter, and Senior Pastor of Riceville Mt. Olive Baptist Church on Houston's Southwest side, got caught up after service, creating a brief panic in the packed theater. Just when I figured it was God's way of bailing me out, the door opened and I made eye contact with Terry's gap toothed grin. In his characteristic Southern church cadence, Terry told the hundred guests in attendance exactly why he was late. It was impossible not to laugh when Terry combined his exaggerated gesticulations with overly enunciated, ebonically infused, syllables. Within seconds, the crowd quickly forgot how agitated they were and fixated their attention on me, Sabrina, and Terry standing at the alter.

Two weeks prior, Sabrina and I sat in Terry's office for last minute premarital counseling, where I revealed it bothered me Sabrina did not value reading books and articles as much as I did. It hurt her, as I assumed it might, but I figured there was no safer place to reveal my concern. Fast forwarding back to the wedding, I realized Sabrina was right - all of life's answers couldn't be found in a book. Love was largely unexplainable and unpredictable. No text could accurately predict if love was enough to overcome our differences. So I looked up and paused in the middle of reciting the vows I had waited until that very morning to write. Burning tears started to well up upon the realization I was surrendering to Sabrina in hopes love would work everything out. "Take your time Meek," one of the elder women shouted. But time waits for no man. In four months I would be a father and there was no way any child of mine was going to doubt my commitment to being in their life everyday. I gained my composure and finished my vows, while audience members dabbed their eyes with tissue. Then it was Sabrina's turn. I sensed an uncertainty in her voice that went undetected by our onlookers. This same uncertainty appeared moments later when Sabrina initially missed her cue to say "I do." Our spectators thought it a humorous slight and Terry capitalized by making a comical remark. Finally, we bowed our heads and made a final appeal to God to bless our union, before kissing to seal the deal.

Afterwards, we turned on the theater's projector to debut a nine minute satire depicting our fateful meeting at the Wachovia ATM eighteen months prior. Sabrina's film production friend, Artis Armstrong, did a great job editing the clip, as the audience continually erupted with laughter. Taking a cue from Martin's Jerome, I played the role of a pimp and Sabrina a saint, before switching to a stereotypical nerd in scene two, with Sabrina playing an arrogant socialite. In the third and final scene we accurately told the story of our meeting. Seeing us on screen, you couldn't tell anyone at the wedding we weren't meant to be together. Joy filled the room, as Sabrina and I hammed it up for the cameras. Strafe's "Set It Off" sent me, Sebastine, Bichar, Venroy, Gerard Johnson, and Lionel Carter to the dancefloor for the Alpha Train. We then locked arms, left over right, to encircle Sabrina and sing the fraternal hymn. "College days swiftly pass, imbued with mem'ries fond / And the recollection slowly fades away." Sabrina and I had finally graduated to adulthood.

There was no money for a honeymoon. Wedded bliss lasted less than two weeks before we were at each other's throats again.

Nesting and frustrated with the pet's summertime shedding, Sabrina begged for me to part with my beloved furballs. When I refused, she accused me of loving the cats and dogs more than I loved her. It didn't matter that they'd been in my life for years before I even met her, she felt they were as expendable as her neglected chihuahua, King, who she left to toil in misery in her parent's backyard. My pets were the most reliable and consistent beings in my life. They provided unconditional love and support, filling emotional voids in my heart's paternal vacuum. Parting with any of them was unfathomable, their cold noses warmed my soul. Owning a home was partially motivated by my promise to get them out of a cramped apartment and into a backyard where they could run all day. Sabrina saw them all as a nuisance, especially the cats who she swore would attempt to smother our baby and suck the milk out of his sleeping mouth when he arrived. "That's some creole voodoo nonsense. Million of people have cats and babies!" I'd contend. But surprisingly her parents were convinced of this outrageous myth as well. Sabrina would put them on speakerphone to explain the unfounded theory. *These people are out of their minds.* "Look, the pets are staying. That's final."

With me refusing to budge on the animals, Sabrina took aim at our other house guest - my mother. "The Bible says you're supposed to leave your mother and cleave to your wife. You don't know what being a man is all about," Sabrina would hurl, igniting rage and resentment. Despite reminding Sabrina time and time again that my mother would be leaving as soon as she completed her nursing degree, Sabrina insisted she leave immediately. Make no mistake, I also desired to live apart from my mother, as it is only natural for adults to have space to themselves. In fact, after leaving the nest early for boarding school and college, it seemed rather apparent I preferred parentless environments. At the same time, I owed my mother a debt of gratitude for busting her butt to put me through school. The least I could do was offer her refuge after deserting her at the age of fourteen. Yet Sabrina, who lived with her parents all her life, and often drove seventy-four miles round-trip to see them weekly, accused me of being a Momma's Boy. Nothing could be further from the truth, though I loved my mother and aimed to free her from the rat race. For the sake of my sanity, I was forced to ask my mother, in the middle of her final nursing school semester, to move in with my sister, at the two-bedroom apartment she rented for her and my niece, Karys. Isolated in the suburbs, surely peace would finally find its way to my home, I figured.

During Sabrina's final trimester we attempted to set aside our differences and focus on the wellbeing of our son. We sat for weekly childbirth classes at the Women's Hospital and I tagged along for each check up with the obstetrician. Name suggestions were hurled at us for months. Whether male or female, Sabrina always envisioned she would name her first child Phoenix, in honor of the mythical flying beast who rises from the ashes of its predecessor. Considering how much I began to despise the University of Phoenix, despite their new policy of allowing employees to work from home, I soured on the name. I thought back to my formative years in The Bronx - padless tackle football behind my building, baseball with Eddie and Louie, epic snowball fights, and my first kiss in the back lobby. I also thought about the things from which I hoped to protect my young, Black, son. I thought about Gary Gonzalez staring blankly into the heavens, while blood pooled under the bench below him from the bullet hole in his forehead. I thought about my father revealing his carnal sin to me and my sister on that same bench and life never being the same again. These were the ashes from which my son would arise. All of these things happened on Hunter Avenue.

Due to complications stemming from preeclampsia, Sabrina's doctor scheduled an induction for November 15, 2011. On that date we arrived at the Texas Women's Hospital in the early morning hours, waiting around all day for the doctor to force labor. As afternoon turned into evening, the clouds gave way to rain. Right before the doctor entered the room to deliver a dose of pitocin, Sabrina's amniotic sac took a cue from mother nature and her water broke unassisted. She elected to go into labor sans epidural. A few contractions later she opted for that same spinal injection she vowed to reject the previous thirty-nine weeks. In the room with us were her mother and paternal grandmother. Sabrina said she didn't feel comfortable having my mother, who had observed hours of labor and delivery during nursing school, in the room. I respectfully informed my mother when she arrived. Fearing I'd never look at her the same, Sabrina encouraged me not to observe the proceedings up close. However I couldn't resist being the first person my son encountered upon entering his new, cold world.

Suddenly, the top of his head was visible. The doctor instructed me to temper my excitement because it might be quite a while before he fully emerged. My instincts told me he was more eager to embrace his new challenge and vacate the womb promptly. My little man exceeded everyone's expectations and was laying on Sabrina's chest in no time. I held him in my arms against my black and metallic gold Vandy tee, relieved he was finally here - Hunter Warren Walker, my son. His middle name was plucked from his grandfather, Sabrina's dad, Joseph Warren Babineaux, who he resembled at birth. Though Joseph had raised his wife's son, Taurus, as his own, he had no biological male offspring. Sabrina and I agreed Hunter's middle name would be a great tribute and sign of our families uniting.

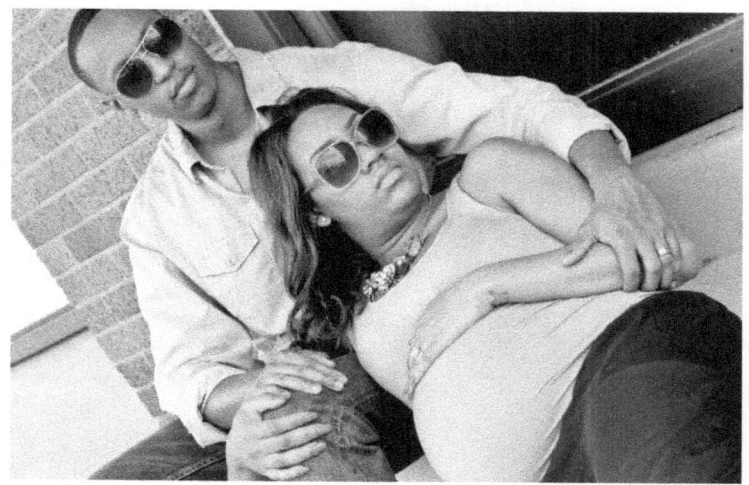

Awaiting Hunter's Arrival

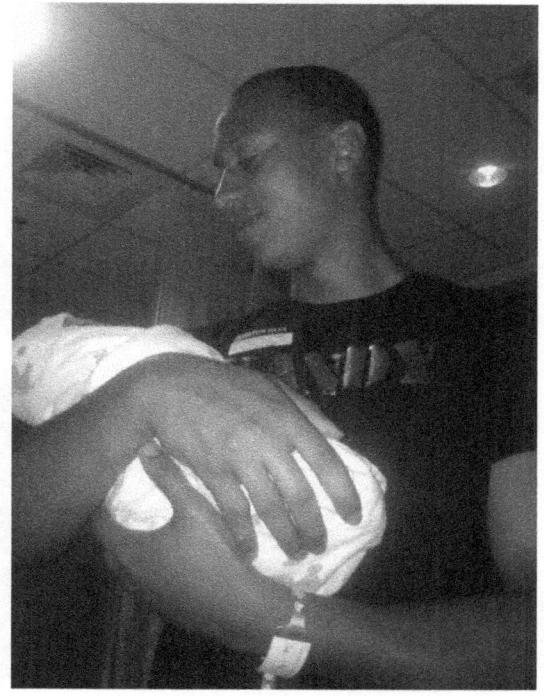

Day One

CHAPTER THIRTEEN

THERAPEUTIC IGNORANCE

> Win my nigga just win
> It's a dirty world but that bitch still spin
> And we don't trust the preachers or the crooked politicians
> The mothafuckers always talking, they don't ever want to listen
> I'm reeking of success you can smell it thru my pores
> And when I build my dream house I'm hiding money in the floors
> You wanna prove me wrong in the end
> Just win my nigga just win
> -Young Jeezy "Just Win"

No one prepared us for how difficult raising a child would be. Prior to Hunter's birth we had a rosy image in our minds of a fun, even-tempered kid who smiled all day because he adored his parents. Nowhere in our thoughts were the uncontrollable meltdowns, disregard for normal sleeping patterns, and persistent need for critical attention. I came to realize parenting required other worldly patience... patience impossible to develop otherwise. Unfortunately patience was in short supply. Sabrina and I butted heads on everything from how soon Hunter should eat meat, to when he should receive his first haircut, and if he should be allowed to play football in the future. There were even disputes about my Pro-Blackness turning Hunter into an angry, Black man, which incensed me because of Sabrina's lack of concern for the Robbie Tolans, Oscar Grants, and Trayvon Martins our son might grow to resemble. We were constantly at odds. I resorted to the silent treatment in an effort to avoid arguing, while simultaneously indicating my displeasure with the arrangement. Days would go by with minimal speech shared. Sabrina hated receiving the cold shoulder and was correct to diagnose it as a sign of emotional immaturity, but it had been employed as my coping mechanism since childhood when I learned to internalize contentious feelings. To avoid interacting with my wife, with whom I felt it was impossible to see eye to eye, I would retreat to my all Black media room (one of the amenities that convinced me I needed to put an offer on the house), to vaporize white widow and experiment with Algoriddim's iPad DJ app.

Growing up I grew accustomed to the sweet but pungent aroma of reefer, yet feared becoming a habitual user, as I associated it with underperformance. A part of me thought it was cool to see my dad and other family members rebel against the status quo and spark up a joint. Still, I knew it was my job to overcome their setbacks, so abstaining from weed seemed a logical approach to breaking the cycle. Like most high school and college students I experimented with marijuana due to social pressures, but I never understood the appeal. I never felt high. Then one day in 2008 I correctly inhaled and it blew my socks off. I gained unparalleled insight, creative thought, and rhythm that had alluded me my whole life. Most of all, it gave me a deeper understanding of my father's mindset, something I constantly sought. I figured joining the lodge would open a bridge for my father and I to communicate more frequently, but that didn't work for more than a year or so. My dad loved weed, and now so did I; I was thrilled about having something to share with him. Even better, the green granted me the rhythm I sorely needed to master the mechanics of deejaying, something I failed at miserably when my father allowed me to play with his turntables as a youngster. Now I had two ways to connect with my dad. In my subconscious pursuit of understanding and relating to my emotionally absent father, I struck gold with ganja. Sabrina swore the only time I was agreeable was when I was high.

When the weed wore off our marriage resumed its dysfunction. Miserable in our union, I appealed to Sabrina to see a marriage counselor. Therapy did us no good. While I spilled my guts and opened up to our blond, female therapist, Sabrina clammed up and kept everything inside... until we got home to argue in privacy.

Running out of options, we thought church might bring us together. Something supernatural was certainly needed to keep our relationship from self destructing. Since we moved in together, I rarely attended Higher Dimension. Not only was the drive far from home, but I soured on Pastor J and the Black church in general. It bothered me that homosexuals were targeted as unnatural enemies destined for eternal damnation in the fire pits of hell. In one of the last services I attended, Pastor J asked for all the boys in the congregation to stand. For twenty minutes straight he berated them for adopting "female tendencies" and not operating as true men:

> "You are a boy! It doesn't matter what you see on TV or hear in the news about gay being okay. God did not put you here to be a homosexual! The devil is busy. Don't let him trick you into doing things that are unnatural."

All my life I'd heard pastors, preachers, and evangelists cite the "clobber passages" to justify their disdain for same sex relationships. In my heart I always felt there was something lost in translation. *Why would anyone choose to be gay? I never chose to be straight. And if people do choose to be gay, why should I care? It's not my genitals. Why should my opinion control the private, consenting lives of others? Most of all, if the church hated gays so much, why did so many effeminate men fill the pews, choir, and staff?* Apparently God was capable of making people Black, White,

Asian, tall, short, gifted, autistic, athletic, disfigured, attractive, unattractive, introverted, extroverted, and straight, but in no way was He responsible for homosexuality. That was the work of Satan himself. It didn't matter if homosexuality consistently appeared in all mammalian populations, God gave people discernment, and according to the church, that special trait was supposed to be used to discern that being gay was wrong. The church's emotionally immature stance on homosexuality angered me. Church was supposed to unite people, not divide them. Encouraging people to pray their gay away was fruitless and destructive. Kids faced bullying, abuse, and neglect for expressing their inner selves. Suicides occurred because people could not cope with the pervasive sin they were unable to escape. It made no sense why the Black church would devote so much energy and hatred towards tearing people down.

Though I disagreed with the church's stance on homosexuality, I still had faith it could turn Sabrina into a submissive, sweet-tempered wife. So back to church we went. Always defiant, Sabrina begged to go to her preferred megachurch, Fountain of Praise, on the south side. She sucked her teeth and rolled her eyes when I drove her to Higher Dimension instead.

"I heard Higher D is shady, I really don't want to go there," she sulked.

"I heard the same thing about Fountain of Praise, so just give it a try one time," I rebutted.

The choir seemed to vindicate me. I smirked and side eyed Sabrina, "I told you they were the best."

Trying to hide her amusement she scoffed, "They're alright."

Then Pastor J finally hit the stage for his sermon. The topic of the day: tithing. *Shit.* Pastor J chastised the congregation for more than an hour about how we were being disobedient to God for not giving a full ten percent of our income *before* taxes to the church. He complained about making guest appearances at other churches and receiving greater "love offerings" elsewhere. It didn't matter that most of his congregants were struggling financially, he blamed our struggle on our refusal to part with more of our finances. He concluded the sermon by asking his deacons to stand up front to collect tithes and offerings in large wicker baskets. Everyone stood and proceeded in a single file line to drop money into the coffers. Once collected, Pastor J asked only the men in the congregation to stand. "You are the men of this church. You're supposed to set the example. God is telling me some of yall have another hundred dollars you can drop in this basket right now. If that's you, I would like you to come on down. Everyone else please remain standing." Two gentlemen dug crispy Benjamins from their pockets and proceeded. Pastor J thanked them then addressed all standing men again, "God is telling me some of yall have another fifty dollars you can drop in this basket right now. If that's you, I would like you to come on down. Everyone else please remain standing." A few more fellas heeded the call. Pastor J continued with his requests, diminishing in denomination each time until he got down to one dollar bills. Embarrassed and feeling exploited, I was so furious that I refused to give Pastor J even one more dollar. I considered kicking his Mercedes or Escalade on the way out the parking lot after service.

"See, I told you they were a bunch of crooks at Higher D," Sabrina grinned. That was the last time I attended service at Higher Dimension.

We tried the Church Without Walls a few streets down from our house in Katy, but didn't feel inspired to become regulars. *Another megachurch intent on building larger facilities to attract even more parishioners and more money.* Church resentment motivated me to begin studying Buddhism and Eastern philosophies, which championed self reflection and personal accountability, cutting out any middlemen to whom I had to appeal for divine intervention. After meeting Dr. Anthony Pinn, author of *Writing God's Obituary: How a Good Methodist Became a Better Atheist*, during a local NBC broadcast on Hip Hop's youth influence, I was turned on to secular humanism. It was the first time I met a Black man who proudly voiced his unbelief. I was invited on the segment to promote my new, fledgling nonprofit, The Black Male Empowerment Institute, which I founded in hopes of encouraging a more entrepreneurial mindset amongst high school and college students who looked like me. I wanted to save them before they committed themselves to plantation life, like I had. Dr. Pinn, who taught a class on the intersection of religion and Hip Hop with Bun B at Rice, echoed my sentiment that rap music's rebelliousness provided opportunities for empowerment. Post broadcast, we exchanged numbers and Facebook info. I was unsure of what my spiritual beliefs were, but certain I needed to do enough research to be as confident as Dr. Pinn once I reached my conclusion.

Sativa elevated my spiritual consciousness, taking my introspection deeper than ever before. It allowed me to recall fond childhood memories of my father, seeing his face light up and head nod when boom bap thumped out of bass heavy speakers. Marijuana permitted me to savour music in three dimensions, not just hearing beats and lyrics, but experiencing the full depth and texture of each note and syllable. I found the key to unlock the rhythm that eluded me all along. I entered a portal to my father's mind and the minds of genius composers and legendary DJs. Just when it would have been easy to forsake the hocus pocussness of spiritual belief, cannabis cemented my realization that there was universal energy, love, and rhythm that existed all around and could be tapped into. Deejaying was the ultimate manifestation of this belief. Mixing on my iPad led me to my coveted role self: DJ Meek Tha Freak, prodigal son of DJ Don C.

No matter how many Black scholars, leaders, politicians, and clergymen dogged Hip Hop for being the "gospel of self destruction," I always found intrinsic value in the therapeutic ignorance of rap music. Rap is the soundtrack to eudaemonia, the embodiment of the African American dream. Rap inspires. Rap heals. Rap transforms. Is rap perfect? No. Misogyny, nihilism, and the spread of economic irresponsibility plague the genre. However, these are merely the symptoms of predominately Black youth navigating a rigged system through emotionally immature vessels. Ignorance is bliss, and nothing could be more blissful than flipping enemies the bird and shouting: "We know!" No matter how perceptively counterproductive it might be, it's exciting to see and hear rappers poetically overcome obstacles, as products of their flawed environments. And the beats are slammin'... inducing spontaneous rhythmic expression, signaling our connection to the universe. In this way, Hip Hop has been as therapeutic to Gen Xers and Millennials as church has been to all generations.

As I graduated from deejaying house parties with my iPad to deejaying clubs with turntables, I embraced the DJ booth as my pulpit, the dancefloor the sanctuary where souls are saved. Pushing patrons to catch the Holy Spirit, evidenced by hands raised to the sky and thunderstruck open jaws collectively shouting "Ohhhhh!!!" I was just as powerful as Pastor J. For myself and the crowd, stress was shed, worries cast away, and optimism renewed in these fleeting moments.

When love between me and my spouse was absent, deejaying gave me respite from the dysfunction. Even if meeting Sabrina's emotional needs was impossible, I was competent enough to bring large groups to frenzied ecstasy, validating my self worth.

Still, Sabrina's lack of support for my newfound career drove the fissure between us even further apart. For hours I seethed with anger, while being devoured by mosquitoes in MacGregor Park after I deejayed a summertime party and Sabrina disappeared with the car. She preferred to hang out with her friend, Othello...

Two months later my friend, James Robertson, the same guy who threw the MacGregor Park party, got me my first real gig at Phil & Derek's restaurant. It would be the first time I used my brand new turntables and mixer. Beyond excited, I invited all my friends and my sister to support me in my new endeavor. As I fumbled with my new equipment and people pretended not to care and danced, Sabrina's presence was notably absent. "Where's your wife?" was asked by every familiar face that walked past the DJ booth. When she finally arrived, right before my set ended, I was dumbfounded by Sabrina's contempt for my dream. Her indifference infuriated me, as I figured my wife should be my biggest supporter and cheerleader. In time, I would establish myself as a legitimate professional, moving from grimey Uptown Hookah to the posh Hudson Lounge in River Oaks, while Sabrina seemed intent on sabotaging my growth in the industry. Yes, I still worked a day job, and Hunter, still in diapers, required extraordinary attention. But I couldn't wrap my mind around Sabrina being unsupportive of my DJ calling, a calling that brought additional income to the household and had the potential to spring me from the plantation, freeing up more time for me to spend at home. The more Sabrina resisted my plan, the more I detached emotionally and pursued it with more vigor. Arguments escalated, culminating in Sabrina tossing one of my turntables over the railing of our staircase. Music my only solace, I considered divorcing my wife and further dedicating my life to Hip Hop, my comforter.

CHAPTER FOURTEEN

JANTEENTH

Waking up in a dream
Sleepwalking on another big stage
You never heard peace 'til you hear people scream
Your name in unison, I'm so far away
From the place I used to be, struggling usually
Look at the newer me, fate pursuing me
I can feel the energy in the air
It feel like I'm supposed to be here
-Kendrick Lamar "Now or Never"

Keenly aware of the data stating two-thirds of Black children were being raised in single parent households, I was determined for Hunter not to be a statistic. Everyone attributed the ills of the Black community to the disintegrating family structure that often turned fatherless, undisciplined youth into juvenile delinquents. Though I was no strict disciplinarian, I most wanted my son to have an emotionally supportive father to encourage him to be his best on a daily basis. Even with my father at home most of my childhood, the invisible wounds inflicted by emotional immaturity and unconscious neglect made a lasting impression. So how then could I leave Hunter to experience the unknown horror of biweekly, court sanctioned visitation if I left his mother? The fear made me drop my initial divorce filing.

Reassessing what truly fueled the dysfunction at home, money was the inevitable conclusion. If I could just earn enough money to stop stressing about bills, I would be able to buy Sabrina the designer wardrobe she coveted, take her on expensive vacations, and spoil her until she had nothing more to complain about. Salary from the University of Phoenix just wasn't going to cut it and I grew to hate the job anyway. Desperate times call for desperate measures, so I knew it was time to do something drastic. Bichar, who moved to Houston following my wedding, had finally settled into a six-figure, commission only sales job, and encouraged me to join him at Vacations to Go. Against Sabrina's wishes for me to stay put and endure the madness at University of Phoenix, I decided to take a shot.

Besides deejaying, traveling to new places was my favorite thing to do. If I was going to defect to yet another plantation, one that required intelligent conversations about polar bear excursions in the Arctic, safaris on the Serengeti, hiking to Machu Picchu, or escorted tours in Europe seemed more ideal. Well versed in a new sales technique, "corporate seduction," which I coined from observing my former University of Phoenix colleague, Robert Pinkney, articulately close deals with baritone flirtation, I enjoyed charming money out of people with disposable income. There was no reason to feel bad about motivating them to expand their horizons by escaping the emotional dredging of American life. Vacations are the highlights of people's lives; I was in the business of supplying life's greatest memories.

But the plantation was shitty. Literally, the plumbing in the old building occasionally caused toilets to back up and spill onto the carpet outside the restrooms. Several floors of the nine-story building often smelled of poop and mildew. Still, the carpets weren't as crappy as the oppressive schedules, juvenile policies, and outdated techniques used to break spirits and keep employees subservient. The company generated massive amounts of incoming leads by misleading the internet's cheapest and/or most computer illiterate web surfers; low hanging fruit, but often headaches other companies tried to avoid. Tuesdays and Wednesdays were technically my days off, days it was difficult to avoid the office due to the persistent customer service needs of my clients. It took me two years of working sixty hour work weeks just to get Saturdays off. When fathers were taking their kids to Sunday sporting events, I was required to be in the office, despite receiving no salary and working purely on commission. Curiously, an Indian woman who started in my training class was given an exception and granted a Monday through Friday schedule after our first year. We both complained to superiors of the difficulty we had maintaining quality of life for our families with young children. However, only her concern was met, despite me outselling her and the rest of the department. She threatened to quit if she didn't receive a schedule that allowed her to cater to the needs of her three-year-old daughter. Black people were so dispensable to the company I didn't dare attempt the same tactic, opting instead to outwork everybody and earn weekends off on my own merit. Two and a half million dollars in sales and the award for top salesman did nothing to convince the higher ups, all White, to consider my case. The schedule left Sabrina home to sulk every weekend with Hunter.

  Though I had finally reached the elusive six-figure income I coveted, life was miserable. All my money went to bills, with nominal assistance from Sabrina, who impulsively spent her paycheck on hair, shoes, clothes, and food. My patience wore thin with the lack of financial discipline I originally attributed to our five year age gap. Though marriage forced me to reverse the financial recklessness I had in my twenties, daycare, car insurance, car notes, cell phones, the mortgage, electricity, cable, and student loans devoured my monthly checks. Making more money than I ever made, yet still struggling to get by was infuriating. Overworked and stressed by bank account hemorrhage, our marriage drowned further.

Penny pinching became my modus operandi. I turned into the dad on Everybody Hates Chris. When I got a text from T-Mobile stating Sabrina's line downloaded twenty-five dollars in new apps, I contacted her immediately to ask why she would do such a thing. Vehemently denying the charges, I pulled up the billing statement to investigate the root of the problem. What I found was mostly, but not wholly unexpected: thousands of calls and texts to unfamiliar, out of state numbers. I dialed the most frequently trafficked to confirm my suspicion - Sabrina sought attention from others in my emotional absence. I knew our marriage was over. My initial reaction was to probe and understand where we went wrong, though the red flags were present before our nuptials. Reflecting on our differences, I convinced myself we were never truly compatible. While I was resentful, peace settled into my heart as I realized Hunter's emotional development would ultimately benefit from being in the presence of two happy parents, even if they lived apart.

I'm thankful for the lessons marriage and divorce taught me about myself, lessons I may not have learned otherwise. My maxes and mins of intellectual stimulation, communication, and isolation were only discovered through weathering the storm. Awareness of my emotional voids, needs, and expectations finally crystallized, so I could confront them.

We are products of our parents' circumstances, mistakes, and insecurities, though I would like my child to be the product of my triumphs. Children become atonement for permanent scars, a way of correcting our legacies. Yet, we should instead aim to free our children from the emotional burdens we carry as the result of previous generations not giving proper emphasis to emotional fulfillment. It wasn't until I read Dr. Lindsay C. Gibson's book *Adult Children of Emotionally Immature Parents: How to Heal from Distant, Rejecting, or Self-Involved Parents* that I learned why Sabrina and I were drawn together in the first place. Dr. Gibson explains how "emotional neglect in childhood leads to a painful emotional loneliness that can have a long-term negative impact on a person's choices regarding relationships and intimate partners."[5] Invisible emotional deficiencies drew us to seek completion in one another. The only problem was, we perfectly complemented each other in the worst ways. We were two emotionally immature individuals of equal and opposite charge, who inherited generations of emotional repression. Like matter in the presence of antimatter, our union could only result in annihilation, since we lacked a true understanding of our motives.

    The wisdom I gained from my failed marriage forced me to examine the emotional motives of everyone around me. It seemed every person I knew was consciously or unconsciously fighting some form of emotional neglect. Many suffered from proximal abandonment, with parents present physically, but emotionally checked out. Some were fully abandoned by a parent, knowing of their existence, but having little or no ability to establish contact. Overwhelmingly, this was true for a sizeable number of my Black and Brown friends. Considering the trend, an examination of our historical roots indicate our unique American experience creates the perfect recipe for stunted emotional growth. Due to slavery's assassination of Black emotions, successive generations have been burdened with overcoming the psychological ramifications of pandemic emotional immaturity. The dehumanization of Black people could only be employed if our emotions were treated as meaningless. Dr. Lindsay Gibson reveals emotionally immature people "fear genuine emotion and pull back from emotional closeness."[6] To survive the trauma of separation, violence, rape, murder, and neglect,

---

[5] **Gibson**: *Adult Children of Emotionally Immature Parents*
[6] **Gibson**: *Adult Children of Emotionally Immature Parents*

Black people have been conditioned to suspend our emotions, instead of coping with them. We project strength even when we're deeply wounded. From an early age Black men learn they must be hard, callous, and ready to fuck somebody up at the drop of a dime. There's no room for being soft, so Black boys often see prison as a rites of passage to manhood. Emotional immaturity is why being educated was considered a weakness by my peers growing up in The Bronx. It's why many of them aspired to spend time at Spofford instead of Harvard. Survival of the fittest gave way to survival of the emotionless. It's the reason 21 Savage "grew up in the streets with no heart." Z-Ro accurately captured the Black male emotional void when he pronounced "ain't no such thing as friends / Only associates." In the famous words of Bone Crusher we lie to ourselves and profess we "ain't never scared."

As a remedy for the void emotional immaturity causes, Black people commit their lives to nurturing institutions like gangs, greek letter organizations, Masonic lodges, sports, church, and Hip Hop. Joining these groups is logical. Being a member minimally confers consistent emotional connection with those under the same banner. Optimally, membership creates connections with those under other banners.

In order for Black people to realize eudaimonia we must overcome the emotional destruction perpetrated upon us by White Supremacy. While racism provides the ideal conditions to nurture Black nihilism, emotional immaturity is the reason we remain trapped in a cycle of self defeat. We have to be emotionally mature enough to schedule regular mental health check ups, the same way we check in with primary care physicians, dentists, and optometrists. We have to be emotionally mature enough to reject homophobia, transphobia, toxic masculinity, classism, and religious fanaticism. We have to be emotionally mature enough to allow each other to be our authentic selves, without judgment. We have to be emotionally mature enough to give Corporate America the finger when we're forced to compromise our integrity by slaving away at plantations who place corporate greed above morality, quality of life, health, safety, and emotional fulfillment. If we are to ever be dangerous Negroes again we have to urgently take control of our own financial destinies by starting, or at least investing in our own businesses.

We have to acknowledge we live in an emotionally immature country that benefits from the divisionary mechanisms of racism, American exceptionalism, and imperialism. According to Dr. Gibson, emotionally immature people "use coping mechanisms that resist reality rather than dealing with it. They don't welcome self-reflection, so they rarely accept blame or apologize. Their immaturity makes them inconsistent and emotionally unreliable."[7] James Baldwin accurately assessed, "One of the results of this is that immaturity is taken to be a virtue too. So that someone like that, let's say John Wayne, who spent most of his time on screen admonishing Indians, was at no necessity to grow up."[8] Only an emotionally immature country would elect a man like Donald Trump to be the leader of the "free" world. Only an emotionally immature country would try to hoard quality education for the privileged. Only an emotionally immature country would downplay the inevitable extinction climate change will cause in favor of short term profits. This country values gun rights over human rights, incarceration over social reform. Only an emotionally immature country would fight incessantly for access to firearms instead of healthcare. Only an emotionally immature country would lock two and a half million people away to suffer greater mental anguish instead of implementing strategies to make these citizens productive members of society.

---

[7] **Gibson**: *Adult Children of Emotionally Immature Parents*
[8] **Peck**: *I Am Not Your Negro*

Stories like Kalief Browder's, which are uncomfortably common, can only exist in an emotionally tone deaf country. Thus, Black and Brown people must go above and beyond pushing for criminal justice reform. The end of mass incarceration can only be guaranteed if we push for the end of prisons altogether. Angela Davis speaks of prison eradication in her book *Freedom is a Constant Struggle*. Davis calls for eliminating the socioeconomic circumstances that create a need for prisons in the first place. As the main ingredient and byproduct of these socioeconomic circumstances, emotional immaturity must be attacked with vigor.

***

The moment I realized I would *never* attain emotional fulfillment working a day job for White Supremacists was the day I sat down to write this book. In order to free myself from the plantation, I had to understand exactly how I ended up there. What was the particular thing holding me back from breaking through the ceiling to liberation? I had to answer that question. I set a plantation escape date of January 31, 2016, the date I would receive half of my ten-thousand dollar bonus, for which I qualified by selling more than two-million dollars worth of vacations. Five-thousand dollars plus the sum of my 401k would surely be enough to open a business and sustain a few months of living expenses, while waiting for profits to roll in. Bichar and I decided we'd open an escape room, after playing several of the sixty minute games around the city, and being sold on the intellectual thrill and group fun they provided. I just had to endure another ninety days on the plantation until I received my bonus.

I stopped coming in on my off days to chip away at the book. In the event of my demise, Hunter needed to know what mistakes and circumstances obstructed my path to liberation. Customer service issues quickly piled up, as my spoiled clientele refused to wait for my return to make outlandish requests, alter reservations, and book complicated air schedules. Exit strategy in place, I feigned concern, but my attitude revealed I was completely over working a ridiculous schedule to accommodate needy, disrespectful, technophobic and mostly White, privileged seniors. One lady felt I was condescending when I asked her where in Europe she would like to visit. "I just want to see Europe. What are your prices?!" she yelled. A year earlier I would have employed "corporate seduction" to sooth her, with the hope she would eventually give me her credit card details. But I had been burned hundreds of times by ungrateful, pestering callers who wasted my time, then booked elsewhere, the rare moment I was out of the office.

"Well it depends on what country or countries you would like to visit, as well as, when you would like to travel. I need more information from you," I dryly disclosed, before pausing to allow her to realize how silly her uninformed request was.

"You're one of those God damned smart niggers I see. Well at the end of the day I'll still be me and you'll just be a nigger!" she fumed.

I laughed and promptly disconnected the call. "That's Negro… dangerous Negro," I spoke into the vacant line.

On January 14th, two weeks prior to receiving my bonus, Vacations to Go, tired of servicing my clients on my off days and sensing my lack of desire to stay with the company another year, let me go. While I wasn't surprised they screwed me on my bonus and monthly commission check, I was disappointed I didn't get to exit on my own terms. Nonetheless, I was as relieved as the slaves in nearby Galveston when General Granger delivered the news of their liberation.

Free from corporate bondage I've had time to find myself, heal hidden emotional wounds, fall in love with an East African girl, and become a better father. My DJ career has blossomed, taking me across North America, opening doors I never imagined. And, in my process of channeling Common, "writing for my life cause I'm scared of a day job," I founded CapitalizeTheB.com to make sure all schools, publications, publishers, websites, and media correctly capitalize the letter B when referencing Black people. After all, the absence of light is black; this does not define me or my people. We are Black - connected by rhythm, roots, and a light that cannot be extinguished. I am a Black man.

I Am A Black Man 290

References

A Convivium Toast to Robert E. Lee. (2012, January 19). Retrieved June 12, 2017, from http://www.kappaalphaorder.org/2012/01/a-convivium-toast-to-robert-e-lee

Gibson, L. C. (2016). *Adult children of emotionally immature parents how to heal from distant, rejecting, or self-involved parents*. Sydney, New South Wales: Read How You Want.

Lewis, M. M. (2004). Scars of the soul are why kids wear bandages when they dont have bruises. New York: Akashic Books.

Peck, R. (Director). (2017). *I Am Not Your Negro* [Motion picture]. USA.

Stiles, T. (2011, April 11). The Commodore's Civil War. Retrieved January 02, 2017, from http://news.vanderbilt.edu/vanderbiltmagazine/the-commodores-civil-war/

www.ingramcontent.com/pod-product-compliance
Lightning Source LLC
Chambersburg PA
CBHW020247030426
42336CB00010B/656